Me Tarzan, You Jane

40 Days to Navigating Your Way
Through the Jungle of Love and Marriage

Me Tarzan, You Jane

40 Days to Navigating Your Way
Through the Jungle of Love and Marriage

Steve & Jane Hutchinson

ME TARZAN, YOU JANE

Unless otherwise noted, all Scripture quotations are taken from the Holy Bible: New King James Version, © 1979, 1980, 1982 by Thomas Nelson, Inc., publishers. Scripture quotations marked NLT are from the Holy Bible, New Living Translation, copyright © 1996, 2004. Used by permission of Tyndale House Publishers, Inc., Wheaton, Illinois 60189. All rights reserved. Scripture quotations marked NIV are from the New International Version, © 1960, 1962, 1963, 1968, 1971, 1972, 1973, 1975, 1977, 1995 by The Lockman Foundation. Used by permission. Scripture quotations marked NRSV are from the New Revised Standard Version Bible, copyright © 1989 National Council of the Churches of Christ in the United States of America. Used by permission. All rights reserved.

ISBN 978-0-9838778-0-6

For worldwide distribution.

Contents

JUNGLE ECONOMICS: CONNECTING FINANCIALLY

JESUS IN THE JUNGLE: CONNECTING SPIRITUALLY

Dedication

To our parents, Ray & Sandra Hutchinson and Al & Harriet Nannarone, who stayed married and taught us many valuable lessons. We are so grateful that we never had to experience our parents divorcing like so many of our friends. Together both of our parents represent over 100 years of marriage. Thanks Mom & Dad! We love you!

To our "amazing" kids... Caleb, Luke, Christianna & Faith Victorya. We are so proud of you! We can clearly see God's wisdom, favor and love coming through you. You guys are really awesome and make us so proud! It is our prayer that this book will help strengthen your marriage one day!

To one of the most amazing people in the world... Steve's grandmother and real boss... Lottie Narewski. There may not be a more giving person on this planet. Thank you for your undying encouragement and support. Thanks for believing in us!

To Steve's brother Tim: I wish you lived long enough for me to see you have a wife and kids. Thanks for being that protective older brother. I love you! I'll see you on the other side!

To our best Friend, our Lord and Savior Jesus Christ: Without your influence and illumination in our lives this book would never have been written. Thank you God for never giving up on us and for loving us in spite of us. Our marriage and life would be lost without you! We are so glad to be your eternal partners, co-laborers, and loyal servants.

Endorsements

Steve and Jane have done a fantastic job of addressing relevant marriage issues and offering time-tested principles that will bring hope and encouragement for any couple. From the standpoint of their own experiences and through honest transparency, this book offers practical guidelines and solutions for staying connected to one another in all levels of relationship, or reconnecting if the marriage partners have drifted apart. This book is a must-read for any couple at any stage of marriage, as well as being a great addition to the resource collection of any marriage ministry.

Jimmy Evans, Speaker & Author
Marriage Today
Dallas, Texas
marriagetoday.com

Steve and Jane Hutchinson have hit a home run with *Me Tarzan, You Jane*. It is one of the best books I have ever read on marriage and relationships. It's engaging, funny, and brilliantly practical and perhaps most importantly, it is REAL! If your marriage is solid, this book will enhance it. If your relationship is in trouble, this book will provide a step-by-step road map for developing the skills necessary to thrive in the jungle of love. A must-read-and-use for those who provide counsel to married couples. I plan to give it to all couples I marry as a gift for their future together.

Dennis Heber, Speaker
Bible Revivals, Inc.
Cleveland, Ohio
dennisheber.org

In order to have a good marriage, you are going to have to put the right ingredients into it to get the right results. When you put the right things in, such as God's Word in God's way, you will have a marriage that will rock the planet and be the witness that God would have you to be to your family and friends. Steve and Jane, in their years of experience, have learned the recipe for a great marriage. Everyone that reads this book and applies it in their life will be blessed by the results.

Jim Cobrae, Pastor
The Rock Church and World Outreach Center
San Bernardino, California
therockchurch.com

Perhaps one of the most prevalent myths among those heading toward marriage is that happiness will just somehow automatically happen. Scripture says, though, that "through wisdom a house is built" (Proverbs 24:3). In *Me Tarzan, You Jane*, Steve and Jane Hutchinson have done a fantastic job of providing a manual for couples wishing to tap into great wisdom that will enhance, strengthen, and improve marriages. Their approach is very down-to-earth, and allows readers to self-evaluate throughout the book. Their work is highly informative, extremely enjoyable, and if their principles are applied, I believe it will be greatly transformative as well. I am pleased to recommend *Me Tarzan, You Jane* to you as a great tool for marriage enhancement.

Tony Cooke
Tony Cooke Ministries
Tulsa, Oklahoma
tonycooke.com

This book provides a creative blend of practical, philosophical, and spiritual perspectives and mandates on marriage. For successful couples, it is full of reminders and encouragement. For those needing some help, there are instructions, ideas, and inspiration.

Dr. William Truby, Superintendent
Lamar County Schools
Barnesville, Georgia

I am blessed to know Steve and Jane on a personal level and I was blown away when I read this incredible book! It is life changing and impacting! I look forward to making it available to my people!

Joe Cameneti, Pastor & Author
Believer's Christian Fellowship
Warren, Ohio
bcfonline.com

This is truly the best book on marriage that I have ever read to date. Rarely do you find people in the ministry that are able to be honest enough to help people in a very sincere, honest and candid manner. In this book, Steve and Jane Hutchinson provide spiritual and practical help for those who are willing to receive it. In a resource that has been written with humility, class, and the fear of the Lord. I believe you will be directed into a new season of marriage.

Antwan Smith, Pastor
Impact Christian Center
Beavercreek, Ohio
impactchristiancenter.us

Steve and Jane, in their breakthrough book *Me Tarzan, You Jane*, give everyone at every level of marital "success or stress" the nuts and bolts necessary to have a marriage that lasts a lifetime! You will love their humor, honesty and transparency that makes this a must read book for all couples desiring a marriage made in heaven that can be lived out on earth. Steve and Jane are not only outstanding marriage authors but amazing marriage and relationship speakers as well!

Dr. Paul Endrei, Pastor
Church on the Rise / Marriage Author
Cleveland, Ohio
churchontherise.net

It's a jungle out there... especially for marriages! As the Hutchinson's point out in their new book *Me Tarzan, You Jane*, the home front is often filled with hurtful separation, rampant divorce, desperate households, lonely little leaguers and cheerless cheerleaders. First Peter 3:7 says, "Husbands dwell with your wives according to knowledge." Many men possess a degree of love, but no knowledge... Jane, with a broken heart, has little positive to respond to.

But wait! There is light at the end of the tunnel... and it is not another train. From the bed to the budget, *Me Tarzan, You Jane* brings hope beyond the scope of human limitation.

As seminar leaders and presenters, Steve and Jane Hutchinson bring in-depth simple concepts and doable content to any faith-based or corporate audience. *Me Tarzan, You Jane* is forty days of proactive steps to take a good marriage to great or breath life and hope into a challenged relationship. It is an honor to recommend the Hutchinson's and their excellent book is simply outstanding.

Van Crouch, Speaker & Author
Van Crouch Communications
Wheaton, Illinois
vancrouch.com

This book is a game changer. Not only is it practical and informative, but it is real - I can relate to that.

Gary Chmielewski, President
Northern Ohio Printing, Inc.
Cleveland, Ohio
nohioprint.com

Our vision of Tarzan is one of him swinging through the jungle on a strategically positioned vine, beating his chest, roaring that distinctive, ululating yell while maintaining possession of his loincloth. Tarzan rescues Jane and in broken Jungle English tells her what she wants to hear and off they go blissfully vine-swinging together. Ah, you've gotta love American TV! But don't panic, I have good news for you.

Steve & Jane Hutchison's *Me Tarzan, You Jane* will give you the answers you need to put the jump back in your jungle and the joy back in your Jane (or Tarzan). While the marriage journey can become challenging – be encouraged, inspired, gain fresh and practical perspectives, and ready yourself to laugh, to learn, and grow together with the love of your life like you have always hoped you could... Let the willing read on!

Lynton & Judy Turkington, Pastors
Celebration Family Church
Raleigh, North Carolina
celebrationfamilychurch.com

Me Tarzan, You Jane flows from the setting of their own marriage as well as real-life experience in helping couples. This read is fun! And Steve and Jane have absolutely loaded it with quality information and insights. You can expect to see value added to your relationship beginning with Day One. Become intentional - give it 40 days. Your best marriage is yet to come!

Brian Del Turco
TrueNorth Publishing
Amherst, Ohio
truenorthpublish.com

Steve and Jane have hit the marriage nail on the head. They bring a fresh and God centered approach to breathing life into marriage. While most married couples avoid issues plaguing their marriage, Steve and Jane provide the tools and courage to face the ongoing issues couples struggle with. This book will turn your "I Do" into "I Can."

Dennis & Lori Cummins, Pastors
Experience Church
Seattle, Washington
experiencechurch.tv

Prologue

Dear Reader,

Me Tarzan, You Jane serves as a marriage manual for couples. We had 4 major goals in mind as we write this book:

- To help you deeply connect with your mate and stay connected (Discover what triggers a disconnect).

- To help you understand why your partner acts and reacts the way they do (Whenever we lack understanding we ultimately judge incorrectly).

- To help you see past your pain (It is true that hurt people, hurt people).

- To help you connect with God deeply (He is our Source of strength).

Me Tarzan, You Jane is written with 40 chapters representing 40 days. We don't believe it takes 40 days to reconnect with your partner, but we also do not believe that it is an overnight, "quick fix" process either. Nonetheless, the reconnecting process can start immediately by simply applying time-tested principles found in this book.

If you have any questions as you read this book or would like to tell us how this book has impacted your marriage, please let us know.

Contact us through our website at MeTarzanYouJane.com or email us at:

office@MeTarzanYouJane.com

It is our prayer that *Me Tarzan, You Jane* will give you an immense amount of hope, encouragement, along with the practical tools for overcoming the relationship challenges every couple faces. We want to see people healed of their relational pain and move forward with confident joy knowing that their best days are ahead.

Enjoy your journey as you experience *Me Tarzan, You Jane*! Not only will this change your marriage, but it will change you!

For your marital success,
Steve & Jane

Introduction

"Enjoy life with the woman whom you love."

~ Ecclesiastes 9:9

"I had enough!" That thought kept running through my mind. I wanted to leave but didn't believe in divorce. "This isn't what I signed up for!" We felt trapped and hopeless. "God, where are you?"

TARZAN THOUGHT...

I felt underappreciated and overworked.

Truthfully, I felt like nothing more than a paycheck. Connecting with Jane became a chore, but it wasn't like this initially. What ever happened? Did she really love me? If she did, then why did I feel at times she just didn't care?

My needs are simple, but I couldn't figure out why everything had to be such a battle even for the simplest of things... things you'd expect to be a given. I felt trapped! Was this it? Were we going to make it or end up like so many couples who just exist together? Did I miss it? Was Jane really the one I was supposed to marry? "God, where are you in all of this?"

JANE THOUGHT...

I felt as if my voice didn't matter.

How could a supposedly godly man come across so harsh at times? Ministry was tough enough. Then to deal with this? He seems to put his work and the kids before me. Honestly, at times I felt trapped. What do I do? Where do I go? I can't leave, but at times I wanted to. We just speak two completely different languages. Is this just God's goal for my life... to be miserable?

CRAZY BEGINNINGS

This is how we felt.

We struggled like so many couples do, especially early in marriage. Not only did we have problems, but our own family network was being ripped apart as well. To top things off, even our own friends seemed to ditch us. It was a lonely time. I had Jane... and Jane had me... and no one else for a season of our lives. We had to learn to get along... and fast. We were all each other had – literally.

Today, people view our marriage as one that is worth emulating, but initially this couldn't have been further from the truth. We had a whirlwind engagement and marriage but didn't receive a lick of sensible counseling. Oh, we asked the spiritual leaders in our lives, but they said we didn't need it. We stressed to them that we thought we really did, but they dismissed it and gave us some shallow advice over the course of a dinner. To our own fault, we should have sought out other counselors from outside our own network. Well... we learned the hard way, but thank God for His mercy and His grace!

"You may have a great marriage and it will get better as you read this book. You may have a lousy marriage and it will greatly improve if you apply what you learn."

This book was written out of the joys of marriage as well as the pain of marriage. Regardless of how painful a past you and your mate have had up to this point, for most people, the joys eventually outweigh the pain.

The pain associated with relational problems often becomes the focal point for many negating the wonderful times they have had together. The biggest initial problem with marital counseling is getting people to see past their pain. Unfortunately, too many people remain stuck in painful events that may have happened years ago. That's why forgiveness is not optional.

Even spiritual people can struggle in their marriage. Take John Wesley, for instance, the father of Methodism. At age 48, Wesley married a wealthy widow by the name of Molly Vazeille and he adopted her four children. This was the beginning of a "30 year war" for the couple.

As Pastor Mark Discroll points out:

"In the final correspondence between the two, John wrote, 'I think it right to tell you in my mind once for all without either anger or bitterness... if you were to live

a thousand years, you could not undo the mischief that you have done.'"

Wow! Talk about pain!

Many couples are living in pain because they are living disconnected and neglected from their spouse. Psychologists have observed that one of the greatest pains we will ever experience is rejection and pain from those who are supposed to love us.

When people tell me they are struggling financially, vocationally, relationally or in any other area of their life, I ask them what book are they reading or what class are they attending that deals directly with the area in question.

That is why we are thrilled that you picked up this book and decided to glean from it. You may have a great marriage and it will get better as you read this book. You may have a lousy marriage and it will greatly improve if you apply what you learn.

Someone once said, "No matter what a person's past may have been, his future is spotless." Don't allow the pain of the past to dictate the future of your marriage. Today is a new day! Today is the first day of the rest of your life. God's mercies are new every single morning. He is truly faithful, and if you rely upon His strength, your future is bright! It is our deep desire that this book will help you see past the pain and connect with your mate in a way you never thought was possible.

No one has ever had a great marriage without overcoming great problems. So be encouraged - your best days are ahead!

"You're not finished when you're defeated;
you're finished when you quit!"
~ Van Crouch

"The brightest future will always be based on a forgotten past;
you can't go on well in life until you let go of your
past failures and heartaches."
~ Unknown

The Jungle of Love & Marriage

~ The Initial Connection ~

Jane and her Tarzan, Steve, tied the knot
on June 24, 1995

CHAPTER 1

It's a Jungle Out There

"Before marriage will make you happy, it will make you grow up."

~ Jimmy Evans

FOUR YEAR-OLD SUSIE had just been told the story of Snow White for the first time. She could hardly wait to get home from nursery school to tell her mommy. With wide-eyed excitement she retold the fairy tale to her mother that afternoon. After relating how Prince Charming had arrived on his white horse and kissed Snow White back to life, Suzie asked loudly, "And do you know what happened after that?" "Yes," said her mom, "they lived happily ever after."

"No," she said with a frown, "they got married!"

Unfortunately, marriage has been getting a bad rap. Recently I just read that four out of ten Americans say that marriage is obsolete.[1] And another 93% of Americans say they want a stable marriage, but only 50% said it is even possible.

Wow! That means only half of all people have absolutely no hope for a happy marriage that will last a lifetime. We want to give couples hope that their marriage can get better and better through time. No matter how difficult your marriage may be or how hurt and disappointed you have been, there is still hope for you.

It has been said that marriage is made in heaven, but so is thunder and lightning. Marriage may be made in heaven but we have to live it out on earth.

When I got married to my Jane in 1995, we were both in our mid-twenties, reasonably mature, people of faith; both of us were well-educated, prepared for our careers, but ill-prepared for marriage.

I heard something recently that out of 150 top executives from major corporations, only one person in the entire group had any training for marriage and it was for only thirty minutes.

When I met Jane I was already pastoring a small church as a single person. Imagine that! When we looked for counseling from an older pastoral couple in our local region (we were in a denominational church at the time), they looked at us during our first counseling session and said, "Look, you're in ministry and you already know all you need to know about marriage - after all, you marry people all of the time."

The day I proposed to Jane on a TWA flight

Jane and I were stunned.

We tried to go to others but they basically said the same thing. Needless to say, we were ill-prepared for one of the biggest decisions of our life. Dr. Dobbins said, "The law requires more training to drive an automobile than is required to choose a mate..."[2]

Then to our amazement we realized after we said "I do," that we really "didn't" know what we were doing. Not only were we getting married, but also we had to deal with a bunch of issues ranging from our vastly different backgrounds, past relationship issues, family issues, balancing marriage and ministry, unspoken and unmet expectations, and how to fight fairly and establishing boundaries just to name a few.

I must admit it was tough. To top things off, we had kids early in our marriage, and yes, some in-law issues too. Welcome to the jungle called marriage. At times we both felt trapped. It looked like a stalemate. What do we do? We could divorce, but what about the kids and our commitment to God?

So, if you haven't figured it out, I am Tarzan (or at least I like to think so) and my wife really is Jane. Without a doubt we knew God put the two of us together. It was so amazing, and no one doubted it ... except maybe a few ex-boyfriends or girlfriends. As we look back, it seemed like we were thrown together and expected to figure out the details later.

It reminds me of a John Wayne western I once watched. In the scene there was a young boy who didn't know how to swim and so John Wayne asked, "So kid, wanna learn how to swim?" "Sure, Mister," the boy replied. The next scene is the gruff cowboy picking up the naïve boy and tossing him in a lake. As the kid is panicking and almost drowning, John Wayne yells out, "Unless you plan on drowning boy, you'd better start flapping your arms in front of you like a dog."

Jane and I felt like that kid; we didn't know if we would sink or swim. Believe me, we needed lots of coaching along the way from key people to keep us from sinking. We faced some tough times, but we also knew divorce wasn't an option. So we figured we'd stay together, but we just couldn't figure out how. The late Ruth Graham (Evangelist Billy Graham's wife) once was asked if she ever thought about divorce. She replied, "Divorce? Never! Murder? Several times!" I think most people can relate. Spouse's have a way of pushing us to our limits.

> *"When your marriage isn't right, your life isn't right.*
> *No amount of 'success' in life can compensate*
> *for a failure at home."*

Marriage is like flies on a screen; some are waiting to get in and some are waiting to get out. There are more lonely and frustrated married couples than ever! Unbelievably, over 50% of first time marriages end in divorce. And you'd think it gets better the second time around but it does not. Around 75% of second marriages are split apart by divorce. Marriage is either a sweet taste of heaven or as bitter as eating brussels sprouts without any seasoning. Most marriages are in big trouble. As a matter of fact, in America marriages last on average 8 years.[3] Amazing! I think it's time to change that statistic.

It didn't take me long in life to realize that a happy marriage means a happy life and an unhappy marriage means an unhappy life. I can't think of many things worse than being stuck in a bad marriage; that's why one of the biggest decisions you'll ever make in life is choosing the right person to marry. Marriage has been a foundation for every society. Although many are trying to redefine marriage, it is what it is and what it always has been – one man and one woman committing to live life in harmony with each other until death do us part.

The fact is many people who are married are miserable or just getting by. The pressures of life, broken expectations, fatigue and infidelity are the ruin of many marriages. Some couples merely exist together hoping for a better day.

When your marriage isn't right, your life isn't right. A poor marriage affects the very core of who you are and will affect your job and your work performance, the way you relate to your kids, your health, and your overall mindset. No amount of "success" in life can compensate for a failure at home.

We must prioritize our marriage and family because the very fabric and well-being of our society depends upon it. We cannot look to the White House to fix all of our problems because they are inept and do not qualify to fix our marriage and our family relationships. We cannot blame our parents or anyone any longer for the state of our relationship. It is time to take responsibility and do something about it.

CONNECTING POINTS

- Do you believe it is possible to have a stable marriage? If not, what is your reason?

- Are you willing to try once again (no matter how many times you have been hurt or have failed trying) and fight for your marriage?

- Will you commit to reading this book (together if possible) in its entirety?

TARZAN & JANE'S FUN FACT!

The average age men marry for the first time is 28.4... For women, it's 26.5.

Source: US Census Bureau, 2009

CHAPTER 2

The Honeymoon Is Over

"The honeymoon is a vacation just before a man gets a new boss."

~ Unknown

A WOMAN WAS WALKING in the street when she heard a voice, "Stop! Stand still! If you take one more step, a brick will fall down on your head and kill you." The woman stopped and a big brick fell right in front of her. The woman was astonished. She continued to walk until she came to a crosswalk. Once again the voice shouted, "Stop! Stand still! If you take one more step a car will run you over and you will die." The woman did as she was instructed and a car came careening around the corner, barely missing her. The woman asked, "Who are you?" "I am your guardian angel," the voice answered. "Oh yeah?" the woman asked. "And where were you when I got married?"

OUR INCREDIBLE BEGINNING

I asked the most beautiful woman in the world if she would marry me and she said "no!" So I asked the most intelligent woman in the world if she would marry me and she said "no." So I decided to ask the most spiritual woman in the world if she would marry me and she said "no." Then finally I asked Jane if she would marry me and she said, "Yes, I don't have the heart to tell you 'no' for the fourth time."

Thankfully, I only had to ask Jane to marry me one time. I proposed to Jane sitting on a TWA airplane which was heading from Saint Louis to Cleveland. I was disguised wearing grungy jeans and a leather jacket. I also grew a beard, wore a long, brown-haired wig my mom had since the 60s, and finished my fashion statement with a funky pair of thick safety glasses. The flight attendants and ticketing agents thought I was crazy, but they loved it and were most helpful assisting me pull off my engagement plan.

Honestly, I looked more like the guy on Wayne's World than someone getting ready to make one of life's most serious, life-altering decisions. Jane and others really got a kick out of my creative proposal. The pilot even announced our engagement over the speaker and sent us to first class with a bottle of champagne (even though I'm not a drinker). We had so much fun.

Ruth Graham was once asked if she ever thought about divorce. She replied, "Divorce? Never! Murder? Several times."

Unbeknownst to us, both of our families surprised us as we walked out of the airport and sprayed us with gobs of silly string. It was crazy. There was even a reporter from the local news station who interviewed us and aired our story on the local news.

We started off with a bang, like a fairytale. Life was good!

I finally met the woman of my dreams. Everything was going without a hitch. But soon, this fairytale was turning into a nightmare and a storm was brewing. It was time to deal with reality. Little did we realize what we had to endure. It was tough, it was painful, but with God's grace we made it!

Like us, no matter what you are dealing with, you can overcome. The catch is this: how much humility will you be willing to demonstrate? Marriage is all about adjusting, growing and learning. Arrogance will destroy everything it contacts. Life may have dealt you a brutal blow, but it's not a fatal blow unless you so choose.

How Did I Ever Get Into This Mess?

No one goes into marriage expecting to disconnect from their life-long mate, or worse, fail and divorce.

Expectation about love and marriage can have a powerful impact on relationships. We go into marriage with lofty ideals and unrealistic expectations. Broken expectations can leave a person hurt, alone and frustrated. It's been said, "If love is blind, then marriage is an eye-opener."

Henry Ford once said, "Coming together is easy; keeping together is progress; working together is success." Marriage is the ultimate team sport and two are needed to cooperate at every level in order to ensure success. In marriage, two become one, but the question is, "which one?" That's often where the battle occurs... the battle of wills, demanding our own way and maintaining our individualism. Marriage is designed to blend two lives into one without ever losing your uniqueness.

Hollywood has lied to us. Most parents and counselors have failed to prepare us. We've received bad advice from well-intentioned friends and now we're in a mess. So what do we do? Just throw in the towel and walk away? No! Running is never the answer in most cases.

On their own, all relationships will disconnect and deteriorate unless we become aware of the relational disconnect triggers and become proactive in our marital relationship. Just like muscles, they atrophy in a short amount of time unless they are exercised. The same is true in your marriage. We must exercise by loving our spouse as they desire to be loved.

So here's what you can do before we get started. Decide today that you will do the following:

THREE THINGS TO COMMIT TO NOW!

Before going on, you must commit to these three steps in order to find lasting marital success. PLEASE do not skip over this part.

1)   Commit to RESPONSIBILITY

   • Read this book in its entirety (Even the parts you don't like).

   • Decide right now that you are going to do all that is in your power to fight for your marriage.

   • Decide to do the right thing even if your partner doesn't.

2)   Commit to HUMILITY

   • Acknowledge your part in any marital mess.

   • Be teachable, honest and vulnerable.

   • Begin to esteem your partner higher than yourself.

3)   Commit to MATURITY

- Commit to changing yourself and doing the right things regardless of what your spouse does or doesn't do. We realize that this can be very difficult, but never allow your partner's poor behavior to excuse you from doing the right thing.

- Apply the principles of this book immediately as you learn them and commit to serving your spouse unselfishly.

- Be the best you... you can ever be!

Are you honestly willing to commit 100% to these three areas? If so, your chances of connecting with your partner will skyrocket! If you harden your heart, you are doomed.

Will You Pray This Prayer Of Hope?

Dear Heavenly Father, I know I cannot be that husband or wife you designed me to be without your strength working in me. Help me right now to overcome every hurt and failure. I repent of my sins and ask your Son Jesus to come into my life and help me! With Your help, God, I commit to responsibility, humility and personal maturity. I ask you to help soften my heart, heal my marriage, and help me to dream again. In Your name. Amen!

TARZAN & JANE'S FUN FACT!

Women are more likely to talk to other women when they have a problem or need to make a decision. Men keep their problems to themselves and don't see the point in sharing personal issues.

Source: Simma Lieberman Associates

Change Is Coming
To The Jungle

~ Preparing to Reconnect ~

Tarzan and Jane

CHAPTER 3

Reconnecting You... To You!

"But let a man examine himself..."

~ 1 Corinthians 11:28

MARRIAGE HAS BEEN DESCRIBED as a three-ring circus. First there is the engagement ring ... then the wedding ring ... and finally, the suffering. Unfortunately, some-times the suffering comes from our own stubbornness and immaturity. That's when marriage goes from being an ideal to an ordeal. Then some start looking for a new deal.

MOVING FORWARD

Your journey towards a great marriage does not start with your mate, it starts with you![4] You cannot control your partner but you can control you. That means your emotions and words must be brought into control. Your partner's poor behavior and attitude is no excuse to justify yours. You must have the courage to face the reality of who you are. You can never change something you are unable to identify or acknowledge; you cannot change what you refuse to confront.

If you fail to acknowledge the problem, you are bound to repeat it. From this point on you must make a bold commitment to no longer justify your negative actions and attitudes. You must recognize how you have contaminated your relationship. It is vital that you become aware of you. You must begin with a strong dose of self-awareness. This is not a time to point the finger at your spouse and say what a screw-up s/he has been, but a time to look within to see how you can change. As my friend Dennis Cummins says, "You don't need a divorce, just divorce the way you've been doing marriage."

Being True To You

Let's get real. At this point in your marriage what you've been doing may not be working at all. It is time to change the world in which you live. I am not suggesting changing your spouse or even relocating. Out of frustration and hurt, people often give up on things that were near and dear to their heart. Have you given up on your marriage? Your dreams? Your purpose in life? Your standards and convictions?

Dysfunction occurs when we depart from what we know is true and foundational. Your marriage won't work right if you're not working right. If you want your partner to change then you begin to change. The truth is he or she isn't the only one who needs to change.

I can't tell you how many marriage counseling appointments we conducted where the whole time the couple wants to blame their vacuous behavior on the other, like two children playing the blame game. It was like watching a tennis match going back and forth with each accusation becoming more and more poignant. The truth is we all have a propensity to play the blame game. Very often we are accusing our spouse of the exact same thing we are doing.

Studies have shown that a single negative thought can rerun in a person's mind 600 times in one day.

You may be living in a mess because you are no longer true to you. You have settled and compromised and reduced your marriage to something less than excellent. You tolerated behavior and attitudes in you, then justified them because your spouse doesn't seem to be holding their end of the bargain. You may have also enabled your spouse's negative behavior through passive-aggressive behavior. Instead of being tactfully honest, you may have acquiesced to things without communicating how you really feel.

It may be time to tactfully but assertively let your spouse know that you deserve to be treated with respect. At the same time, your spouse also deserves to know that they deserve equal respect and treatment. When you assertively act on a whole new level, you will notice your partner and even those around you relate to you differently.[5] It is time to relate to your spouse from a position of strength and not weakness.[6] To do this you must commit to change... real change.

Stagnancy in relationships is dangerous. I love how Francois Fenelon puts it,

"There is nothing that is more dangerous to your own salvation, more unworthy of God and more harmful to your own happiness than that you should be content to remain as you are."

Counselor Dr. Richard Dobbins believes,

"Until the pain of remaining the same hurts more than the pain of change, people usually remain the same."

Healthy change is necessary to being true to yourself and to reconnect you with you!

"But my spouse won't change!" Maybe not, but you can. Your change just might inspire your partner to change. I can almost guarantee you this: Your spouse will feel rather foolish seeing you full of zest, living in confidence while they are wallowing in self-pity and sulking in bitterness. Let the change start with you.

So, here are some quick points on how to facilitate change in your life.

CHANGE YOUR MIND

The word "repent" means to change your mind, think differently, and reconsider.

You may need to change your mind on certain behaviors and attitudes you have been carrying and quit justifying them. You must remember that your marriage problems are not 100% your partner's fault. Are you justifying your sour attitude? Are you justifying your self-centered reasons for a divorce? Have you resolved in your heart to live a separate life from your spouse? Have you become a pop-in-jay where no one is going to tell you anything anymore? Has vilifying your mate become your favorite pastime? It is time to get real with yourself. That's what repentance is all about.

Repentance means confessing before God and your mate your selfish behavior, sour attitudes and hidden agendas. This involves a great deal of humility and brokenness on your part. This is the starting point for true reconciliation. Repentance will soften your heart and have a positive effect on your partner as well. No amount of counseling will change your heart, only repentance can (Revelation 2:4, James 5:16).

Change Your Diet

You must change what you've been feeding on. It may be bad advice from others. You certainly wouldn't want to go to Hollywood for marital advice. It may be wrong thoughts you've been dwelling on all day or poor reading material. According to a psychological study, one negative thought reruns in a person's mind on average 600 times in one day. People become what they dwell on. Your whole mood and attitude can change based on what you are feeding your mind (Romans 12:2, 2 Corinthians 10:3-5).

Change Your Friends If Necessary

Yes, you may need to change some of your friends.

I have realized over the years that a vast majority of people felt pressure from their friends to get out of a relationship. I remember one lady who befriended another woman who was going through a nasty divorce and was part of what I call the "I Hate Men Club." It didn't take long for this lady to pick up the same sour attitude and the next thing you know she's divorcing her husband, with the encouragement from her bitter friend.

Always be careful what counsel you receive and from whom. Remember, poor relationships can be fatal. "Bad company corrupts good behavior" (1 Corinthians 15:33). Just because someone is interesting doesn't make them a candidate to be a good friend. There may be no greater relational gaffe than surrounding yourself with the wrong company. What does your coterie look like? No human relationship is more valuable than the one you have with your mate (Psalm 1, Proverbs 13:20).

Change Your Words

Change the way you speak. Your words are powerful! (Proverbs 18:21).

You can change the whole course of your life just by changing the way you speak... especially to your partner (James 3). Your words are so powerful that they can create an atmosphere in your home and marriage. What kind of atmosphere? Well, that depends upon you. Some of us would have been fired from our jobs if we spoke to our boss in the same tone as we addressed our spouse. Words can bring healing or further the schism between you and your mate.

CHANGE YOUR ROUTINE

When is the last time you did something for the first time? It has been said that a rut is nothing more than a grave with the walls knocked out. Do something spontaneous with your partner. Refuse to live in the status quo day after day. By the way, the root meaning of status quo literally means "for the mess we're in."

Refuse to leave your marriage in a mess. Changing your habits has a way of motivating us to go to new levels in life. Do something fun and spontaneous with your spouse.

CHANGE THE WAY YOU RELATE TO YOUR CREATOR

I would be remiss if I failed to mention this last point. God is a real Being who wants to help you throughout life. When God is respected, positive change occurs. The Bible tells us that people do not change because the fear (respect) of the Lord is missing in their life (Psalm 55:19). When God is first place in your life, it facilitates change; it keeps you from remaining stagnant. Make no mistake, God created marriage and He knows how to fix it and give you the wisdom to maintain it. Without God, success in marriage is quite difficult, if not impossible.

Conference speaker Joyce Meyer, in one of her conferences pointed out that, "The most mature person will do the right thing first." So here's my question to you: "Are you willing to go first and be the catalyst of change?" I think you and your marriage deserve it!

"Therefore take heed to your spirit, and let none deal treacherously with the wife of his youth." ~ Malachi 2:15 NKJV

CONNECTING POINTS

- Has my spouse repeatedly mentioned something that I need to change? What is it?

- Can you Identify three bad habits you've had for more than two years?

- What percentage of the problem is attributed to you? Your spouse? Your parents? Your career?

- What is something I need to change now?

- What is something my spouse needs to change now?

TARZAN & JANE'S FUN FACT!

Men think it's sexy when their wife has an occasional blonde moment... Women think it is sexy when their husband does housework.

CHAPTER 4

Problem Number One: You!

"Success in marriage does not come merely through finding the right mate, but through being the right mate."

~ Barnett R. Brickner

M Y SISTER WENT TO THE DEPARTMENT STORE to check out the bridal registry of our niece whose wedding was coming up soon. When my sister returned from the store, she tossed the gift list on a table and declared, "I think she's too young to get married." "Why do you say that?" I asked. "Because," she said, "they registered for Nintendo games."

WHERE DID I GO WRONG?

Well, to start with, you didn't get in this mess all by yourself, you had some help. The odds are stacked against you. Society at large is working against your marital success.

For many of you, your parents, with all due respect, were of no help at all. They may have lived in the same house together, but they may not have had much of a marriage. Of course statistically the majority of your parents ended their marriage in an ugly divorce. Your home life growing up may have been filled with turmoil, dysfunctional behaviors, sour attitudes, verbal or physical abuse, and God only knows what else.

The fact is most of us were never taught how to be successful in relationships or how to handle our emotions. We never had a class on how to choose the right partner for life or even who qualifies to be our mate. No one ever told us that your success in life is largely determined by how well we relate with people.

No one has ever entered marriage with the intention of ending it or getting their spouse so angry that they left you. Either way, the stats on divorce are staggering and stubbornly refuse to go below 50%. Whatever we've been doing as a society isn't working. Enough is enough!

Take Responsibility

Our perspective can become like tunnel vision. We become so focused on our own hurts, our own needs, and our own pursuits, that we become negligent and irresponsible with our spouse. At the same time we fail to realize how difficult we are to live with too.

The truth is not easy to hear, that's for sure. You must be willing to be brutally honest with yourself and humble enough to admit your shortcomings. You have to refuse the temptation to get defensive and fall into denial and blame your partner for all the problems you are having as a couple.

"Just because your spouse did something that caused anger in you doesn't mean the spouse caused the anger."
~ Jimmy Evans

When you see yourself as others see you [especially as your partner sees you], you are well on your way to connecting.[7] If your marriage has morphed into a stagnant stalemate, then it's time to do something about you.

You must realize how you have been sabotaging your relationship. You must accept responsibility for your part in the problem. It takes two to tango. No one creates a relationship mess all by themselves. The road to your marital recovery does not start with your partner, it starts with you! You must get yourself into a place of wholeness and only then can you be an asset instead of a liability in your marriage. You must be more concerned about your own flaws than your partner's.

When you learn to love your spouse as yourself, you position yourself for successful relationships and a more peaceful life. When you consistently live in this posture you not only energize yourself, but you have the ability to inspire those around you. You will notice that people, including your spouse, will relate to you on a whole new level. You cannot give what you do not possess. If you lack self-love, you won't be able to give real love in return.

Notice the ancient Scripture passage in Matthew 22:39: "Love your neighbor AS YOURSELF" [emphasis mine]. You must begin loving others by loving yourself in a healthy way without becoming narcissistic.

> "God designed marriage so that
> it wouldn't work for selfish people."

The changes in you will without a doubt spark changes in your spouse. You must decide right now that your spouse's wrong behavior will not dictate or promote wrong behavior in you. You are the "master" of your world and no one else. You must take charge of your life and quit making excuses for your inappropriate behavior or a bad attitude. Dr. Phil McGraw insists:

> "You cannot have a bad relationship unless your lifestyle is characterized by stress, pressure, distraction, and a harried and chaotic existence. Moreover, if you are living in a dysfunctional relationship with another person, it's because you have been dysfunctional yourself... A bad relationship cannot exist if it is not fed and nurtured in some way."[8]

It is not up to your mate to make you a better person; that is up to you. It is your choice no matter what you are going through. Townsend and McCloud remind us all, "We are responsible to each other, but not for each other... When we do loving responsible things, people withdraw from us. When we are unloving or irresponsible, people withdraw from us."[9] We must act responsibly even when our spouse isn't. You cannot control what they do. Rabbi Shalom Arush aptly observes:

> "Every married individual should feel that he or she alone bears responsibility for the peace in the home. Both partners in the marital union must learn their respective responsibilities and obligations and do their utmost to fulfill them. Neither should police the other; a person that's preoccupied with finding fault in someone else fails to see his or her own faults."[10]

I believe wholeheartedly that by the time you finish this book you will inspire your partner's actions and attitudes beyond your wildest dreams.

HOW DID I GET HERE ANYHOW!

Have you ever felt so frustrated, overwhelmed and hopeless that there seemed to be no way out? If you believe marriage is for a lifetime, but you feel like getting out because your spouse doesn't show any signs of changing, yet you know this would violate your core beliefs and be devastating to your kids - this is known as feeling trapped.

How can two people who were madly in love, who used to spend half the night talking on the phone, who would do anything just to spend some quiet time alone, now drift miles apart, full of resentment, seething anger, and wanting out?

The bottom line is this: if you want to see change in your relationship then you must start by changing yourself. Your relationship didn't go south all by its self. You actually helped nurture the problem like a weed that has grown out of control. Each one of us is culpable to some degree. Each one of us is naturally selfish and needs to learn to live beyond ourselves. If we don't our marriage is doomed. God designed marriage so that it wouldn't work for selfish people.

Often we have learned to function in our dysfunction. Our bad thinking, our selfishly sour attitudes and infectious wounds from the past have created a world of deception we've learned to function in. You never dreamed of this on your wedding day but here you are nonetheless. You must deal with reality.

If you want to reconnect with your partner then you need to reconnect with yourself – your core values, inner convictions, and self-respect. The truth is, you most likely have compromised and you've learned to live with it.

Compromise comes when we accept what we do not believe because we refuse to fight for what we do believe. Life can have a way of wearing us down, and if we're not careful, we will learn to function in our dysfunction. Phil Munsey once said, "Tolerance of compromise and complacency is accepting defeat in slow motion!" We can become so familiar with our problem that we simply adjust our life and accept it without a fight. Fight for your marriage... I truly believe the best is yet to come! Don't give up!

> *"Search me, O God, and know my heart; Try me, and know my anxieties.*
> *And see if there is any wicked way in me, and lead me in the way everlasting."*
> ~ *Psalm 139:23-24 NKJV*

> *"But let a man examine himself..."* ~ *1 Corinthians 11:28 NKJV*

Truthfully, most of your marriage problems may have little to do with your partner. If truth be told, you may have been deeply damaged by your dysfunctional upbringing, past relationships, abusive parents, poor thinking patterns, and sabotaging behavior.

Your partner just may be the recipient of your hurtful and unreasonable behavior and is suffering in silence, unwilling to openly discuss with you out of fear of you hurling insults and withholding more of your soul. You may be pointing the finger at your spouse, but you are merely projecting the exact same things you are accusing them of doing. It's time to look in the mirror and ask yourself, "How have I been hurting my spouse and how can I change?"

"You must become more deeply concerned about your own issues than our spouse's... When we do loving, responsible things, people draw close to us. When we are unloving or irresponsible, people withdraw from us." ~ John Townsend & Henry Cloud

CONNECTING POINTS

- Have I been easy to live with? If not, explain why.

- Have I brought some ugly baggage into this marriage?

- How have I sabotaged my relationship?

- How have my parents affected the way I relate to my spouse?

- How has my ex-spouse or ex-lovers influenced the way I treat my spouse?

TARZAN & JANE'S FUN FACT!

Men are attracted to a woman's positive outlook, cheerful disposition, and beautiful smile... Women are attracted to a man's confidence, humor, ambition and good hygiene.

Source: Multiple Surveys

CHAPTER 5

The Beauty of a Teachable Spirit

"If you are teachable, you are reachable."

THERE IS A STORY OF A MAN who was driving down the freeway and his wife called him on his cell phone. She said, "Henry, be careful, be very careful. I just saw on the news that there is some crazy man driving down I-271 going in the wrong direction." Henry replied, "Not just one, Henrietta, there are hundreds of them driving the wrong way."

Being teachable is essential to having a solid marriage. When it comes to self-revelation and self-awareness, our spouse will teach us more about ourselves than anyone else. Sometimes our spouse knows us better than we do.[11] We all have blind spots that must be addressed. Marriage has a way of surfacing our weaknesses and blind spots. Most relationships we have are basically pretty shallow even if we say otherwise. A true friend is one whom you can share honest feelings without jeopardizing the relationship. Your spouse ought to be your best friend.

We all possess weaknesses and blind spots, but they often are noticed by everyone but ourselves. Your spouse is divinely positioned to help you become a better person... that is if you can take the heat of constructive criticism.

No one likes to be corrected. But somehow we must overcome our pride and look objectively at ourselves. We all come into marriage with baggage. Some of that "baggage" is our family background. We may have adopted poor habits, racist attitudes, unhealthy thinking patterns, quirky mannerisms, harsh tones, and sometimes, bizarre viewpoints that need to be adjusted or changed altogether. The atmosphere you grew up in has given you a certain bent that is apparent to everyone else, but often unnoticed by you.

We all start off in life at the same point... ignorant and clueless! John Wooden said, "Everything we know we learned from someone else." Only the truly teachable will continually aspire to new levels.

> *"You cannot help anybody who thinks you are their problem."*
> *~ Jimmy Evans*

So many times I listened to all of the professional pundits but neglected my wife's voice. She wisely observed poor decisions I was making even though the "experts" said otherwise. It is painful for a spouse to witness their mate ignoring glaring idiosyncrasies that need to be addressed. After enough failure, I decided to listen up and look within. This is having a teachable spirit!

CHARACTERISTICS OF AN UN-TEACHABLE PERSON[12]

THEY HAVE CHRONIC FAILURE

Areas we succeed in are areas we've been teachable. Now, if you insist on doing something you are not gifted or trained for, it may be a result of an un-teachable spirit. If you are on the same level as you were 5 or 10 years ago, it may be due to the lack of growth which often indicates you've stopped learning. If you stop learning, you'll stop growing.

If you continually repeat the same mistake it shows you are not learning from it. John Maxwell insists that we should "Never pay the price twice for the same mistake."

"As a dog returns to its vomit, so a fool repeats his folly." ~ Proverbs 26:11

THEY ARE ARGUMENTATIVE AND DEFENSIVE

I (Steve) worked with someone where everything turned into a big issue. She was very intelligent and a hard worker, but teachable she was not. It had to be her way or no way. If it wasn't her idea it was a bad idea. I have encountered people who will take the opposing view, even if they didn't agree with it, just to be difficult. This person would get defensive at anything I didn't agree with her on. Needless to say, this individual remained stagnant and in an immature state.

Defensiveness is often the first sign of denial. Ask yourself: Why do I get angry and defensive? Often it is because people are afraid to look within and take an inventory of themselves.

Some are so unteachable that they never take advice, change or accept truth. It has been said that "Fools never change even in the presence of truth." A fool is defined as one who is defiant, stubborn and rebellious.

Here are some questions you must honestly ask yourself:

- How do you respond to correction?

- Does correction put a stain on the relationship?

- Does correction, even if you disagree with it, end the relationship?

"Whoever corrects a mocker invites insult; whoever rebukes a wicked man incurs abuse. Do not rebuke a mocker or he will hate you; rebuke a wise man and he will love you. Instruct a wise man and he will be wiser still; teach a righteous man and he will add to his learning." ~ Proverbs 9:7-9

"The foolish woman is loud; she is ignorant and knows nothing." ~ Proverbs 9:13

It's hard to live with a person that never admits they are wrong.

Early in our marriage, it was always Jane's fault and I had to win every argument. I was like some super-lawyer that had to find a loophole in every argument until I finally got what I wanted and "win" the argument. The times I thought I won, I actually lost. It's hard to live with a person you cannot talk to and debate in a healthy way. Thankfully, I learned a few things since then.

THEY ARE ISOLATED AND WITHDRAWN (AN INDEPENDENT SPIRIT)

People who believe they can survive on their own are truly self-deceived. We all need people! We cannot do life alone. Many people go through life without one single close friend.

The value of mentors in our lives can save us from needless mistakes. I knew a pastor who had no affiliations, no mentors, did no networking with other pastors or business leaders; he was all alone. The result? His ministry failed very quickly.

Another tactic an unteachable person may use is to claim that "God told them" to do such-n-such. Now I adhere to the belief that God speaks to His people even to this day in a variety of forms. However, when people claim God told them things that contradict His Word and His standards, then it clearly was not God talking. An unteachable person will sidestep wise counsel, pursue his own means and try to come across more spiritual than they actually are.

"The one who lives alone is self-indulgent, showing contempt for all who have sound judgment. A fool takes no pleasure in understanding, but only in expressing personal opinion". ~ Proverbs 18:1-2 (NRSV)

THEY LOVE TO PLAY THE BLAME GAME

Jimmy Evans insists, "You cannot help anybody who thinks you are their problem." It is easy to blame others for the reason you are going through what you are going through. Instead of looking in the mirror, this person loves to play the blame game. This is a way of justifying oneself and refusing to change or grow.

Adam did this when he ate of the forbidden fruit in the Garden of Eden. Sure, his wife took the initiative and coaxed him into disobeying God, but the fact remains, Adam chose to do this. Adam, when confronted by God, did what all of us have done at some point... blame our spouse. Adam refused to take responsibility for his own actions.

> *"If we desire real change, then we are going to have to take all the necessary steps to learn."*

The man said, *"The woman whom you gave to be with me, she gave me fruit from the tree, and I ate." ~ Genesis 3:12 (NRSV)*

In reality, Adam wasn't just blaming Eve, but God as well: "The woman YOU gave me..." Blaming is another tactic people use to get the focus off of themselves and onto others.

THEY SURROUND THEMSELVES ONLY WITH THOSE WHO AGREE 100% WITH THEM

Take an assessment of the people with which you have surrounded yourself. What are they like? Do they have marriages and lives you aspire to? Do they ever challenge you? Would you consider yourself the smartest one of the pack? Do they inspire you to live at a higher level?

If these are in question, you may want to enlarge your circle of friends. The wrong group of friends will lead you down the wrong path. It happens slowly and subtly, but it happens nonetheless. You begin to pick up their values, their way of thinking, and yes, their nasty habits as well.

I knew a young man who would leave a church every time he received counsel with which he disagreed. Then he would return once he made his predetermined decision. He suffered in marriage, career, and reputation because of his poor decision making. He would spurn wise counsel and go to his peers who lacked wisdom, credibility and life experience.

Real friends won't tell you what you want to hear and a wise person is not threatened by differing opinions. There are people who search for a counselor who will tell them what they want to hear and won't be content until they find it.

"But Rehoboam rejected the advice the elders gave him and consulted the young men who had grown up with him and were serving him." ~ 2 Chronicles 10:8 (NKJV)

"He who walks with the wise grows wise, but a companion of fools suffers harm." ~ Proverbs 13:20 (NKJV)

Get around people who can challenge you to go to the next level.

THEY NEVER SEEM TO "GET IT"

John Maxwell says, "All the good advice in the world won't help you if you don't have a teachable spirit."[13] Every boss, coach, pastor, manager will have a team member who never gets past first base. In other words, they never seem to learn the basics.

You can train them, remind them, re-train them, model to them, try numerous approaches, and still, they never get it. Sometimes it can be boiled down to a problem with how things are being communicated by the trainer. But some will never "get it" even if you have excellent communication and training simply because they choose not to. They may have a differing agenda and certainly an unteachable spirit.

"Just because someone is in pain doesn't necessarily mean something bad is happening." ~ John Townsend & Henry Cloud

Pride has a blinding effect (Obadiah 1:3) and keeps us from seeing who we really are. Pride also has a way of excusing ourselves and rationalizing our laziness and unwillingness to change. If we desire real change, then we are going to have to take all the necessary steps to learn. Based on years of counseling and marital intervention, marriage expert Jimmy Evans attests:

"In marriage counseling, I never had a problem helping a couple who were willing to learn. As I gave instruction to a couple and give them books to read and assignments to do between our sessions, I never once have had a problem with those who really studied and applied themselves. However, in every single case of a failed marriage, being too proud or too lazy to learn was the major contributor." [14]

GO BEYOND STUCK

Jesus said a lack of understanding can come from a hardened heart (Mark 6:52). A hardened heart keeps people from understanding and seeing past their pain and weakness. This lack of understanding keeps people stuck at a level and never goes beyond what they were designed for.

Remember this final point: If you are teachable, you are reachable.

CONNECTING POINTS

- In what area(s) have you demonstrated an unteachable spirit?

- Are you open towards your spouse's input?

- Describe those closest to you. Do they ever challenge you? Do they go along with everything you say even if it violates commonsense or biblical values?

- Who do you tend to blame when things go awry?

TARZAN & JANE'S FUN FACT!

There is a chemical that is released in men whenever someone is abrupt with them and makes them more aggressive.

Source: Steven Stosny & Patricia Love

THE TEACHABILITY TEST: HOW TEACHABLE ARE YOU?

1. I am an agreeable person (as opposed to being argumentative and defensive).

2. I am able to receive correction.

3. I connect with others (instead of isolate myself or withdraw) during difficult times.

4. I tend to take responsibility for my actions without blaming others.

5. I can handle disagreements without feeling threatened.

6. I have someone who can speak into my life directly without becoming offended with them.

7. I seem to learn from my past mistakes.

8. I usually aologize rather easily.

9. I go to people who will speak honestly and truthfully to me.

10. I listen intently to those in authority without "talking over" them.

11. Am I open to other people's ideas?[15]

12. Do I listen more than I speak?[16]

13. Am I open to changing my opinion based on new information?[17]

14. Do I readily admit when I am wrong?[18]

15. Do I observe before acting on a situation?[19]

16. Do I ask questions?[20]

17. Am I willing to ask a question that will expose my ignorance?[21]

18. Am I open to doing things in a way I haven't done before?[22]

19. Am I willing to ask for directions?[23]

20. Do I act defensive when criticized, or do I listen openly for the truth?[24]

SCORING: HOW MANY "NO'S" DID YOU ANSWER?

0-2	You have a teachable spirit
3-5	You have some blind spots
6-10	You are a difficult person to work with
11+	You are a stubborn as an old goat

Sabotage In The Jungle

~ Discovering the Disconnection ~

Jane's parents, Al & Harriet Nannarone, were married for
over 50 years and together had 6 children.

CHAPTER 6

Tarzan & Jane's Big Disconnect

"So God created... male and female..." ~ Genesis 1:27

"...and they shall become one flesh." ~ Genesis 2:24

THERE WAS A MAN WHO WAS HIRED by a big firm for a fairly prestigious position. The new corporate "big shot" saw someone coming to his office so he wanted to act important since he was basically doing nothing at that moment. So he picked up the phone and begins talking as a stranger walked through the door of his elaborate office. Motioning to the stranger that he'll be just a moment he proceeds with his charade.

"Yes, Mr. President, I'm right on that. Anything else, Mr. President? Absolutely, not a problem. I look forward to golfing with you soon. Goodbye." Turning to the man waiting for him, he asks, "How can I help you?" The man replies, "I'm just here to connect the phone lines."

We can't pretend to be connected when we're not. We don't have the time, energy or acting skills to fool people long enough. It is usually pretty telling when a couple has faced a big disconnect. You can see it in their body language, not only what they say to each other, but what they don't say to each other. There is a lack of honor, value and true heartfelt connection.

Your relationship can disconnect even when neither one of you do anything wrong... it's as natural as muscles; if left alone, they atrophy all by themselves. Couples may disconnect over a single issue or multiple ones. In this chapter we will look at some of the biggest reasons couples detach themselves from one another. Often, the "disconnect" is made unconsciously, not maliciously. There is incredible loneliness we feel when we are disconnected from our spouse. So get ready to identify where you and your partner have disconnected.

Areas That Cause Marital Disconnection

FEAR & ANXIETY

When we fear someone, we have a natural tendency to avoid them. Sometimes we instill fear in our partner by our reaction (or overreaction) to pressure, disagreement, or sensitive issues. If you blow up and act like nothing has happened, then you just started the disconnection process.

Women are generally unaware how fear and anxiety affects them. It may drive her to be a chronic worrier or an aggressive controller. Fear and anxiety keep women in abusive relationships and causes them to be timid or passive-aggressive. For women, fear is their greatest source of pain due to the insecurity she feels.

> *"The problem with most relationships is that they live on the brink of relational bankruptcy."*
> *~ Steve Kelly*

Fear can be good in the sense that it can keep us out of harms way, thus keeping us safe. Shame can also be good in the sense that it keeps us moral and is a reminder to stay on the straight and narrow.

We all experience fear, but women in particular struggle with this more than men. Women literally live on the edge of fear. Generally speaking, women are more prone to fear than men. Case in point: ever see how a typical woman acts when a mouse scrolls across the floor? My wife and I were talking in the kitchen and literally a mouse came out from under the dishwasher and circled her feet then scampered across the floor. My wife went ballistic. Imagine a guy acting like that? (Unless we're talking about Ross-the-Intern or Richard Simmons).

Understanding this is particularly important for men to realize a woman's natural tendency to fear. The way he speaks to her, his body language, his ability to substantially support her and the kids is essential to her well-being. Fear for women may be the greatest point of disconnect. If she doesn't feel safe and secure around him, she without even realizing it, disconnects from her husband.

SHAME & INADEQUACY

Shame is having a sense of embarrassment, failure and guilt. It is also feeling disgraced, dishonored and discredited. Whenever a spouse feels shamed by you, immediately there is some type of disconnect.

Men are generally unaware of how the sense of shame and inadequacy affects him. It may drive him to be very timid or very aggressive. Shame and inadequacy allow men to be controlled, guilt-ridden or verbally abused by his wife. I (Tarzan) overworked out of shame, inadequacy and the fear of failure. Little did I realize, at least initially, that was my motivation. For men, shame is their greatest source of pain due to the inadequacy he feels.

Adam felt incredible shame right after he sinned in the Garden of Eden. He hid himself and was afraid. The word shame means to conceal or hide. Since that time men in general had to fight being passive, timid, and full of shame.

Now all of us feel shame, but generally speaking, men are more prone to shame than women. As a matter of fact, they live on the edge of shame. For example, men rarely would return a hamburger at a restaurant if it was cold or under-cooked. Men feel like they would be acting too sensitive or think to themselves, "Just take it like a man, a little raw meat won't kill anyone."

Feeling shame is another reason why men hate asking for directions. Men may think they aren't smart enough to figure out where they are and which direction they should be going. They think, "Any idiot can figure this out and right now I'm feeling like one, but if I ask everyone will think that too."

Men grew up in an atmosphere where men should never cry. If he does, he's acting like a girl. They compare the size of their penis with their friends at an early age. They put lock stock and barrel in what they do (not for whom they are) and how much money they earn. Men constantly ask themselves if they truly measure up.

A woman can shame a man in an instant. A man can be shamed by the guys at work and his boss, but nothing is more stinging than shame from the love of his life. This can completely devastate a man. Men have run into another woman's arms simply because his wife shamed him repeatedly. If a man feels shamed by his wife, he will disconnect from her and build an impenetrable wall of resentment.

IGNORING PRIMARY NEEDS

One of the biggest complaints I hear from people I have counseled (and Jane and I were no exception) is that "My spouse doesn't hear me."

The reason your spouse doesn't hear you is because s/he is not connected to you on a heart-to-heart level. I am sure you, like many couples, may be married, but are you really connected spirit, soul and body? Wives, if you don't connect with your husband sexually, I promise you he will tune you out. Husbands, if you don't connect emotionally with your wife, I promise you, she's not going to hear you. As partners, list your top five marital needs. Then ask each other which one they feel is deficient and begin to address them immediately. When primary needs are ignored, it is easy to disconnect.

DEPRECIATION

Marriages today seem to depreciate as fast as cars do. Appreciation on an asset is one worth investing in and your marriage is the biggest investment of all... greater than your house, automobiles and stocks. So in order to bring appreciation to your marriage investment, you must start depositing value into it.

All relationships require making deposits into them. Deposits are the positive things we can do for our mate. Deposits come in the form of meeting needs and mending wounds.

Withdrawals are also necessary from time to time. "Withdrawals" are corrections, disagreements, and hurts that happen on occasion. Pastor Steve Kelly of Wave Church in Virginia Beach, Virginia has said, "The problem with most relationships is that they live on the brink of relational bankruptcy."

That means one negative comment, correction or disagreement makes the relationship feel like it is at a point of devastation. When there is a paucity of needs being fulfilled, it pushes a relationship into further separation. Whenever couples proactively make regular deposits, then the occasional argument won't send them into relational bankruptcy.

It is so important to proactively resist disconnecting with your mate. Once you can identify points of disconnection, then you can begin to bring necessary repair and healing.

Please visit our website www.metarzanyoujane.com and take the State of Your Union Marriage Health Assessment to pinpoint problematic areas in your marriage.

CONNECTING POINTS

- What would you say are the top two greatest areas that causes you to disconnect in your marriage and why?

- What would you say is your biggest area of disconnection right now in your marriage?

- What makes you feel connected to your spouse?

- What causes you to quickly disconnect?

- What ways do you try to re-connect with your mate?

TARZAN & JANE'S FUN FACT!

Men have a deep need to be honored and respected...
Women have a deep need to be loved and accepted.

Source: Ask any man or woman.

CHAPTER 7

When Differences Disconnect

"The goal of marriage is not to think alike, but to think together."

~ Robert C. Dodds

A HUSBAND READ AN ARTICLE TO HIS WIFE about how many words women use a day... 30,000 to a man's 15,000. The wife replied, "The reason has to be because we have to repeat everything to men. The husband then turned to his wife and asked, "What?"

Differences are good! If we were identical then one of us is unnecessary.

God created us and matched us up with someone who is different from us. Differences were created because none of us have all we need to be self-sufficient. Differences are meant to complement or complete each other, not compete with each other. Differences don't have to disconnect us but unfortunately they do, often out of immaturity. Marriage is a conflation of two lives with one mission: To promote the happiness and well-being of each other.

DIFFERENCES

... Are meant to complete or complement each other.

… Give us an opportunity to selflessly love outside of our comfort-zone.

... Are part of life.

... Are God-given.

Gender Differences

Men and women differ physically and psychologically. For instance, men have short-term memory causing them to forget things like birthdays and anniversaries. On the other hand women can remember details and conversations from years ago. Men are typically taller and physically stronger than women. Women typically are more emotional than men and often have better communication skills. Men are typically more structured and punctual than women. Men have larger lungs than women, but women can multitask much better than men.

Generally speaking, men like to talk but women like to talk more. Women like sex, but men like sex more. Women are analytical, but men rely on logic over emotion. Men are emotional, but women tend to be more emotional.

> *"If both of you were identical, then one of you wouldn't be necessary... appreciate your differences."*

Little girls are drawn to dolls and baby buggies. They are innately more nurturing. Boys, on the other hand, are drawn toward toys like guns, trucks, and balls. They are innately more aggressive. My daughters love to play teacher, while my boys loved to play coach. Teachers are calm, sweet and patient. Coaches tend to be more rough, impatient and demanding. Boys love to boast about their accomplishments in sports, at school, or how much money they saved. Girls love to bond with their friends and share in detail about their connection with them. These differences are innate and with good purpose.

Personality Differences

There are four basic types of personalities. They each have inherent strengths and weaknesses. You may be the more serious type, but your partner is the more humorous, carefree type. Differences can be either appreciated or viewed as a nuisance. It's hard to appreciate the differences in personalities unless you know what their purpose is and the strengths each brings. Here's a rough sketch of each personality type:

CHOLERIC (LIONS)

- Strengths: Likes a leadership role, take initiative, does the difficult, persistent
- Weaknesses: Hurried, dominate, harsh, insensitive, inflexible, forceful

- Under Pressure: Autocratic

- Personal Motivation: Challenge, results

- Ideal Job Environment: Challenge, freedom, change, authority

- Needs to Improve On: Listening

- Needs to Trust God For: Love and patience

- Preference: The bottom line and results

SANGUINE (OTTERS)

- Strengths: Influences and inspires others, ability to communicate

- Weaknesses: Impulsive, can be too optimistic, lacks follow-through

- Under Pressure: Attacks

- Personal Motivation: Recognition, desire to help others

- Ideal Job Environment: New and exciting, freedom from details, opportunity to motivate others, social interaction

- Needs to Improve On: Pausing and reflecting

- Needs to Trust God For: Discipline and discernment

- Preference: Things that are new and exciting

PHLEGMATIC (GOLDEN RETRIEVERS)

- Strengths: Loyal, works well with people and implementing plans

- Weaknesses: Non-initiating, resists change, avoids conflict

- Under Pressure: Acquiesce

- Personal Motivation: Appreciation, relationships

- Ideal Job Environment: Area of specialization, working with a group, consistency, opportunity to help others

- Needs to Improve On: Initiating more and personal confidence

- Needs to Trust God For: More goal orientation and facing confrontation

- Preference: Relationship and empathy

MELANCHOLY (BEAVERS)

- Strengths: Insures quality, detailed, methodical

- Weaknesses: Overly cautious, too detailed, pessimistic

- Under Pressure: Avoid

- Personal Motivation: Quality, to be right

- Ideal Job Environment: Role to be clearly defined, requires precision, limited risk, methodology and structured

- Needs to Improve On: Declaring

- Needs to Trust God For: Joy and optimism

- Preference: Details, quality and methodology

Knowing personality differences can help us understand others without judging. This awareness can help us relate with others on a whole new level. For free online personality tests you can go to www.humanmetrics.com.cgi-win/jtypes2.asp.

Background Differences

Your home life growing up may vastly differ from your partner's. Family habits or lack of it, holiday traditions, boundaries, moral standards, work ethic, education level, dietary habits, and so on can affect couples as they attempt to mesh their lives from two into one.

Cultural Differences

Each nationality can carry with it its own baggage. The Irish are known for their tempers. The Italians are known for their hand gestures when they speak. Although there are a slew of Polish jokes, the Polish are known for their hard work ethic and producing many sensational athletes. The Scots have been stereotyped for their stinginess. The point is, even though these are stereotypes, each nationality possesses cultural differences that can either be a blessing or can come across as an irritant.

Gift & Talent Differences

Maybe you are artsy, but your spouse is more analytical. You may be a good writer, but your partner is a good conversationalist. You can be good working with your hands, but your spouse would rather focus on organizing. Whatever the case, what we're good at can differ like night and day.

DESIRE & STYLE DIFFERENCES

Maybe you like things that are progressive, but your spouse is more traditional. You are the country, outdoorsy, athletic type, but your spouse is more of the city type who'd rather take a mall over a camper any day. You love sports, but your spouse views them as a threat to your time. Can you learn to appreciate these differences?

DEEP NEEDS THAT DIFFER

Men and women have differing core needs that are just that... needs. Without these we tend to feel shame, fear and insecurity. Here is a quick run-down of his and her needs.

HER NEEDS

- Relational & Financial Security

- Romance and Affection

- Meaningful Conversation

- Protective Leadership

- Commitment to Family & Home

HIS NEEDS

- Honor, Appreciation & Respect

- An Exciting Sexual Partner

- An Attractive Spouse

- A Recreational Companion

- Domestic Support (Homemaker)

When a partner lacks understanding regarding the needs of their spouse, it can create frustration and can quickly remove the underpinnings of the relationship. If you are unaware of the existing needs of your partner, subsequently you won't prioritize them which will further frustrate your mate. Study your mate and appreciate their God-given differences.

Love Languages

Even how we perceive being loved can vary drastically. Dr. Gary Chapman reveals the top five love languages.[25] We usually have one or two dominant love languages in our life. The problem occurs when we love our mate the way we like instead of learning what our partner likes. Even if we love our spouse, they must feel loved. If not, we're missing it. Here are 5 practical ways that people feel loved:

- **Quality Time:** Love is felt when time is given sacrificially.
- **Gifts of Appreciation:** Love is felt when something tangible is given.
- **Non-Sexual Touch:** Love is felt when physical touch is expressed.
- **Acts of Service:** Love is felt when something deliberate is done on your behalf.
- **Words of Affirmation:** Love is felt when kind words are genuinely expressed.

Learn your spouse's love language and remind yourself daily until you habitually demonstrate it without being prompted.

Different Doesn't Have To Mean Difficult

Different isn't synonymous with difficult unless you choose to let it be. These differences become even more amplified when couples already feel a disconnection from each other. The secret is to recognize each other's uniqueness and respond accordingly.

Refuse to allow immaturity to rob you and your partner of connecting with one another just because differences exist. Allow your differences to complement and complete each other, not compete with each other. God put them there for a reason.

"Be patient with each other, making allowances for each other's faults because of your love." ~ Ephesians 4:3 (NLT)

"Too often men and women see the differences between each other and make each other wrong, rather than appreciating how they can benefit from those differences." ~ Simma Lieberman

CONNECTING POINTS

- What is your personality profile?

- What is your partner's personality profile?

- What 3 differences in your spouse really bless you?

- How can you handle differences without becoming defensive?

TARZAN & JANE'S FUN FACT!

Women focus on building rapport, by sharing experiences and asking questions. Men like to tell and give information rather than ask questions. They often share experiences as a way of being one-up.

Source: Simma Lieberman Associates

CHAPTER 8

Identifying Destructive Behaviors

"Humble people don't think less of themselves... they just think of themselves less."

~ Norman Vincent Peale

A MAN LOOKS AT HIS WIFE who happens to be hard of hearing on their 50th wedding anniversary and sweetly and passionately says: "After 50 years I find you to be tried and true!" The wife sits there emotionless and once again he says: "After 50 years I find you to be tried and true." Then she replies: "Well, after 50 years of marriage, I'm sick and tired of you too!"

The following behaviors can etch away at the core of your relationship if not dealt with properly. Each type of behavior, if left unchecked, can be a grating habit that will disconnect you from your partner. We cannot excuse ourselves and use our personality, nationality, background, or gender as an excuse for destructive behavior that not only annoys our spouse, but I can assure you, those around you as well. Please be open, humble, and honest and locate at least two areas you need to work on. If we didn't list yours then feel free to write it in.

Destructive Ways People Sabotage Their Marriages

DESTRUCTIVE BEHAVIOR #1: THE DOMINATOR

Characteristics:

- Demonstrates superiority and intimidation.

- Refuses to show any weakness or vulnerability.

- Ultra competitive in everything.

- Given to jealousy and envy.

- Often are drawn to very passive people.

- Over-bearing and defensive in nature.

- Often demands perfection.

- Controlling and domineering.

You know you have this problem if...

- You try to control everything your spouse does.

- You feel people have to "check-in" with you first before making simple decisions.

- You are a micromanager and refuse to empower people including your spouse.

- You have a hard time with authority.

- You always have to be in charge.

- You love having people feel dependent upon you.

- Everyone must agree with you on everything.

- Things center around you, your agenda, and your preferences.

- You are harsh and austere.

Why is it a problem?

- It squelches your spouse's uniqueness.

- It sucks the life right out of your partner.

- People around you don't feel heard.

- It makes people feel guilty doing things that aren't centered around the dominator.

- It destroys relationships.

- People around you feel devalued, under-appreciated, and squelched.

- People are hurt and will avoid you.

- People feel manipulated and controlled.

How does a person get this way?

- Choleric personality.

- Poor examples growing up.

- Unhealthy view of masculinity or femininity.

The remedy?

- Practice self-awareness.

- Learn humility in its truest sense.

- Develop a servant's spirit.

DESTRUCTIVE BEHAVIOR #2: THE JELLYFISH

Characteristics:

- Passive and/or passive-aggressive.

- Dishonesty.

- Submits to the wrong people.

- Lacks backbone.

- Suffer needlessly.

- Loves to play the martyr.

You know you have a problem if...

- You falsely label stronger personalities as controlling because you refuse to stand up for yourself.

- Conform to the image of others while denying your own uniqueness.

- You get talked into doing things you don't want to do.

- You are afraid to rock the boat.

- You are easily controlled by others.

- You like stronger personalities but only from a distance.

- You will compromise principles for peace.

- Intimidated and acquiesce too easily.

Why is it a problem?

- It creates an atmosphere of dishonesty.

- It can turn into a passive-aggressive personality.

- Passive people will compromise to please others.

- Enable poor behavior in others.

- Provides weak leadership.

- If in men, can encourage role reversal in marriage.

How does a person get this way?

- Phlegmatic personality.

- Fear of man.

- Poor examples growing up where honesty and expression were not encouraged.

The remedy?

- Boldness and confidence.

- Get around and learn from confident people.

- Establish boundaries and stick with them.

DESTRUCTIVE BEHAVIOR #3 - THE PLAYBOY/PLAYGIRL

Characteristics:

- Sex-crazed.

- Perpetually sexually immoral and unfaithful to your spouse.

- Lazy and irresponsible.

You know you have this problem if...

- You do not have healthy boundaries with the opposite sex.

- Chronically lustful: You view the opposite sex as something to conquer.

- Cannot control your eyes, thoughts or behaviors.

- You are flirtatious and must be the center of attention with the opposite sex.

- Sex has become the focal point of your life.

- You are hooked on pornography, dial-a-porn or go to strip clubs.

- You are irresponsible and chronically dishonest in order to fulfill your addiction.

Why is it a problem?

- Immorality of any kind destroys relational intimacy with your mate.

- May destroy your marriage.

- Distorted thinking and an unhealthy view of "normal".

- Unfairly comparing spouse to ex-lovers or pornographic images.

- Cannot seem to be sexually satisfied.

- Your spouse won't trust you and it will make them feel jealous and insecure.

How does a person get this way?

- Pleasure seekers: lives for self and never deprives self from any pleasure.

- Undisciplined thought life.

- Sexual rejection from their mate.

- Immoral friendships.

- Laziness.

- Trying to avenge past hurts.

The remedy?

- Develop a life of moral purity.

- Meditate on the Scriptures.

- Choose friends and entertainment wisely.

- Guarding your eyes is a key to guarding your heart.

- Establish relational boundaries with the opposite sex.

DESTRUCTIVE BEHAVIOR #4 - THE WORKER BEE

Characteristics:

- Overwork.

- Overachieve.

- Discontentment with lifestyle: The quest for more and more.

- Works well over 60, 70 or even 80 hours a week on a regular basis.

- Chronically neglects marriage and home life.

You know you have this problem if...

- You are driven to the point of exhaustion and continual burnout.

- You are known as a work-a-holic.

- Even fun things turn into work.

- You have too many hobbies, interests, or pursuits.

- You are chronically fatigued and suffer burnout.

Why is it a problem?

- Creates a life of imbalance.

- Creates shallow and superficial relationships.

- Spouse and kids may begin to dislike you.

- Judges others as lazy and unproductive.

- Career becomes the center of your life.

- Creates rebellion in your children.

- May turn your spouse into a worker bee out of frustration.

How does a person get this way?

- Self-worth is determined by what one does in life and what one possesses.

- Poor examples growing up.

- Unresolved conflict in the home.

- Perverted values and misplaced priorities.

- Idolize money, job and position.

- Materialism and the lust for more.

- Greed.

The remedy?

- Learn balance.

- Learn to prioritize.

- Learn your true identity.

- Honor the Sabbath Day.

- Have a "no technology" day once a week.

- Make home and marriage are the highest priorities second to God.

- Being a husband/wife or father/mother is more honorable than any position from any company.

- Adjust your lifestyle.

- Turn your worries over to God.

DESTRUCTIVE BEHAVIOR #5 - THE SNAPPING TURTLE

Characteristics:

- You blow up at the smallest things.

- You are known for your harsh, critical spirit.

You know you have this problem if...

- You suppress your true feelings.

- You fail to communicate honestly.

- Your reactions don't match the offense.

Why is it a problem?

- These sharp comments and explosions may be an unconscious way of avoiding intimacy.

- You create shame or fear in your partner.

- You are driving your spouse away.

How does a person get this way?

- Mental or physical burnout.

- Negative mindsets.

- Perfectionist attitudes.

The remedy?

- Think before you speak - be intentional.

- Ask your spouse how well you come across and brace yourself for an honest answer.

- Ask yourself two questions: Why am I really angry? Is it really worth arguing over?

- Use "I" statements in lieu of accusatory "you" statements.

DESTRUCTIVE BEHAVIOR #6 - THE NARCISSIST

Characteristics:

- Unteachable.

- Unapologetic.

- Know-it-all.

- Extremely hurtful.

- Negligent.

- Has to be the center of attention, especially with the opposite sex.

- Has a sense of entitlement and extremely ungrateful.

You know you have this problem if...

- You are unaware of your problem due to deception that is associated with arrogance.

- You continually refuse to take responsibility for your behavior.

- You are unbendable and rigid.

- Refuse to hear your spouse when s/he tries to talk to you.

Why is it a problem?

- Failure to see your own blind spots.

- Expect people to cater to you.

- Unaware of your own vulnerabilities.

How does a person get this way?

- Narcissism.

- Only child syndrome growing up.

- Poor thought patterns.

- Self-centeredness.

The remedy?

- Develop and model humility.

- Listen when others point out your weak points.

- Esteem others higher than yourself.

DESTRUCTIVE BEHAVIOR #7 - THE LAZY LOVER

Characteristics:

- Lacks manners and common courtesy.

- Lack of excellence in demeanor and disposition.

- Over-familiar with your spouse to the point that you are being hurtful and negligent.

- Relationship is stagnant and you are in love with comfort and refuse to change or be challenged.

- Not energizing or stimulating to your spouse.

- You've let yourself go in one or all of the following: emotionally, sexually, conversationally, in appearance, etc.

- You have no personal motivation to better yourself and have nestled in a comfort zone with no plans of changing.

You know you have this problem if...

- If you do not have regular dates with your spouse.

- You rarely, if ever, make your spouse feel uniquely special.

- You forget birthdays and anniversaries.

- You fail to celebrate your spouse and your marriage.

- Deep conversations are laborious and even boring to you.

- Emotionally you are on cruise control.

- You are completely out-of-touch with your partner.

- You leave it up to your partner to keep the marriage exciting and fresh.

Why is it a problem?

- You are not being responsible for your marriage relationship.

- There appears to be no motivation for improving oneself.

- Others seem to be a higher priority to you than your spouse.

- You may be unknowingly hurting your spouse with an uncaring attitude.

- Your attitude and actions can make your spouse feeling rejected.

How does a person get this way?

- Often the couple was sexually active or lived with each other before marriage.

- Unresolved issues or being selfishly absorbed in your own little world.

- Respect and honor are rarely exhibited towards your mate.

- Over-familiarity: Forgetting that your spouse is not only your husband or wife, but best friend, lover, and confidante.

The remedy?

- Celebrate and honor one another; make each other feel special.

- Have a date night scheduled (no kids) for at least twice a month.

- Romance each other and take time connecting on a daily basis.

DESTRUCTIVE BEHAVIOR #8 - THE QUITTER / RUNNER

Characteristics:

- Always in a posture that is ready to bolt and run; often rooted in a volitale home life growing up.

- The inability to handle pain, tough seasons and times of crisis.

You know you have this problem if...

- You have had numerous intimate relationships.

- You go from friendship to friendship.

- Your spouse has to be on his or her best game to keep you secure.

- You hate seeing your spouse's shortcomings.

- You are easily discouraged and lose all hope.

- Frequently use the "D" word... divorce.

Why is it a problem?

- It creates insecurity in your spouse.

- Your spouse may catch on and take a preemptive approach to avoid getting hurt by you.

- You remain in an immature state by refusing to persevere through marital struggles.

- Your spouse will insulate themselves from you.

How does a person get this way?

- Poor examples from parents.

- May be suffering from one or more personality disorders.

- Fear of rejection and disappointment.

The remedy?

- Develop a covenant mindset.

- Counseling in order to get the root of your tendency to run.

- Deal with inner fears and past hurts.

- Refuse to see the current problems in light of past problems.

DESTRUCTIVE BEHAVIOR #9 - THE STUCK-IN-THE-PAST PERSON

Characteristics:

- You subconsciously try to come to terms with an old problem.

- You are often mistrustful, suspicious and refuse to become vulnerable out of fear of being hurt.

You know you have this problem if...

- You see your spouse in light of your ex or father/mother.

- Old problems and hurts still fester within you from a long time ago.

- You feel instant anger, fear or shame whenever the subject is brought up.

- You can cry at the drop of a hat when thinking or talking about the past.

- You are plagued by fear of rejection.

- You have a dossier on your spouse and cannot let go of a past event.

Why is it a problem?

- You put your spouse in a negative light regularly.

- You sabotage intimacy with your spouse thus causing them to mistrust you.

- You read into things that simply do not exist.

- Thinking you have your spouse all sized up (incorrectly judging).

- There may be a root of bitterness in you.

How does a person get this way?

- Hurts from a former relationship.

- Deep wounds that have never healed properly.

The remedy?

- Solve the issues of your past and immediately forgive the people who have deeply hurt you.

- Refuse to transfer your feelings of past relationships on to your spouse.

- Are there any unresolved issues between you and your parents or ex's?

- Refuse to compare your spouse to any other person.

Connecting Points

- What two sabotaging behaviors do you have to address or keep under control?

- What two sabotaging behaviors does your spouse need to address or keep under control?

- Are there any underlying issues that motivate you or caused you to struggle in these areas?

- What practical steps will you take to ensure you won't repeat sabotaging behavior?

TARZAN & JANE'S FUN FACT!

Women think the sexiest parts of a man are his eyes and smile... For men? What do you think?

Source: Multiple Sources

Jungle Love

~ Reconnecting Without Words ~

Don't announce the new and exciting
changes in your marriage. Just do it!

Chapter 9

When Sex Talks, Who Needs Words?

"Sex is emotion in motion."

~ Mae West

A MINISTER DECIDED to do something a little different one Sunday morning. He said "Today, in church, I am going to say a single word and you are going to help me preach. Whatever single word I say, I want you to sing whatever hymn that comes to your mind."

The pastor shouted out, "CROSS." Immediately the congregation started singing in unison, "THE OLD RUGGED CROSS." The pastor hollered out, "GRACE." The congregation began to sing "AMAZING GRACE, how sweet the sound." The pastor said, "POWER." The congregation sang "THERE IS POWER IN THE BLOOD." The Pastor said, "SEX." The congregation fell into total silence.

Everyone was in shock.

They all nervously began to look around at each other afraid to say anything. Then all of a sudden, way from in the back of the church, a little old 87 year-old grandmother stood up and began to sing "PRECIOUS MEMORIES."

Has your sex life been reduced to nothing more than precious memories? Is your marriage being neglected sexually? An overwhelming seventy percent (70%) of couples in America are frustrated with their sex life.

People are flocking to chat rooms, night clubs, the Playboy channel, pornography, romance novels, and strip clubs. But why? I believe it is because it is more exciting for many couples than going in their bedroom with their mate. If people aren't committing actual affairs they are having affairs of the heart.

Is your sex life as dead as Lazarus? Well, good news! You have the ability to resurrect it!

Ambiance may be the store for lovers, but the Bible is also a book for lovers. If you don't believe me, read Song of Solomon, Proverbs and 1 Corinthians just to name a few. God created sex and wants you to have fun as married couples. Remember, sex is for your mate, not for your girl/boy friend, lover or significant other. Sex is a barometer of your marriage. It can be a revealing factor of your health as a couple.

Patricia Love and Steven Stosny assert,

"When the relationship is on the rocks, the rocks are in the bed. No relationship issue has the ability to stir fear and shame like sex… Sex always makes the top-four subjects couples fight about. The reason is simple: Sex is a powerful source of pleasure and a powerful source of pain. It can easily evoke fear in women and inadequacy in men, which makes it difficult to see each other's point of view or be rational about the subject."[26]

As a matter of fact, when a couple's sex life is deprived it often becomes over-emphasized making it the focal point of conflict.

Men are deeply hurt and angry when their wife isn't there for him sexually. This anger can come out in so many ways. Many women wonder, "What is he so angry about?" She may ask her husband, but rarely will he be forthright about this subject because of the deep shame he feels when his sexual advances are rejected. Often this anger he feels can be traced back to the marriage bedroom and the lack of sexual connection he has with his wife. As a result, men can hurt women with their anger, making it impossible for her to feel sexual toward him. She will simply disconnect because of his anger, making this a vicious cycle of hurt.

Men emotionally disconnect from a wife who rejects him sexually. This is very dangerous to a marriage given the importance of sex, not only for men, but for the marriage itself.

He may have to fight temptations from outside and will feel guilt and more shame when he feels temptation, or succumbs to it. When a wife isn't available to her husband sexually, as HE needs, NOT as SHE thinks, what she is really saying to him is this: "I expect you to be exclusively faithful to me, but don't expect me to meet your sexual needs."

When married couples are not sexually satisfied, it is devastating to a marriage. If one partner is dissatisfied it affects the couple as a whole. Marriage is the ultimate team sport. Sexual neglect will build a wall of resentment and will disconnect you from your partner resulting in a downward spiral of endless frustration... unless some action is taken.

"70% of couples in America are frustrated with their sex life."

One man, although quite embarrassed, admitted to me that he turned to solo sex because he couldn't face another rejection from his wife. She refused to have sex with him for five years and was hooked on porn. He wasn't proud of his behavior but it was safer for him than to face the constant shame from his wife's refusal.

Women, like men, are not out to destroy their marriage, but like anything else, we can destroy out of neglect and ignorance. In some cases, pure selfishness is a root cause, coupled with careless, cavalier attitudes. Men find it extremely cruel whenever their wife withholds sex from him. It is emotionally devastating for them more than most women will ever know.

How Did The Sexual Disconnection Happen?

PHYSICAL & EMOTIONAL EXHAUSTION & STRESS

Work, kids, care for the home, financial problems, and life itself can wear you down. Fatigue is a huge factor for many. People are getting used to living life in the fast lane while burning the candle at both ends. People are working more and more and connecting less and less. We find it easier to connect via email, phone calls, texting, chat rooms and Facebook. Why? It's easier.

Many people work on the way to work and on the way home from work trying to get ahead. In times past it seemed like your work was pretty much complete at the end of the day. Nowadays one person is hired to do the work of three. We must find a way to simplify our lives and get back to the basics.

If your job is too demanding, then you might need to find a new job or career. I know of a surgeon who is actively developing his own business so he can change his career despite all of his schooling and student loans. Why? Because of the stress and strain it puts on his wife and family. Being overly committed and doing too many things can bring on adrenal exhaustion. Learn to pace yourself and by all means rest.

PHYSICAL PROBLEMS

Sometimes a person's sex drive (libido) can be lowered due to hormonal imbalance in the body. Hormonal imbalance, adrenal exhaustion, low metabolism, low energy levels, etc. can decrease the libido in men and women. It is important to have a healthy diet and exercise. Exercising alone will boost your metabolism and sex drive!

DEPRESSION

According to the National Institute of Mental Health, over 20 million Americans suffer from depression every year. Depression causes a person to live in a vacuum without hope, energy or vision for life. De-pression causes people to detach themselves from relationships and lose interest in activities they would normally enjoy.

UNFORGIVENESS

A bitterly offended heart will take its toll upon a person if left alone. Unforgiveness causes an individual to focus and accentuate on the negative. Prolonged unforgiveness causes people to be offended, bitter and resentful. Offended people slowly construct an impenetrable wall that seeks to exclude the one who hurt them, or the one they perceived to have hurt them. This will certainly affect a couple's sex life.

AN UNSAFE ENVIRONMENT

The safer the environment, the more connected couples feel. The more sex men have in marriage, the safer they feel and they will be more emotionally connected. Sex and romance are deep forms of intimacy, but alone they are deficient. Couples need both sex and romance to achieve the highest form of intimacy.

I often wondered why God made men and women so differently. I believe the main reason is to learn to love each other unselfishly. Since marriage doesn't work for selfish people, it means when we learn to become sacrificial in our marriage, that's when great things happen. A good example of this sexual difference between men and women is demonstrated in the following graph.

A husband's arousal:

A wife's arousal:

Women need to understand that men can be quickly aroused (usually 3-4 minutes) and then come crashing down. Women typically need more arousal time then men. Men need to be more understanding of this. Since women need more time to reach orgasm (usually 10-11 minutes), men can mistakenly think this means that she isn't attracted to him. Women can mistakenly think he is only interested in his own desire when he arouses so quickly. Sex requires understanding, patience and some communication.

Men are like two stroke engines that start and rev up rather quickly. Women, on the other hand, are like diesel engines. My brother has a diesel truck and I learned that before you can even turn the key to start the engine, you must wait for the glow light. Diesels remind me of a woman. You must first wait and be patient for her glow light to turn on. In other words, many women are not interested in sex until they are actually having sex. It goes without saying, but most men are interested in sex all of the time!

Most men have up to 40% more testosterone than women, thus explaining their intense sex drive. But interestingly, approximately 20% of women have a stronger sex drive than their husband. This can also leave a wife feeling frustrated, unwanted, and alone.

Sex is a great way to improve your marriage without talking about it. Make sex a non-issue by regularly incorporating it into your marriage. Why not take some time for each other this week?

"Sex is like golf, more people are talking about it than actually doing it." ~ Dr. Phil McGraw

"Silent suffering is not patience."
~ John Townsend & Henry Cloud

CONNECTION POINTS

- How does it affect you when your spouse is not there for you sexually or emotionally?

- Can you identify what has caused a sexual disconnection between you and your spouse?

- How often do you desire to be sexually intimate with your spouse each week? What about your spouse?

- What can you do practically to improve your sex life?

TARZAN & JANE'S FUN FACT!

Alcohol effects women twice as hard and fast because men have a higher water content, larger blood supply, and bigger liver. Men also possess a liver enzyme that women do not produce, which helps breaks down alcohol and detoxify the liver,

Source: Discovery Channel's, "Science of the Sexes".

CHAPTER 10

How Approachable Are You?

"People will marginalize you if you lack approachability."

ONE TIME JANE AND I WERE AT A RESTAURANT and our waitress was, to put it mildly, annoying. Now, we believe in tipping well even when people may not deserve it. We also believe in treating those who wait on you with kindness and respect. But this time this woman was testing our attitude and generosity.

We had to repeat everything. If we didn't have any utensils, we'd have to ask her three times. If we needed napkins, she was bugged and needed several reminders. Each time we had a simple request, she was annoyed. Her body language was clear: "You annoy me and I wish you'd leave already." Clearly this waitress wasn't there to serve us nor was she giving credence to that establishment. She was put off and put out by everything. You could say she wasn't the approachable type.

I am wondering how many times we come across this way towards our mate? If we treated our boss the same way we treat our spouse, most of us would be fired! Our harsh words and sour-ish attitudes can destroy the very thing we are trying to build... our marriage! We all can come across with a rotten attitude that is aloof and put out. I know we all have our moments, but some people actually live in "Sourville."

Your ability to connect with people and stay connected with your spouse will be directly determined on how approachable you are. People will marginalize you if you lack approachability. Your spouse will disconnect from you if s/he cannot trust you, if you are moody or come across with a chip on your shoulder. If people cannot trust the consistency of your moods and attitudes, they simply will not trust you. One of the main reasons you fell in love and were married is because you both felt safe with each other. There was a time you felt you could talk about anything; you never turned down a time to be romantic and lovey-dovey. How about now? How approachable are you?

I'd like to point out three primary modes people operate in that Stosny and Love have outlined. Examine yourself and see what mode you use when relating with your partner.

What Is Your Approach Mode?

APPROACH MODE

When we are in approach mode, we are connecting with someone while giving positive energy. When we say someone is approachable we mean they are easy to connect with, engaging, open to new ideas and information, friendly, personable, and genuinely interested. It means we seek to connect by being open, available, cooperative, and accessible.[27]

> *"In 'approach mode' you*
> *make it easier for your partner to connect with you."*

In approach mode we disarm our partner and present a safe, caring atmosphere that fosters trust and intimacy.

AVOID MODE

When we endeavor to avoid someone, we give little of ourselves. We are trite and keep interaction to a minimum. To avoid means to give no energy at all.

In this mode you are about as interesting as a trigonometry test. In avoidance mode you are trying to get away from someone. You may distract yourself from the source of your problem through over-working, over-entertaining yourself, or over-activity.

When we distance ourselves from our mate, we tend to justify that behavior by rationalizing that we have more "important" things to do. This is often unconscious behavior we demonstrate in order to "numb out" the pain, hurt and disappointment from another person. Avoidance means we are unwilling to engage, participate or cooperate. We show no interest and are cutting the other person off.[28] Avoidance has a negative effect on your marriage.

ATTACK MODE

In attack mode we are intentionally hurtful and out to destroy... yes, destroy. When we attack our spouse (often out of hurt or guilt) we devalue, harm, incapacitate, and seek to instill shame and fear. In this mode the goal is to put our partner in his or her place. There is an air of superiority which seeks to destroy the other person's worth, confidence and uniqueness.[29]

In attack mode we are angry, judgmental, critical, defensive, bitter, and out to punish.[30] This mode is very destructive to a marriage and communicates...

- "I am better than you."
- "I am more knowledgeable than you."
- "I am more talented than you."
- "I am more original and creative than you."
- "I am not interested in your perspective."
- "My needs and interests are more important than yours."

You can be in attack mode and not even raise your voice. As a matter of fact, you can be in attack mode and not even say a word; it may be a sour, disrespectful attitude. Our body language can say:

- "You are bugging me and annoying to me."
- "Leave me alone, I don't like you."
- "I am not here for you, so please don't bother me."

As a general rule, being approachable allows for connection and reduces fear and shame. Avoid and attack mode increase fear and shame. Even your dog or cat can know what mode you're in.

IMPROVING YOUR APPROACHABILITY

MASTER SELF-AWARENESS

Know yourself and your tendencies.

Examine your body language, words, tone of voice, and overall attitude. I knew someone who really was a nice guy, but he looked like he was mad all of the time and people tended to avoid him. Listen to what others are saying and give someone permission to critique you and speak into your life without getting offended.

PROACTIVELY DEMONSTRATE TO OTHERS THAT YOU REALLY CARE

Here are some practical things you can do:

- Eye contact
- Ask a question
- Show genuine interest
- Mirror back what is said
- Call people back in a timely manner
- Slow down and seek connection not just impression
- Don't be in such a hurry
- Stick around and talk to people

The person in all of history we respect the most is Jesus of Nazareth. He had to be the most approachable person on earth. Even nasty sinners felt comfortable coming to him. He loved the unlovely. He touched the untouchable. And he comforted the hurting. He reached out to the poor and outcasts, not just the rich and famous. He has changed the world as we know it because of his approachability. He was more interested in showing grace than judgment.

In approach mode you make it easier for your partner to connect with you. As the old adage goes, "It's easier to catch bees with honey."

CONNECTING POINTS

- How can you be more approachable towards your partner?
- What areas seem to put you in an avoid or attack mode?
- How can you be more conscious and aware of hurtful behaviors and attitudes?
- When do you feel most approachable?
- Will you give your spouse permission to speak truthfully but gracefully in your life without becoming offended?

TARZAN & JANE'S FUN FACT!

You burn 26 calories a minute by kissing.

Source: Discovery Channel's, "Science of the Sexes".

CHAPTER 11

Love Is An Action Word

"If you can really make a man believe you love him, you have won him."

~ Dwight L. Moody

WHAT IS LOVE? Just ask kids... A group of professional people posed this question to a group of 4 to 8 year-olds, "What does love mean?" The answers they received were broader and deeper than anyone could have imagined. See what you think:

"When my grandmother got arthritis, she couldn't bend over and paint her toenails anymore. So my grandfather does it for her all the time, even when his hands got arthritis too. That's love." ~ Rebecca, age 8

When someone loves you, the way they say your name is different. You just know that your name is safe in their mouth." ~ Billy, age 4

"Love is what makes you smile when you're tired." ~ Terri, age 4

"You really shouldn't say 'I love you' unless you mean it. But if you mean it, you should say it a lot. People forget." ~ Jessica, age 8

"When you love somebody, your eyelashes go up and down and little stars come out of you." ~ Karen, age 7

Love! It's on everybody's mind. We all want to be loved and accepted for who we are. There is no greater pain in life than to feel rejection and hurt from those who are supposed to love us the most.

Talking without being connected can be a fruitless endeavor. That's why studies have shown that two-thirds of couples who went to counseling were no better off and even in a worse condition a year later. Talking does nothing without connection. People assume the only way to connect and deal with problems is by talking about it. Talking about problems without connecting will only add fuel to the fire and make things worse.

But I know what you're thinking, "That's the problem! We can't connect because there are problems." Face it! We'll always have problems to some degree, but that doesn't mean we can't connect as a couple. Love in action is the best way to connect. The old saying "actions speak louder than words" cannot be underestimated.

"In our culture, 'love' is used too loosely. We love our dog, we love pizza, and oh yeah, I love you too."

Since we overuse the word love and put it on equal footing in practically every area of our lives, love itself is misunderstood and diluted in its meaning. However in the Greek culture, there are different words for love. Here are the main four:

Phileo

This is simply friendship love. As a married couple, continuing to build upon your friendship should be of grave importance.

Storge

This is love demonstrated by family affection. We all have a natural affection towards our children and mate. Only those who suffer deep emotional illness do not have normal family affectionate love.

Eros

This is sexual love. Most of society banks on this to sustain them in marriage, but eros was never meant to stand alone. This is important, but it's not the foundation of a marriage. When asked "What is love?" One teenager put it this way: "Love is a feeling you feel when it is like a feeling that you've never felt before." If we based our commitment on feelings alone, we are destined for heartache and long-term disconnection.

Agape

Agape love is 100% unconditional, unmerited love. That's right! No strings attached. It is the highest form of love because it is the God-kind of love. In other words, it is showing actions and attitudes of love even to those who don't deserve it.

It is the kind of love that makes it through any hurt, disappointment or betrayal. It is the love that will take the high road even when your spouse takes the low road. Agape love does NOT suggest being a doormat, but it does show the kind of love it hopes to receive in return. It is the kind of love that operates independently of feelings or past experience and has incredible resolve and resilience.

There are some people who will refuse this type of love because it makes them vulnerable. Yet, when we walk in this type of love, it moves God to act on our behalf.

When it comes to love, we place many conditions on it. Conditions like: "I'll love you if you meet my needs." "I'll love you if you make me happy." "I'll love you if you never challenge my behavior." That is not real love.

Love Is Risky Business

Love is the greatest risk you'll ever make in life! You can never truly love someone without a risk. You risk being misunderstood, rejected, and not receiving the same level of love in return. But true love expressed develops you into a person of strong character often leading to a strong marriage.

Jesus risked it all for us. He chose to die a horrific death on a cross in hope that people will turn to Him for the forgiveness of their sins. What a huge risk, but one that has paid off for multitudes.

Learning to love people will be a life-long endeavor. Loving other people is both risky and rewarding. True agape love will always take a risk and pay the price because the outcome is incredible.

Connecting Points

- What are some ways you can show your spouse agape love?

- How is it possible to have unresolved marital issues and still remain connected to each other?

- Why isn't talking about the problem rarely the way to solving the problem?

TARZAN & JANE'S FUN FACT!

Men like it when their wife builds him up with her words... Women like it when their husband makes her laugh.

Source: Multiple Sources

Jungle Lingo

~ Reconnecting With Words ~

Steve's parents, Ray & Sandra Hutchinson, have been married since 1962 and together have 7 kids.

CHAPTER 12

Lost In Translation

"There is no lonelier person than the one who lives with a spouse with whom he or she cannot communicate."

~ Margaret Mead

A DISGRUNTLED WIFE WENT TO AN ATTORNEY and said: "I want to file for a divorce." "What grounds do you have?" asked the attorney. "About an acre." She replied. "No! Do you have a grudge?" "No, we have a car port." "No! Does he beat you up?" "No! I'm usually up before he is." Frantically the attorney asks, "Then why do you want a divorce?" She said, "Because we just can't communicate."

Do you ever feel like you are speaking a foreign language? Communication is not the mere exchange of words; it is an exchange of meanings. What is said can quickly turn into what wasn't meant. Communication involves three critical things:

What is said?

What is heard?

What is interpreted?

In the book Men are Like Waffles, Women are Like Spaghetti, Bill & Pam Farrell humorously communicate what s/he says versus what s/he really means.

WHAT SHE REALLY MEANS ...

IF SHE SAYS...	SHE MEANS...
It's your decision.	The correct decision should be obvious by now.
Do what you want.	You'll pay for this later.
You're so manly.	You need a shave and you sweat a lot.
This kitchen is so inconvenient.	I want a new house
Do you love me?	I'm going to ask you for something expensive.

WHAT HE REALLY MEANS ...

IF HE SAYS...	HE MEANS...
I'm hungry.	I'm hungry.
I'm sleepy.	I'm sleepy.
I'm tired.	I'm tired.
Do you want to go to a movie?	I'd eventually like to have sex with you.
Can I take you out to dinner?	I'd eventually like to have sex with you.
May I have this dance?	I'd eventually like to have sex with you.

Real communication takes place when we are in tune with each other. Here are some practical tips.

BOOST YOUR CONNECTION THROUGH WORDS

NUMBER ONE: FIND THE RIGHT TIME

Sometimes timing can be everything. Don't wait till you both are exhausted and spent or when the kids need your attention or when your spouses' favorite show comes on TV. Some things are more urgent then others but use wisdom with your timing. One thing we NEVER do as a couple is try to talk about serious or depressing issues over any meal. It's a good way to get indigestion.

NUMBER TWO: DEVOTE A SPECIFIC PLACE TO TALK

Atmosphere can be everything. I cannot study in a cluttered office. I cannot exercise unless the atmosphere looks like and smells like a gym. In the same way, designate a place with minimal distractions in order to talk. It could be a walk around the block, your bedroom, a park, or at Starbucks. Find what works for you. Men usually love to do some activity while communicating such as walking or even driving. Women want focused, undivided attention. Find your balance as a couple.

NUMBER THREE: TAKE YOUR TIME AND GIVE YOUR ATTENTION

One of the reasons we usually aren't attentive is because we are in such a hurry. Time communicating with your partner is time well-spent and should be a high priority on our things "to do" list.

NUMBER FOUR: MIRROR BACK WHAT IS SPOKEN TO GAIN CLARITY

Mirroring back is simply a way to ensure the other person that you are listening and that you understand what is being communicated. One way of doing this is saying, "So, what you're saying is that..." and repeat what was already said in a courtesy way. This is also a great time to affirm your partner of your commitment to them and that you value their feelings.

NUMBER FIVE: ASK PENETRATING QUESTIONS

Questions are powerful because it shows that you are really interested. It also implies humility and a desire to connect. A penetrating question is one that involves more than a yes, no or I don't know response. By the way, this is a great way to get a man to open up - just ask for his advice or opinion.

WORDS, TONE AND BODY LANGUAGE

USE THE RIGHT WORDS

Words are powerful so be very selective. Too many times we can be lazy and flippant when it comes to our spouse. One dubious remark can bring a relationship to a screeching halt. Death and life are in the power of the tongue (Proverbs 18:21).

USE THE RIGHT TONE

You can actually say some difficult things if you carefully use the right tone. If your spouse isn't responding this could be a good indicator that you are using a harsh tone.

USE THE RIGHT BODY LANGUAGE

According to research, our words influence about 7% of our conversations, our tone influences 38% of our conversations but an overwhelming 55% of our conversation is determined by our body language. In other words, you can have the right word choice and tone but negative body language can ruin your communication efforts.

COMMUNICATION TABOOS

We'd like to highlight four communication faux pas we learned from Jimmy Evans.

DISTRACTION

If you are avoiding eye contact, being distracted by the TV, keep looking at your watch or yawning, this sends a clear signal to the other person that you are just not that interested and that you have bigger and better things to do. Learn to give your spouse your undivided attention, using eye contact, and appropriate body language.

DISHONESTY

This also includes exaggeration which is a form of lying. Lying immediately breaks trust, hurts your credibility and creates suspicion. There is never a time to use lying, convenient omissions, and stretching the truth. Steve's good friend and mentor Dennis Heber says, "The more you stretch the truth, the more people can see right through it." Dishonesty will create a barrier that may take years to overcome.

"Men have been punished in the past for being honest, so they have learned to grunt and bare it."

DIRECT ATTACKS

Men have been punished in the past for being honest, so they have learned to grunt and bare it. As a result they have become emotionally reserved. Women, on the other hand, have been victims of verbal attacks from their husband. This causes women to be anxious and turned off sexually from their husbands. Attack mode will never deepen your connection with your partner nor inspire intimacy.

DEMEANING ATTITUDES

Beware of "you" terms like "You should have... You could have... etc." The "coulda, woulda, shouldas" never help. Hindsight is always 20/20. Instead use "I" terms like "I feel..." or "I believe..." or "I like..." Your feelings aren't necessarily wrong; it's just the way you feel. Avoid using accusatory remarks or being too direct; it will kill quality communication and marital connection.

FIVE LEVELS OF COMMUNICATION

Communication is simply an exchange of information and feelings. Communication ranks high on the list of marital problems. Below are the 5 levels of communication in order to help identify where you are in relation to your partner.

LEVEL 1 – CLICHÉ

This is the shallowest form of conversation that often requires no thought or dialogue. Things like, "How's it going?" And they reply "Fine!"

LEVEL 2 – REPORTING FACTS

Repeating things they already know. Often it is chattering about the trivial things such as the weather, the ballgame, politics or the like.

LEVEL 3 – IDEAS & SOLUTIONS

At this level you may share ideas but with a careful eye; it's just a peak of the real me. If your spouse opens up to you and they see you yawn, get distracted, roll your eyes, or look bored they'll go back to level 2.

LEVEL 4 – FEELINGS & EMOTIONS

Real ideas and feelings are shared on a deeper level. If there is any form of disconnection then they'll quickly revert back to level 3.

LEVEL 5 – DEEP PERSONAL COMMUNICATION

This is known as "symphony of the soul" where there is total transparency. There is absolutely no fear of rejection and complete vulnerability. When a couple reaches this level of communication they will often empathize with one another and truly feel their pain and joys.

Communication involves two people who take turns listening and speaking. If you want your spouse to open up and respond with positive energy then it is going to take humility, understanding and some tenderness.

"Good people enjoy the positive results from their words..." ~ *Proverbs 13:2 (NLT)*

CONNECTING POINTS

- What holds you back from sharing your true feelings with your spouse?

- When is the best time to have an in-depth conversation with you and your partner?

- What is one of the most important aspects of being a good communicator?

- How do you respond when you don't feel like you are being heard by your partner?

TARZAN & JANE'S FUN FACT!

Men like a wife that is respectful towards him...
Women like it when her husband functions as a leader.

CHAPTER 13

Communication Killers

"Great communication comes when we learn to talk to each other instead of at each other."

~ Jeff McElory

J ACK WONDERS WHETHER IT WOULD BE ALRIGHT to smoke while praying. Max replies, "Why don't you ask the priest?" So Jack goes up to the priest and asks, "Father, may I smoke while I pray?" But the priest says, "No, my son, you may not. That's utter disrespect to our religion."

Jack goes back to his friend and tells him what the good priest told him. Max says, "I'm not surprised. You asked the wrong question. Let me try." And so Max goes up to the priest and asks, "Father, may I pray while I smoke?" To which the Priest eagerly replies, "By all means, my son. By all means."

Here's the moral of the story: You can get farther by simply rephrasing what you say.

Society is conditioning people to talk less. Things like texting, emails, Facebook, Twitter, chat rooms, and the like are being substituted more and more to ensure less personal contact with others. It is not unusual today to see four people in a car or at a restaurant where no one is talking to each other because they're too busy texting. Although all of the aforementioned means of communication can be effective tools for business, it can be disastrous for marriage and home life. There is simply no substitute for face-to-face and heart-to-heart communication.

The breakdown in communication will eventually lead to a breakdown in the relationship unless we do something about it.

According to hundreds of therapists, counselors and even divorce attorneys, communication problems continue to remain the number one predictor and reason for divorce.[31] Without healthy communication couples will disconnect rather easily.

It is amazing how one dubious comment can ruin a boatload of good. As a matter of fact, marital researchers Cliff Notarius, Howard Markman and John Gottman, have estimated that one negative comment can erase as much as twenty positive ones.[32] These powerful words penned ions ago still apply now more than ever:

"Dead flies will cause even a bottle of perfume to stink! Yes, an ounce of foolishness can outweigh a pound of wisdom and honor." - Ecclesiastes 10:1 (NLT)

"Those who love to talk will experience the consequences, for the tongue can kill or nourish life." - Proverbs 18:21 (NLT)

When we married, we may have had a good amount of character and intellect, but very few us possessed the communications skills and strategies needed to succeed in marriage. Unfortunately, many learn by trial and error. This can be detrimental to a marriage due to the devastating trail of damage our mouths can leave behind. We all know the hurtful feeling of being the victim of ill-advised words from our mate... it can hurt beyond words. To make matters worse, often we are totally oblivious of how caustic our words are and how much hurt we have done to our partner.

We are warned over and over in Scripture to guard our tongue. Here are just a handful of them:

"The wicked are trapped by their own words, but the godly escape such trouble." - Proverbs 12:13 (NLT)

"Some people make cutting remarks, but the words of the wise bring healing." - Proverbs 12:18 (NLT)

"Good people enjoy the positive results of their words, but those who are treacherous crave violence." - Proverbs 13:2-3 (NLT)

"The talk of fools is a rod for their backs, the words of the wise keep them out of trouble." - Proverbs 14:3 (NLT)

"Everyone enjoys a fitting reply; it is wonderful to say the right thing at the right time." ~ Proverbs 15:23 (NLT)

"The godly think before speaking; the wicked spout evil words." ~ Proverbs 15:28 (NLT)

"A good person, produces good words from a good heart, and an evil person produces words from an evil heart. And I tell you this, that you must give an account on judgment day of every idle word you speak. The words you say now reflect your fate then; either you will be justified by them or you will be condemned." ~ Matthew 12:36-37 (NLT)

COMMUNICATION KILLERS

Here are some communication killers you will want to avoid and/or diffuse as quickly as possible due to their damaging effects.

SARCASM

Sarcasm can be described as a sharp, bitter, or cutting expression or remark; a bitter jibe or a taunt. It is essentially another way of getting back at your spouse; it is a "creative" way of belittling and hurting your partner. The Bible tells us:

"A hothead starts fights; a cool-tempered person tries to stop them." ~ Proverbs 15:18

"Avoiding a fight is a mark of honor; only fools insist on quarreling." ~ Proverbs 20:3 (NLT)

Sarcasm is essentially laying the gauntlet down and daring your spouse to engage in warfare. Sarcasm is fighting below the belt; it is an attempt to etch away your partner's dignity. The use of sarcasm causes your spouse not to trust you, furthering any disconnection you already may be experiencing.

Sarcasm is used contemptuously, directly or indirectly, and in a form of irony. An example of direct sarcasm would be: "What a great husband you turned out to be." Or, indirectly like this [to a lazy student]: "Make sure you don't study too hard today." Here are some others:

Husband to wife: "Aren't you just a ray of sunshine?"

Wife to husband: "Feel free to make yourself at home and do the dishes."

"You're not the sharpest tool in the shed are you?"

Sarcasm is a hostile form of communication. Sarcasm comes from a Greek word *sarkasmos* that means to tear flesh, gnash the teeth, and to speak bitterly.[33] There is no success in marriage without learning to be gentle with our words.

SILENCE

Sometimes silence is golden, but not when it is time to respectfully communicate your thoughts and feelings with your spouse.

Silence is a way of punishing your spouse. Communication is the "lifeblood" of any relationship, therefore, prolonged silence will starve it. Your partner may withdraw through silence often out of fear: fear of rejection, fear of an outburst, fear of being put down or belittled. Some fear dealing with reality and bearing the nakedness of their soul possibly due to family upbringing, past hurts and rejection. Learn to open up your heart and confidently share your feelings, thoughts and dreams with your spouse.

John Townsend and Henry Cloud have noticed:

"Some do not leave physically, but they leave emotionally. They forsake the relationship by taking their heart out of it."[34]

Relational starvation through silence can severely damage your marriage.

ESCALATION

Escalation can be described as:

"When partners respond back and forth negatively towards each other, continually upping the ante so the conversation gets more and more hostile."[35]

It is important to stop the escalation process before an all-out war erupts. Maybe the greatest problem with escalation is that things are said that threaten the very fabric of the marriage. Often little things erupt into an inferno that leaves partners with little hope for the future. It really is fighting "dirty."

Escalation also occurs when one partner uses intimate knowledge of the other as a weapon during arguments that really hurt and add fuel to the fire.

Abraham J. Heschel observes:

"In a controversy, the instant we feel anger, we have already ceased striving for the truth, and have begun striving for ourselves."

King Solomon reminds us:

"Beginning a quarrel is like opening a floodgate, so drop the matter before a dispute breaks out." ~ Proverbs 17:14 (NLT)

Recognizing and stopping escalation in its tracks will save you a plethora of heartache.

INVALIDATION

Invalidation can be described as:

"A pattern in which one partner subtly or directly puts down the thoughts, feelings, or character of the other." [36]

These painful put-downs scar a relationship. Invalidation comes in the following forms:

An attack on character: "You're just like your father/mother."

An attack on intelligence: "You just don't get it, do you?"

An attack on emotional well-being: "You're just overreacting." Or, "You need to see a counselor or get some medication."

An attack on your spirituality: "Relax and let the Lord handle it."

An attack on your physical stature: "You really need to lose some weight; you're reminding me of your Aunt Helen."

An attack on your sense of significance: "Why don't you get a real job?"

An attack on your worth: "Just what is it you do all day?"

Invalidation will cause deep pain in your mate and will cause them to disconnect from you. You may ask: "How can I validate my partner if I don't agree with them? Wouldn't I be enabling them?" Everyone deserves the right to be respected and heard whether you agree or not. Respect the feelings, character and thoughts of your spouse. Validating your spouse has nothing to do with agreeing with them or enabling bad behavior.[37] It is simply listening, understanding and giving them the respect they deserve.

NEGATIVE INTERPRETATIONS

Negative interpretations can be described as:

"When one partner consistently believes that the motives of the other are more negative than is really the case." [38]

If these negative interpretations continue to exist, nothing will change it. Not even positive things. Your perception is truly your reality. Sometimes people will only see what they want to see. The negative interpretations will overshadow any good (past, present or future) in the marriage.

The University of Denver researchers point out:

"When relationships become more distressed, the negative interpretations mount and help create an environment of hopelessness and demoralization."[39]

A negative interpretation is the lens through which a partner views everything you do. Any poor behavior from you further reinforces their mindsets, even if they are misunderstandings, wrong assumptions or inaccurate judgments of another. When negative interpretations exist, mind reading is an accepted form of judging. Mind reading is when you are convinced you know what your partner is thinking, his or her motivation, and all of the reasons for their actions.[40]

Negative interpretation can come through a multitude of "lenses." A lens is a filter in which we view life, our situation, or our partner. A "lens" can stem from family background, expectations, our emotional state, fatigue, stress, beliefs, memories, view of men and women, and so on.

GOSSIP

Gossiping is essentially the art of confessing someone else's sin or perceived sin. Just because something is true gives you no right to repeat it. Learn to put a muzzle on your mouth.

"Communication is more than just talking, it is listening intently."

More homes, churches, business, and relationships have been destroyed by the coyness of gossip maybe than by anything else. Repeating unnecessary things your spouse did or didn't do to your friends, parents, or siblings can cause great damage. If nothing else happens, you just altered the way others will view your mate from that point forward by divulging privy information to others needlessly.

For example, Sally loves to tell her mother everything. That day Sally and her husband, Larry, got into a heated argument. So Sally runs to her mother, Rita, to tell her how Larry said Sally was lazy and taking things for granted. Sally's mother then gets furious with Larry because she knows how hard Sally works balancing home and career. Sally makes her mother swear she won't say a word to Larry. She agrees.

But when Larry sees his mother-in-law, he is going to get the cold shoulder once again, but he can't figure out what he's done to deserve such treatment. Unfortunately, Sally forgot to tell her mother that Larry apologized for his nasty comments. She also "forgot" to mention that she started the fight by calling Larry a selfish slob. Gossip is very destructive.

"A troublemaker plants seeds of strife; gossip separates the best of friends."
~ Proverbs 16:28 (NLT)

HARSHNESS

A sharp tongue is toxic to your marriage. It causes people to either attack or avoid each other. Yelling, name-calling, the use of profanity, belittling, threatening language, and the like, are all forms of verbal abuse. God's Word instructs us to do the following:

"Don't use foul or abusive language. Let everything you say be good and helpful, so that your words will be an encouragement to those who hear them. And do not bring sorrow to God's Holy Spirit by the way you live. Remember, he has identified you as his own, guaranteeing that you will be saved on the day of redemption. Get rid of all bitterness, rage, anger, harsh words, and slander, as well as all types of evil behavior. Instead, be kind to each other, tender-hearted, forgiving one another, just as God through Christ has forgiven you."
~ Ephesians 4:29-32 (NLT)

"The hypocrite, with his mouth, destroys his neighbor." ~ Proverbs 11:9 (NKJV)

Using harshness will NEVER get your spouse to connect with you on any level. Learn to soften your tone and walk in humility in its truest sense. Your words can deflect a potential conversational implosion.

"A gentle answer deflects anger, but harsh words make tempers flare." ~ Proverbs 15:1

SECRECY

Secrecy is something that is concealed and is often rooted in self-preservation. Marriage is a relationship where transparency should be the norm, not the exception. The more secrecy you have in a marriage, the less intimate connection you'll experience. Ask yourself, "Why do I keep key information from my partner?" Is it out of fear of rejection or another heated argument?

It may be worth noting that there is a distinct difference between secrecy and confidentiality. Secrecy is something you conceal often to protect yourself, while confidentiality is something concealed to protect someone else. There are some things I keep from my wife, Jane, in order to protect her. Things such as conflicts with another couple in the church or sins of others that I know about that are only going to cause her to lose sleep. I also attempt to protect the reputation of the guilty party as much as I possibly can. Secrecy in marriage is never a good idea.

VAGUENESS

Some people hate to be pinned down on anything. They can be likened to trying to hold a fish in your hand; they wiggle out as fast as they can. Vagueness is often a sign that you're hiding something.

You may tell your spouse that you'll be home around 7 or 8 o'clock or thereabouts. The truth is, you plan on meeting your buddies at the pub at 6 o'clock on the way home and you are giving yourself a little leeway without your spouse knowing about it. Learn to be crystal clear and speak honestly with your partner. Vagueness creates suspicion and breeds mistrust. Vagueness is often a vice people use to avoid accountability.

QUESTIONS

Yes, questions can be secret weapons in warfare. Questions can be posed as innocent, but actually be traps that lead to another argument. According to our friend and life coach Bishop Joey Johnson, "Questions can be clever, coercive, or concealed ways of either offering opinions or manipulating others."[41] Here are seven most commonly used pseudo-questions people use:

The Leading Question: "Don't you feel that...?" "Wouldn't you rather...?" These questions put limitations on the responder. It is often a way to force a person to make a commitment or an admission.[42] Steve admits he has been fairly "proficient" at doing this.

The Punishing Question: "Why did you say (do or try) that? This is a way to arouse conflict and is a way to punish the other person by attacking their character, consistency or motive.[43] Jane admits that she's had to work on this area.

The Demanding Question: "When are you going to do something about this?" This is a demand or a hidden command although it may appear to be an innocent request.[44]

The Dreaming Question: "If you were in charge here, would you rather...?" It is a hypothetical question that is out for a hypothetical answer. It may seem harmless but it seeks to criticize and devalue.[45]

The Needling Question: "What are you waiting for?" or "What did you mean by that?" This is an attempt to interpret the intentions of another. This question leaves no one-level answer and can have multiple choice meanings.[46] No matter what answer your spouse gives, it can be misconstrued and spun with a negative interpretation leaving your mate in a "catch 22."

The Setting-Up Question: "Didn't you once say that...? This maneuvers your mate into a vulnerable position, ready for the hatchet.[47]

The Rhetorical Question: "Do you think I'm an idiot?" or "Would you rather die in a fire or fix these smoke detectors?" This is way of belittling and insulting the intelligence of another. These types of questions are a way of laying down the gauntlet ready to attack.

"Why" questions are also another way to gain control. "Why" questions are often accusatory in nature and can be a covert way of judging the motives and intentions of others. As a pastor for nearly two decades I have learned that some times people ask questions, but they really aren't looking for an answer. They're looking for an argument.

David Augsburger puts it this way: "Love gives up the concealed weapons called questions and makes a clear statement like: I care about you. I need you. I want your help. I want your respect. Love is honestly open in conversation. Love sets no traps."[48]

NOT LISTENING

Communication is more than just talking, it is listening intently. When one or both parties stop listening to each other, it can cause a relational downward spiral. Practice the art of active listening. Bishop Joey Johnson says, "Be a heart with ears." Use good eye contact, mirror back what is said, and give your spouse your undivided attention.

CONNECTING POINTS

- What causes you to close up like a turtle?

- What can you do to create a safe haven for your mate?

- What have you done in the past to destroy that sense of a safe environment?

- What are some "hot topics" you and your partner have a difficult time discussing civilly? (e.g., finances, sex, in-laws, career, etc.)

TARZAN & JANE'S FUN FACT!

Stanford University researchers found that women have a classier sense of humor than men. The researchers gave men and women humorous cartoons to look at while having their brains monitored with an MRI. Men showed a lot less activity in their brains than women. Men expected the cartons to be funny and started laughing sooner without much thought. Women evaluated the cartoons with much more thought; their brains showed that they experienced more delight with each cartoon.

CHAPTER 14

Communication Builders

If you claim to be religious, but don't control your tongue, you are only fooling yourself, and your religion is worthless.

~ James 1:26 NLT

HERE ARE SOME PRACTICAL STRATEGIES we can use to diffuse poor communication with our spouse.

LISTEN UP!

Listening is just as important, if not more so, than speaking. Listening says, "I care about you and I value your feelings." Learn to give your spouse your undivided attention. That means no TV, no Facebooking or any other distraction. Listening involves eye contact, approachability, welcoming body language, and mirroring back what is said.

"Dear friends, be quick to listen, slow to speak, and slow to get angry. For your anger can never make things right in God's sight." ~ James 1:19-20 (NLT)

Oftentimes we are quick to speak, slow to listen and even quicker to get angry. Listening communicates more than words sometimes. I heard a saying many years ago I have never forgotten: "Since God made you with two ears and one mouth, you should do twice as much listening as speaking." Great advice!

SPEAK UP!

Praise your spouse every day. Most marriages are starving from the famine of indifference. We must intentionally communicate our love in the form of praise. How easy it is to let our partner know when they've blown it, but how many times do we neglect to praise them when they did things right or pleasing to you? High doses of praise will only encourage your spouse to be more responsive to you. They will also build up their self-confidence knowing that you believe in them.

Praise has a way of drawing your spouse closer to you, connecting with you on a deeper level. Just remember, your spouse doesn't have to earn praise from you any more than they have to earn your love. Don't let a day go by that you don't communicate your love for your mate in word, letter or deed.

"Encouragement is the oxygen of the soul."
~ John Maxwell

Don't let a day go by that you don't look your spouse directly in the eye and tenderly tell him or her "I love you." Do this even if you don't feel like it. There is plenty of research that tells us that feelings follow words.

OPEN UP!

There is no true depth of conversation without transparency. Some, out of hurt, have grown cold and live in a perpetual state of guardedness. Self-preservation is the first law of selfishness. I wonder how many arguments have been caused by things we've kept inside out of fear of being rejected by our spouse. When you both have created a safe atmosphere for one another, you must let down your guard and share your deepest thoughts, feelings and dreams. Find special times where you can engage in the sharing of your soul.

SHUT UP!

That's right! Learn when to keep your mouth shut. I once heard it said, "Better to remain silent and be thought a fool than to open your mouth and remove all doubt." It is impossible to retrieve a word once it has left your mouth. Spewing forth needless vitriol will only demoralize and destroy. Guard your mouth and carefully screen every word that proceeds from your lips. The health and strength of your marriage depends upon it.

MAN UP!

This means to take responsibility and immediately apologize quickly for EV-ERY disparaging remark no matter how small you might think it is. In the heat of the battle words can roll off our tongue like a missile from an F-14 fighter jet. When words fly recklessly, they can do irreparable damage unless you act immediately. There is no excuse for failing to control your tongue and hurting your mate.

WISE UP!

If in-depth conversations with your mate continue to be volatile, then it's time to wise up and change your approach. A little wisdom can go a long way. If what you've been doing isn't working, why continue with the same approach? Put to use the strategies given in this section on communication.

T-H-I-N-K Before You Speak

Here is a simple acronym that will help you filter your words before they exit your mouth.

T – IS IT TRUE?

Is your communication accurate and completely forthright?

H – IS IT HELPFUL?

Is it edifying or tearing down? How is your conversation going to help your marriage?

I – IS IT INSPIRING?

How will you inspire your partner through your words?

N – IS IT NECESSARY?

Just because something is true does not mean it is worth repeating.

K – IS IT KIND?

How we come across will either foster connection or divide. Our own mental and emotional state is nourished whenever we are kind.[49] When is the last time you told your spouse you love them or are proud of them? Look for opportunities to freely give kind words.

No More Excuses

Quit making excuses for being difficult and possessing a disagreeable attitude. Use your words to draw your partner in lieu of repelling them. Your words will either heal or tear down. Words have the ability to create a strong connective bond between you and your partner or create a wall of separation and deep pain.

Beware, because one mindless comment can ruin everything. I would venture to say that more relationships have been destroyed by caustic words than by infidelity. Your words will produce something good or bad, and according to Joyce Meyer, words are containers of power. PLEASE USE THEM WISELY.

Encouraging Your Spouse

I heard John Maxwell once say that "Encouragement is the oxygen of the soul." Everyone thrives off of encouragement. We are all naturally drawn to those who encourage us the most. Here are some practical things you can do to encourage your spouse.

GET EXCITED ABOUT THE THINGS S/HE IS EXCITED ABOUT

Be your partner's best friend and be their biggest cheerleader. Show interest in your partner's interests… isn't that what friends do?

DON'T BE JEALOUS OF THEIR SUCCESS OR FAVOR

Recently I had a getaway for a few days and spent it in a friend's condo in south Florida. I was able to plan and of course relax while I was there. It was actually going to be a surprise for Jane but my mom couldn't watch the kids that week. So… I decided to go myself.

Yes, I had been working very hard the past year and I looked forward to breaking away from the daily routine. However, Jane had been working hard too and was taking care of Faith, our five month-old daughter. Truthfully, she needed the getaway more than I did, but not once did she ever try to make me feel guilty or express any jealousy.

To top things off, the day I got to Florida there were five inches of snow that fell and continued all week. When I called, I was at the pool in 80-plus degree weather and she was taking care of four kids and battling the snow. But all that came out of her mouth was how happy she was I was able to get away for a much needed break. Wow! Not one complaint, only happiness over my happiness. That builds trust and I can't wait to surprise her soon. This time my mom promised to watch the kids! If not, I will.

ASK PENETRATING QUESTIONS ABOUT YOUR SPOUSE'S INTERESTS, PROJECTS, OR LIKES AND DISLIKES

Questions clearly say, "I am interested in you." Now there is a difference between interest and interrogation. When your spouse hears you ask a question, do they get defensive? It may be in your approach such as your body language or tone of voice or even the words you use.

GIVE THEM THE FREEDOM TO PURSUE THEIR INTERESTS

Don't nag him every time he wants to watch football and don't get ugly every time she wants to watch a sappy movie. If he likes to take self-defense class, don't make him feel guilty for that. If she likes to take an aerobics class, don't make her feel guilty for that either.

COMPLIMENT. COMPLIMENT. COMPLIMENT.

A recent study discovered that complimenting another person three times a day will produce a happier life.[50] Words will either breathe life into your relationship or death but the choice is up to you. It is nearly impossible to take back the effects of an ill-advised word or comment. Do not go a single day without complimenting your spouse on something. It could be the way they dressed, their hair, how hard they work, how they act around the kids, how well they take care of themselves... the list is endless. Be consistent and genuine. Make no mistake: a marriage that is suffering is deficient in compliments and life-giving words.

Remember to keep your words sweet because one day you might have to eat them.

"Don't use foul or abusive language. Let everything you say be good and helpful, so that your words will be an encouragement to those who hear them."
~ Ephesians 4:29 (NKJV)

CONNECTING POINTS

- How can you be a better listener?

- Do you take responsibility and apologize immediately for any disparaging remarks?

- What can you work on in order to create a safe environment for your spouse?

- What do penetrating questions communicate to your partner?

- What is the difference between penetrating questions and interrogation?

TARZAN & JANE'S FUN FACT!

Boys have cooties!

90% of women wash their hands after using a public restroom; 75% of men do.

Source: American Society for Microbiology

Girls have cooties!

70% of men shower daily. 57% of women shower daily.
Source: Harris Interactive

BONUS SECTION

Power Struggles

GOD SANCTIONS MARRIED COUPLES to be joined or literally to "cleave" to one another. The word *cleave* is a Hebrew word that literally means:

> *To impinge, cling, adhere, to stick, to glue, catch by pursuit, abide, fast, cleave, fasten together, follow close or hard after, be joined, overtake, keep, pursue hard, stick, take.*

In other words, when God tells us to cleave to our spouse, it means to pursue him or her with great energy and intensity. This is not meant to be a one-time occurrence but a way of life.

Remember the beginning stages of your relationship when you were dating or engaged? Do you recall the incredible amount of time and forethought you took for your new found love? You may recall the long, long phone calls that lasted two, three, even four hours - the conversation to you seemed like 30 minutes tops. Then there were the dates that were carefully and creatively planned. There was the goodbye kiss that was full of passion and you hoped would never end.

It's been said that marriage is where two become one, but the question is, which one? Arguments are often petty in nature, so why do such simple things turn into an all-out fight? The Bible tells us why:

> *"Pride leads to arguments."* - *Proverbs 13:10 (NLT)*

Pride is often a result of self-protection. We guard ourselves and do the bare minimum out of fear of being taken advantage of or feeling shame or fear. When we operate in pride, we do not submit to one another (Ephesians 5:21) as BOTH husbands and wives are instructed to do. Note: The wife is instructed to submit to her husband's LEAD, but the husband is to submit to his wife's NEED. There is mutual submission. Power struggles are rooted in fear and pride.

Stosny and Love sum it up this way:

"In a nutshell; power struggles happen when two people fight to protect them-selves from shame and fear. She wants him to do what she wants so she doesn't have to feel anxious, and he wants her to give in so he doesn't have to feel like a failure. They try to control each other or even force the other to submit. Because human beings hate to submit, power struggles always result in more resentment and hostility, which will only aggravate fear and shame." [51]

When it comes to Jane's areas of expertise, I submit to her opinions 99% of the time. When we are in a gridlock on an issue, we make a decision based on consensus or I (Tarzan) can make the final decision after seeking the Lord intently. If it is a huge decision, we may also acquiesce to the safest route unless the Lord directs us otherwise. Although God has given the husband the responsibility as leader, marriage is a team sport that requires equality, never dominance.

It's Getting Hot
In The Jungle

~ Connecting Physically ~

Bring on the heat!

CHAPTER 15

25 Excellent Reasons To Have Sex

"Marriage is honorable among all, and the bed undefiled..."

~ Hebrews 13:4

A 92 YEAR-OLD MAN WENT TO THE DOCTOR to get a physical. A few days later the doctor saw the man walking down the street with a gorgeous young lady on his arm. A couple of days later the doctor talked to the man and said, "You're really doing great, aren't you?" The man replied, "Just doing what you said Doctor, 'Get a hot mamma and be cheerful.'" The Doctor said, "I didn't say that. I said you got a heart murmur. Be careful!"

The following reasons are legitimate reasons to have sex. All but two of them are from the British Medical Journal. This incredible God-given gift has some huge benefits on our health and well-being.

1. **Sex is fun!** Do you need any other reason?

2. **Sex helps you feel good about yourself.** A sexually satisfied man or woman has an extra spring in their step and a sense of confidence and acceptance.

3. **Sex reduces depression.**[52] A hormone found in semen called prostagandin, actually adjusts female hormones. An orgasm releases endorphins which produces a sense of well-being.

4. **Sex heightens your sense of smell.**[53] Sex produces prolactin that produces new neurons in the brain's smell center.

5. **Sex can bring pain relief.**[54] Oxytocin, the hormone that triggers an orgasm, is a natural pain reliever. It can also cure headaches. So if she says she can't due to a headache, let her know you have the cure... doctor's orders!

6. **Sex helps you sleep better.**[55] The calm after sex is better than any sleeping pill. Studies report that after sex people are more at ease, happier and handle stress better.

7. **Sex increases blood flow.**[56] Blood oxygenates your body and helps remove toxins.

8. **Sex helps you look younger.**[57] Sex can slow down the aging process because it lowers Cortisol levels in the bloodstream.

> *"When it comes to sex and the needs of your partner,*
> *create a "yes" environment."*

9. **Sex will help you lose weight.**[58] Sex can burn at least 200 calories which is equivalent to fifteen minutes on the treadmill.

10. **Sex helps you have a healthier heart.**[59] Sex protects from heart disease in women with the production of estrogen. What a great cardio workout.

11. **Sex can help cure the common cold.**[60] Sex, even once a week, can increase the amount of immunoglobin A, which boosts the immune system.

12. **Sex helps keep the prostate healthy.**[61] Urologists link the lack of ejaculation and prostate cancer.

13. **Sex has a calming effect.**[62] Sex is ten times more potent than Valium with no side effects.

14. **Sex boosts your immune system.**[63] Sex releases endorphins that fight disease.

15. **Sex helps hair to shine and skin to glow.**[64] Estrogen makes hair shine and serotonin gives skin that glow.

16. **Sex can unblock a stuffy nose.**[65] Sex is a natural antihistamine that can combat hay fever and asthma.

17. **Sex can help firm your tummy and butt.**[66] The workout from sex will help you look good and improve your posture.

18. **Sex helps protect from Alzheimer's and osteoporosis.**[67] The more sex a woman has the more estrogen her body produces which fights these nasty ailments

19. **Sex can give you a natural high.**[68] God gave us a gift in marriage that will help alleviate depression, stress and any negative emotion. Isn't God good?

20. **Sex gives you better bladder control.**[69] Sex strengthens pelvic muscles that control the flow of urine.

21. **Sex helps you forget.**[70] Having a bad day? Sex is the answer! The hormone released during sex, oxytocin, literally helps you to forget. The parts of your brain that manage stress, fear and anxiety are turned off during an orgasm. This memory lapse can last up to five hours. For men, sex can help them forget the huge riff he had with his wife. Weeks of carrying a weight of anger and frustration seem to be lifted off after being intimate with your spouse.

22. **Sex rewires you for pleasure.**[71] Your brain learns to associate your spouse with pleasure.

23. **Sex puts the passion back into your marriage.**[72] Sex is a barometer for your marriage. There is no such thing as a passionate marriage when times of sex are few and far between.

24. **Sex is something you should do with your mate because you said you would.**[73] When you said "I do" it was understood that you made a commitment to that relationship and sex was part of that commitment.

25. **Sex will help you live longer.**[74] One study insists that having sex three times a week will increase your life by 50%.

Something To Think About

When it comes to sex and the needs of your partner, create a "yes" environment and be an approachable partner. In other words, communicate to your mate that you will do everything in your power to be available and give "due benevolence" even when I may not have the urge or desire to do so at the moment. This is the kind of atmosphere in which a marriage will thrive.

"The husband should fulfill his wife's sexual needs, and the wife should fulfill her husband's needs. The wife gives authority over her body to her husband, and the husband gives authority over his body to his wife. Do not deprive each other of sexual relations, unless you both agree to refrain from sexual intimacy for a limited time so you can give yourselves more completely to prayer. Afterward,

you should come together again so that Satan won't be able to tempt you because of your lack of self-control." ~ 1 Corinthians 7:3-5 (NLT)

CONNECTING POINTS

- Why is sex so important?

- How does sex connect married couples?

- How do you plan to connect sexually with your spouse?

TARZAN & JANE'S FUN FACT!

British men waste 6 million hours of driving each year (burning gas and polluting their environment) because they do not stop to ask for directions.

Source: http://bestfunfacts.com/human_gender_differences.html

CHAPTER 16

When A Husband Disconnects

"My wife is a sex object. Every time I ask for sex, she objects."

~ Les Dawson

"GRANDMA HOW OLD ARE YOU?" asked her young granddaughter. "Never you mind, Sweetheart. You're not supposed to ask those questions," Grandma gently replied. "Grandma, how much do you weigh?" she asked again. "Never you mind. Some things you're not supposed to ask people," Grandma protested. "Grandma, I found your driver's license and I now know your age. You are 62 years old. You weigh 140 pounds and you got an "F" in sex."

Is your sex life failing to make the grade?

Unfortunately, many husbands would give their wives an "F" when it comes to sex. Most husbands fantasize about their wife initiating sex and flirting with him with her bedroom eyes. The fact is most women do not like being the initiators of sex with their husband. Statistically speaking, women love to feel pursued by their husband. This means that men need to make it easy for their mate to initiate sex with them.

Women have incredible power at their disposal - it's called sexual attraction. It's no secret that men are stimulated visually and typically have a much higher level of libido than women. In the Bible, men are referred to as fountains and women as wells. Fountains are under pressure but wells must be primed. The point is most women will never fully understand the male sex drive. For a woman to say she understands her husband's sex drive is like a man saying he understands pregnancy. For women, sex is more of a "want" but for men it is a legitimate "need." One study has shown that the typical woman desires sex every 10 to 14 days, but for men it was every 3 to 5 days (usually 3 depending on age and health).

This chapter is just for women. Please be open-minded because many married men are quietly struggling in this area of sexuality and are being left vulnerable to temptation. But there is good news: you and you alone have the power to help him enormously. You are the only legitimate source he has to express his sexuality and it becomes a huge source of frustration if he feels rejected and misunderstood by you.

"Sex is a powerful act that can either build up your marriage or destroy it rather quickly when it is withheld."

For some women, sex is only viewed as a necessary evil. This may be due to sexual trauma she may have received in her childhood such as rape, incest, a promiscuous background, or an unhealthy view of men. In any case, sexual trauma is serious and can affect your marriage relationship unless healing occurs. Jane and I counseled one woman who refused to have sex with her husband. She was remorseful and admitted, "Sex to me was only a reminder of the pain of my past." Unfortunately, her husband left her because his needs went unfulfilled.

The temptations to look or stray are magnified today. From the lower neck lines and fashions, to billboards, grocery lines, television, movies, magazines, to the skimpy-dressed girl at the office … men are totally bombarded with sexual images that can stimulate their sexuality in an instant, especially if he is left in a sexually vulnerable state. Some men feel a sense of entitlement towards pornography and other sexually destructive behavior when their wife flat-out rejects him sexually. Sexual rejection empowers temptation and weaponizes lust.

In the book of Wisdom (Proverbs) a comparison is made between a Worthy Wife and a Shameful Wife. A Worthy Wife brings joy to her husband and is his crown. A crown is something a king wore proudly and was a symbol of respect and honor. When a wife is honoring it gives great strength to her husband beyond what any words can ever say. A sexually fulfilled man possesses great inner strength, happiness, confidence and self-respect.

A Shameful Wife is one who creates insecurity and saps her husband's strength (Proverbs 12:4). A sexually deprived man is a man without focus, depleted inner strength, and is struggling with self-worth. He will end up physically and emotionally drained; not a good recipe for what you'd want in a husband. Sexually-fulfilled husbands are very responsive to their wife. Sex is a good segue for men to open up emotionally.

Your husband probably feels duped. When you were engaged and on your honeymoon you most likely came across as very sexual. Then shortly after marriage, you settled in and the hormones waned and now you wonder why your husband is so horny. The truth is he didn't change. You did! He was expecting you to be the same way you were on your honeymoon and early on in marriage, available and very sexual. Although most women are not wired the same way as men, it also cannot be an excuse not to be available for your husband. What you treat as common becomes common. But what you treat as valuable remains something special, as sex should be.

The male sex drive is a powerful thing. Here are some statistics that reveal the "sex-crazed" male:[75]

- At age 17 a male peaks sexually. Incredibly, he is able to have an orgasm 4 to 8 times within a 24 hour period.

- In a man's 20s his sex life continues to be extremely strong.

- In his 30s the decline begins but he still prefers sex once in a 24 hour period.

- In a man's 40s and 50s the sex drive declines more but the desire sex at least once a week. Some men are capable of more.

- Men in their 60s and 70s experience a drastic decline in their sex drive and some hardly desire it at all.

The marital picture is often one of a man sexually-starved and a woman feeling overwhelmed by her husband's "obsession" with sex. Years ago Jane and I were "discussing" this subject, she looked at me intently and said, "Something must be wrong with you. This can't be normal." I said, "Yes there is something 'wrong' with me… I'm male!"

Marriage was never meant to be a graveyard for sex. According to a German study, a women's libido drastically plummets once she enters a secure relationship, and 20 years later less than 50% of women wanted regular sex. A female's initial sex drive helps bond the couple.[76] To top things off, the smallest thing can set a man off. He can be minding his own business then all of a sudden – wham! He wants sex in an instant. These triggers can be things like:

- A tight dress

- A woman's cleavage

- A whiff of perfume

- The sight of a pair of sexy legs

- A glance of a well-shaped behind

- A flirtatious gesture

- A risqué billboard, television show, internet ad or magazine cover

Women, never underestimate the incredible power and influence of a man's sex drive. If you make a habit of dressing and undressing in front of your husband, you are sending him strong messages even if you aren't meaning to. Ladies, you have been warned!

One man admits, "I am 37 and my wife is 39. If I can persuade her to have sex with me twice a week, I am happy; but she gives me a hard time accepting." Unfortunately, many men feel this way. As a wife, if you make sex a big deal, it will wind up being a big deal to him. Interestingly, studies have shown that when marriages are struggling, sex registered very high on the problem list.[77]

Conversely, when couples say their marriage is very happy, sex rarely comes up in conversation. Why? When couples are sexually content, sex is a non-issue; it's just a regular part of the rhythm of life. If it seems like sex is over-emphasized by your husband, then be easily accessible to him and you'll see him make sex a virtual non-issue. If men don't have this security from their wives it makes them irritable, unfocused, untrusting, even controlling, and left feeling a sense of shame and inadequacy.

Unfortunately, many women have a poor view of sex for several reasons:

- They may have a low level of libido due to health problems, depression or stress.

- They may have been sexually abused and sex is a reminder of the pain of the past.

- They may have been sexually promiscuous and associate sex as something shameful, even unconsciously.

- They have a poor view of men in general because of an abusive father or ex.

Sex is a powerful act that can either build up your marriage or destroy it rather quickly when it is withheld. A wife can immediately sabotage her marriage if she shames her husband sexually. Men can tolerate a lot of things but this is one area that is near and dear to their heart. Can your husband trust you with his heart? Can he trust you with his greatest vulnerability, his sexuality? Can he trust you to be available to him without an attitude, pre-conditions or without making him feel guilty for wanting the incredible, beautiful woman he married?

Want to change your husband? Then change your bedroom! Make it hotter than ever; help him feel secure and vulnerable with you. Friend, Pastor and author Paul Endrei puts it this way:

"When a man experiences sexual rejection from his wife, he shuts down emotionally and will unconsciously stop meeting his wife's emotional needs." [78]

When you are available for him sexually, there is a significant chance he will be there for you emotionally and show you the tenderness most women desire. A sexually contented man will feel confident, energized and more sensitive to his wife. A sexually contented man won't come across like a raging stallion in heat. Ladies, if you feel "overwhelmed" by your husband's sexual needs, then remember this: A sexually contented man will be more "sexually balanced." In other words, if you make it difficult for him, it will only get worse. Men often have a sense of entitlement towards pornography and other promiscuous behavior whenever a wife turns a cold shoulder towards his sexual needs.

God's Word reminds husbands and wives to give each other "due benevolence" (1 Corinthians 7:3). The word *due* means to be obligated, bound, indebted, and ower. The word *benevloence* means to be agreeable, kind, well-minded in thought, feeling, will, or understanding. This is a picture of a safe environment that seeks to please each other to the best of their ability.

For men, sex is more than just a physical release. Men, like women, need an emotional connection to their physical attachment for sex to be fulfilling. That's why prostitution or pornography will never satisfy men sexually. As a matter of fact, it only creates an insatiable desire for more intensity and frequency of sex because he is longing for something that can only be found and tamed by his covenant partner... his wife!

"Let your wife be a fountain of blessing for you. Rejoice in the wife of your youth. She is a loving doe, a graceful deer. Let her breasts satisfy you always. May you always be captivated by her love. Why be captivated, my son, with an immoral woman, or embrace the breasts of an adulterous woman?" ~ *Proverbs 5:18-20 (NLT)*

"Parents can provide their sons with an inheritance of houses and wealth, but only the Lord can give an understanding wife." ~ *Proverbs 19:14 (NLT)*

CONNECTING POINTS

- Ask your husband how often he desires sexual intimacy? (Don't assume you know)

- What holds you back from him sexually?

- Do you know how your husband reacts whenever (if) you reject his sexual advances or make it difficult for him?

- Will you initiate sex with him today? Practice role reversal: For the next two weeks, initiate sex with your husband 3 times a week.

TARZAN & JANE'S FUN FACT!

14% of 25-34 year-old men live with their parents. 8% of 25-34 year old women live with their parents.

Source: US Census Bureau, 2009

CHAPTER 17

Is There Sex After Marriage?

"Always be intoxicated by her love."

~ Proverbs 5:15

O NE DAY A MAN WAS FILLING OUT JOB APPLICATION and on the application was asked to check sex. The man wrote "not lately."

We spend one-third of our life sleeping in bed. The bedroom can not only affect your sex life but your entire life. Sex is the only unique feature of marriage. We can shop with others, hang out with others, have fun and laugh with others, but we only have sex with our spouse. Sex says, "I am committed to you." When sex is withheld, it says "You don't really care about me," even if you do.

You may have heard of the acronym DINKS which stands for "Dual Income No Kids." There is now a new acronym: DINS ... "Dual Income No Sex." There are many "sex-less" marriages today. The average married couple in America has sex only 68.5 times a year according to the National Opinion Center at the University of Chicago. And that stat has been consistent for a decade.[79] An article in the USA Today reported that 40 million married couples have little or no sexual contact with their spouse. There are approximately 113 million married Americans and many are frustrated with their sex life. Some psychologists have estimated that 15 to 20% of couples have sex no more than 10 times per year.[80] Dr. Les Parrot observes that "marital celibacy is real."[81] Margaret Carlson claims that for many couples "sleep is the new sex."[82]

The absence of sex will build an impenetrable wall of disconnection between couples because sex was designed to keep couples bonded to each other. The Latin root for sex means "to cut off or sever."[83] In other words, sex drives us to connect to that which has been severed. Sex is meant to keep married couples connected on a deep physical, emotional, and spiritual level. The French Sociologist Jacques Ellul views our modern sex-crazed attitudes as a sure sign of a breakdown of sexual intimacy.[84]

"When you value each other, you will have the urge to merge."

According to studies, couples have turned to "solo sex" for sexual release. According to statistical studies, 90% of all men and 65% of all women masturbate on occasion.[85] Another study suggests that 96% of males under 20 sexually relieve themselves regularly, on average 14 times per month. This happens to be the same for married men. Teenage boys do this as often as most married men. Studies conclude that the frequency remains relatively consistent in males from adolescence throughout adulthood.[86] A high number of women also reported as experimenting with self-pleasure on a regular basis.

So what is really happening?

SEX BUSTERS

There are some reasons couples have a sex life that looks more like a flickering candle than a blazing fire. Here are some of them:

OVER-WORKED

Stress and fatigue are huge factors for the lack of intimacy. Physical and emotional exhaustion can turn even the most hormone-crazed man or luscious-lipped woman in to a frigid, withdrawn, low-energy lover. Intimacy must be prioritized. Work is important but don't allow it to become an excuse for the lack of sexual closeness.

According to Stosny and Love:

"Men and women in the United States work longer hours than in any other industrialized nation, including Japan, which gave us the term 'karoshi', meaning 'to drop dead from overwork.' We actually work longer hours than the serfs did in the Dark Ages. And now with telecommunication, work doesn't stop when you leave the workplace. Evening and weekend hours that used to belong

to the individual and family are increasingly considered fair game for getting caught up at work." [87]

OFFENSE

The best way to kill any sexual desire towards your spouse is to stay upset with them. An unforgiving spirit will breed feelings of contempt and words of sarcasm. Be sure to address all anger and unresolved issues before the sun goes down (just try not to wait until midnight to talk about things). A women's libido can significantly drop whenever there are unresolved emotional and relational issues, even if they are little ones. Learn to deal with disagreements quickly and peaceably. Your bedroom will get hotter (in a good way).

OVER-FAMILIARITY

It is so easy to take for granted those we are closest to. Over-familiarity can breed laziness in any relationship especially in marriage. Remind yourself of using proper manners and simply remember how you used to act when you first started dating. Courtesy and respect were commonplace, not an anomaly.

OFFSPRING

Kids can really put a damper on things some times. I swear my kids knew exactly when to wake up, throw a fit, or suddenly want to come and sleep in mommy and daddy's bed… How could they possibly know this was the time mommy and daddy waited for all day, and now you need mommy and daddy at 1:00 a.m.? You were perfectly fine the last 5 days, why now? Oh, and by the way, make sure you have a dead bolt on your door!

OTHER LOVERS

Studies suggest there is a tendency to become less satisfied with your mate physically and emotionally the more sexual partners you had prior to marriage. [88] Couples who were not promiscuous before marriage are much more satisfied compared to those who were. [89] Due to this propensity of human nature, this means, depending on your sexual past, you may want to be proactive and intentional at demonstrating love and affection towards your mate regardless of feelings.

Turning Up The Heat

Here are a few suggestions that will help your bedroom heat up!

JUST DO IT!

People with a low desire actually get into the mood while doing it. The high-desire person needs little or no prompting. Usually one spouse is much more sexually aroused than the other. Make a commitment with each other that you will have sexual intimacy with each other as much as you are able.

DRESS FOR SUCCESS

What you wear in private can also be a big turn-on as well. Wearing lingerie and practicing good hygiene is also a huge plus.

EXERCISE REGULARLY

Yes, working out can not only change your body shape, but it can change your metabolism and your libido as well. When you exercise, you begin to feel good about yourself and develop confidence. The last thing women in particular feel like doing is having sex when they have a poor body image. When a man doesn't feel good about himself, the opposite is true - sex makes him feel better as a person.

FORGIVE

It is virtually impossible to have a great marriage and sex life with bitterness, resentment and unforgiveness present. Ruth Bell Graham once said, "A good marriage is the union of two forgivers." When your hearts are open towards each other it is easier to express your body and bare your soul with one another.

VALUE

Esteem one another daily. Sex is a beautiful way to communicate value to your mate. Sex is so powerful that it is like powerful superglue that binds you together spirit, soul and body. When you value each other, you will have the urge to merge. When physical intimacy is lacking, your partner believes "you simply don't care about me."

"Create anticipation and excitement... try something new."

PROTECT

A healthy, vibrant sex life will help ward off would-be predators. Temptations decrease when marriage sexual intimacy increases. Protect each other by meeting the most basic of marital needs. Protect your time together and allow nothing to stop you from connecting regularly.

PRIORITIZE

No one on their deathbed says, "Gee, I wish I worked harder and more hours." It's usually just the opposite. We can prioritize our job, kids, school, and parents sometimes above our spouse. Sexual intimacy is a way of prioritizing your mate. Dr. Phil McGraw says, "A good sexual relationship can make you feel more relaxed, accepted, and more involved with your partner."[90] There are times to be spontaneous and there are other times you need to schedule (yes, schedule) your time together. Build anticipation and make each other feel special by prioritizing one another. We must learn to slow down and major in the majors. Unfortunately, many Americans suffer from "hurry sickness" or sheer marital laziness. You should always have something you are looking forward to as a couple. Don't put your marriage on autopilot hoping things will change. Prioritizing makes a strong statement that says, "You are the most important person in my life and nothing will come between us."

VIVE LA DIFFERENCE

Create anticipation and excitement and try something new. For more information read Kevin Leman's book called *Sheet Music*.

ATMOSPHERE

Involve all of your senses. Use scented candles, romantic music, chocolate, etc. Atmosphere can create anticipation and help your mate get in the mood.

WOO YOUR PARTNER

Remember to entice your mate by luring him or her just like you did early in your relationship. Never lose that romantic edge.

CONNECTING POINTS

- Which one of the sex busters do you need to work on the most?
- What can you practically do to be more sexual with each other?
- Are there any sexual hang-ups? It may be spiritual, emotional, or physical. If so, what is being done about it?

TARZAN & JANE'S FUN FACT!

Does size really matter? According to multiple surveys, no! Men nor women are deeply concerned about the size of "certain" body parts although Hollywood may try to make us think otherwise.

BONUS SECTION

Bedroom Etiquette

"Marriage is an alliance entered into by a man who can't sleep with the window shut, and a woman who can't sleep with the window open."

~ George Bernard Shaw

ONE DAY TWO MEN WERE MOURNING over the state of the economy and their stock investments. The first man said, "My stocks have tanked and I haven't been able to sleep in weeks." The second man replied, "My stocks have tanked, too, but I sleep like a baby." "Really?" said the first man, "how is that?" The second man said, "I wake up every hour and cry like a baby."

We spend roughly one-third of our life sleeping in bed so let's make the most of it! The bedroom will not only affect your sex life but your entire life. Here are some simple tips for improving your sex life and intimacy level.

GO TO BED TOGETHER AT THE SAME TIME

If you are going to bed at different times on a regular basis, you are robbing each other of quality bonding time. Make it a point to go to bed together regularly. I knew one couple where she went to bed at 10:00 p.m. and he would stroll into bed around 3:00 am. Needless to say, they had serious intimacy issues. Going to bed together can promote intimate conversations and emotional connection besides the sexual connection.

LIMIT CHILDREN SLEEPING IN YOUR BED

One couple we counseled always had a little one sleeping in their bed since having children. Once again, they too, had serious sexual problems. They placed their children above their own relationship which will always spell disaster for couples. One of the biggest intimacy robbers is allowing children to sleep in your bed on a regular basis. Now occasionally when there is a bad thunderstorm or when a child is sick or teething, sometimes this rule is broken. But this is to be short-lived and the exception, not the rule. Your marriage and emotions won't wait for your kids to grow up.

REMEMBER YOUR BEDSIDE MANNERS

Passing gas, belching and other bodily functions are part of life and many couples joke around, but remember not to overdo your practical jokes. Over-familiarity can stifle intimacy in a heartbeat. It's good to be relaxed around one another and be yourself and instill a little humor (if you find that hilariously funny), but remember to value your partner and put your best foot forward. Make your spouse feel special and honor your bedtime togetherness. Don't allow over-familiarity spoil times of intimacy.

JUST DO IT!

Sometimes just begin to romance each other. You may be tired and may not even feel like it, but like Nike says, "Just Do It!" Sex begins by prioritizing each other. Whether you feel like it or not you must remember that sex is a powerful way for a husband and wife to connect to each other and keep the passion alive. If you are a high-desire person then this won't be a problem. Low-desire individuals don't feel like having sex until they are in the act of sex.

THERE'S A TRADE-OFF

Women complain because their husband's sex drive is wearing them out and that their husband is not very emotional. Men complain that their wife is ignoring them sexually and that she isn't sexual enough. Listen, here's the trade off: Ladies, if you want your husband to be more emotional? Be more sexual! Guys, if you want your wife to be more sexual? Then be more emotional! Before you touch her body, be sure to touch her heart.[91]

The goal of sex is connection. It is the only part of our being where we can connect spirit, soul and body... that's the power of sex.

Connecting Points

- Have children come between your marriage? If so, what can you do about it?

- What can your mate do to help promote a better "love life"?

- How have your sleep patterns affected your life and marriage?

Jungle Romeo

~ Connecting Romantically ~

Life is sweeter in the jungle when you are
connected with your Tarzan or Jane!

CHAPTER 18

Romeo, Romeo... Where Art Thou?

"Husbands must give honor to your wives. Treat her with understanding as you live together. She may be weaker than you are, but she is your equal partner in God's gift of new life. If you don't treat her as you should, your prayers will not be heard."

~ 1 Peter 3:7 NLT

SAM TOLD HIS WIFE MARYLOU HE WOULD TAKE HER OUT to dine royally. Later MaryLou reported, "We started out at Burger King and wound up at the Dairy Queen." Do you still give your wife the "royal" treatment? Do you treat her like the queen she is? And I'm not talking about fast food dates either. Women need to be pampered from time to time.

This chapter is geared just for men. Admittedly, us men need help in this area of romance just as women need prodding when it comes to sex. Romance is not the same as sex. Romance is what makes you and your spouse feel special. Romance is defined by Websters as "a love affair, atmosphere, attitude or tendency characterized by a sense of remoteness from or idealization of everyday life." In other words, it is time focused on your spouse: getting out of the mundane of everyday activities.

Romeo, Romeo, where art thou? What ever happened to the one I married? He used to be Mister Romeo now he's more like Mister Rogers. She used to be

Juliet, the great lover. Now she resembles an Ice Queen. Why did the flames die so quickly? Maybe you feel like mere roommates sharing the same house. I can recall a time Jane looked at me and with intensity in her voice said, "I feel like I am nothing more than your business partner; I just want to be your wife." It took a little time, but she got my attention and I began to change.

Many wives feel they've been dealt a sleight of hand. During courtship, the engagement and early in marriage you were such a romantic stud. She was thinking you'd always be like this. Then you settled into marriage and became complacent. The chase is over and now you've got the cat in the bag. She is left feeling hurt and frustrated - Romeo has disappeared. The truth is, Mister Romeo was being flooded with hormones related to an infatuation stage. These rush of hormones turn men into smooth-talking Pepe LePew's. Unfortunately, this hormone bath only lasts for a short season. After that, men must work at being Romeo again.

> ### "Identifying the source of your problem is the first step to rectifying it."

Romance for a man involves nudity. For women, romance is a slow process of in-depth conversation, non-sexual touching, watching a chick flick, and much anticipation. Sex for her is a destination; for men that's usually their starting point.

Jimmy Evans says,

> "Failed marriages are like cars that have rusted out and been banished to the junk yard. At one point they were shiny and new, but eventually the owner stopped maintaining it. All it took was one little spot of rust. How can we keep our marriages from rusting out? One of the best methods for treating marital 'rust' is to practice the art of romance." [92]

Let's stop the marital rust by being proactive. The truth is sometimes we are more in tune with the condition of our cars than our own wife! Let's learn today how to "rust-proof" our marriage.

Now the flames of romance don't have to be a blazing inferno everyday, but we all need to see some flames putting out some kind of heat. Unfortunately, that fire may be a mere flicker. So what happened? We believe life happened. We get so caught up working, paying the bills and chasing the American dream, that we forget what is most important. We don't want to obtain some grandiose vision and dream unless we can be united every step of the way. We don't want to gain wealth, fame and success at the expense of my marriage and family. There is nothing in the whole world that is worth sacrificing my marriage and family for.

When we read the Song of Solomon, we envision lots of romance, fun, laughter, creativity, excitement, and passion. Now that's the kind of marriage we want, how about you? Chances are, your marriage is suffering from a romance deficit. Let's look at some reasons as well as the remedy for a lack of romance.

Romance Busters

Identifying the source of your problem is the first step to rectifying it. Awareness precedes change. I believe there are four main areas that deflate the air in our romantic balloon.

FAMILIARITY

There is an old saying, "Familiarity breeds contempt." We also believe it breeds laziness. We all have been a bit cavalier regarding our marital connection. What we once prized has become "old hat." Remember how we treated that new car or home? Many times after the chase is over, we coast in the relationship. We need to guard against attitudes of over-familiarity and begin to prize each other again. What we treat as common becomes common, but what we value becomes preciously valuable.

We wouldn't have dreamed of being late for our date early in the relationship. But now it may be a common practice. We wouldn't dream of being late for work or keep our boss waiting, but often we can have no regard for our partner. We should never treat others with more respect than our own mate.

It is important to feel comfortable and at ease around each other, however it is vital that we don't lose "the chase" just because you are married. Don't lose all of your manners, thoughtfulness, kindness, courtesy, chivalry, care for your body and respectful words just because the chase is over and you have him or her in the bag. Many times we treat strangers better than those closest to us. Keep your marriage alive by guarding against over-familiar attitudes with one another.

FATIGUE

People no longer work nine to five – it's more like seven to seven nowadays. Not only that, but according to Focus on the Family, approximately 60% of wives are working outside the home. In 2006, 6% of couples who filed for divorce sited the reason was due to their spouse being a workaholic.[93] Then to top things off many kids are involved in nearly every sport or extracurricular activity.

I remember when Jane and I were first married we would go for a walk at midnight or go to a movie theatre at 11:00 p.m. just to play Pac Man or have fun at 3:00 am. Now with a house full of kids, are you kidding? There are days we are so exhausted even sex sounds like a chore (well, maybe not for Tarzan!). When we were dating, we'd talk to the wee hours of the morning over the phone. Now it can be hard to stay awake past ten. Physical exhaustion can mess with our romantic side because we lack the energy needed to be creative when facing fatigue. The question is, "How long can we last on this fast-track?" Bill Hybels says:

"The problem arises when you spend too much time in crisis mode. That's when crisis mode goes from being a season of life to becoming a way of life." [94]

Couples are going at a pace God never designed for us to maintain. In a USA Today poll, eighty-nine percent of Americans say they have little or no free time. In a world of text messaging and eating on the fly, we're in a hurry going nowhere. John 10:10 says,

"The thief comes only to steal and kill and destroy; I have come that they may have life and have it to the full."

The word "kill" literally means to breathe hard. Many people are out of breath due to the crazy lifestyles they have been living. The enemy Satan is likened unto a roaring lion that tries to keep us on the run 24/7. Love is spelled T.I.M.E. and that's one thing we don't seem to have enough of. We are over-extended and burning the candle at both ends. What is it going to take for us to get off this train? We need to simplify our lives, slow down and prioritize our marriage.

Dr. James Dobson has observed:

"An explosion was just as matter of time, because each of us was too exhausted to consider the needs of the other."

Sometimes we are overly-committed doing too many things at once. Do you really have to do three projects all at once? Do you really have to work 80 hours a week on a regular basis? We must consider our ways for our own health, but for the health of our marriage.

FINANCIAL PRESSURE

As never before we have more couples in a deep financial pit. In the early days of our grandparents they had ten to fifteen-year mortgages, cars that were actually paid off in two or three years and hardly any debt. The easy credit has brought heavy burdens upon our lives. Two car payments, mortgage plus an equity line, student loans, daycare costs, kid's expenses for school and extracurricular activities can be monumental.

Financial pressure equals marriage pressure. Many believe money problems are the number one reason for divorce. So if that is the case, we need to do everything possible to keep ourselves from being strapped in a financial prison. I could remember times when I wanted to buy my wife flowers until I looked at my checking account balance. Those were some hard days. Be unified in your spending, have a budget and pay down your debt. Avoid emotional spending and be a giver as well as a saver. If necessary have a side a job where you can use that money to either pay down debt or pay cash for things you'd normally put on credit.

UNFORGIVENESS

You will never be romantically affectionate and intimate with your mate when unforgiveness is present. In this case, you can never "fake it till you make it." Jimmy Evans guarantees, "Unforgiveness is like a dead rat in the attic; it makes the entire house stink." [95] Unforgiveness not only punishes your spouse, but it will punish you as well. Unforgiving attitudes invite emotional and physical problems. It is impossible to truly connect with your partner as long as an unforgiving spirit persists.

What Women Want

Women crave tenderness as much as a man craves sex. Wives want their husband to show tenderness especially when he isn't wanting something else in return (wink, wink). A husband who shows tender affection inspires his wife to be more sexual towards him. Although most women (90%) desire tenderness, for men the opposite was true. Only 25% of men desired this same tenderness from their wife.[96] Men, it is important for your wife to know that you will show this gentle tenderness towards her and be more emotional even when you don't feel like it; just as you desire your wife to be there for you sexually even when she doesn't feel like it. This tender attitude will undoubtedly and unequivocally influence your wife's attitude towards you. If you have been harsh towards your wife for years, don't expect her to warm up to you immediately, but she will certainly love this new change in you. Your tenderness just may bring the healing needed to connect you to your "Jane." Why not show her today?

Connecting Points

- Ask your wife what she needs from you to be more romantic? (If she tells you that you should already know, then reminisce about what worked in the past).

- What prevents you from being more romantic? What will you do about it?

- Do you know your wife's birthday, your anniversary, your song and other important things?

- Do you make sure the kids honor her on her birthday, Mother's Day, Christmas, etc.?

- Learn your wife's "Love Language" and act according.

- Will you do something romantic for your wife today? What will you do?

TARZAN & JANE'S FUN FACT!

Men get sick twice as often as women, although women tend to be more concerned about their health.

Source: http://peoplerelationships.syl.com/battleof-sexes/differences

THE ROMANCE TEST

1. Does your mate feel like you are meeting his/her needs?
   Yes   No

2. Do you initiate romance by meeting the needs of your spouse?
   Yes   No

3. Do you know your spouses' love language?
   Yes   No

   If yes, name them: _____

4. Have you given your spouse flowers, gift, a love letter, or some kind of surprise over the past 30 days?
   Yes   No

5. Do you go out of your way without any prompting and without asking anything in return to make your spouse feel good about themselves?
   Yes   No

6. Could your marriage be described as fresh, exciting and passionate at some point in the past 3 months?
   Yes   No

7. Does your mate know that s/he is valued above anyone or anything?
   Yes   No

8. Are you creative and try new things?
   Yes   No

9. Have you had two date nights with your spouse in the last 30 days?
   Yes   No

10. Can you name the 5 basic needs of your mate?
    Yes   No

    If yes, list them: _____

SCORING: HOW MANY "NO'S" DID YOU ANSWER?

0   You're a romantic love machine (Pepe LePew)

1-2   Need more consistency

3-4   Your spouse is probably frustrated with you

5+   You are romantically deficient and hurting your spouse (get help!)

CHAPTER 19

Balancing Sex & Romance

"I am my beloved's and my beloved is mine."

~ Song of Solomon 5:2

A YOUNG MAN WAS PROPOSING to his girlfriend: "Honey, I love you, but I wish I could give you the things my friend Benny has: boats, cars, airplanes." She replied, "I love you too, baby, but tell me more about Benny."

Truthfully, there are many people, some we have counseled, who would admit they'd trade all their wealth for a good marriage.

> *"I hate to be a failure. I hate and regret the failure of my marriages. I would gladly give all my millions for just one lasting marital success."*
>
> *~ J. Paul Getty*

The accumulation of things will never bring true happiness nor does it imply a better sex life or romance. Statistics just might show the complete opposite.

There is a difference between sex and romance. Sexual intercourse is powerful, but romantic affection is just as powerful. You see, neither sex nor romantic affection is designed to stand alone. Balancing sex and romance (tenderness and affection) is essential to experiencing physical and emotional connection.

Romantic affection is non-sexual touching, flirting, and communication. Truthfully, everything we do in marriage is "foreplay" or a precursor to the marriage bedroom. Romantic affection is how a couple relates to one another on a daily basis. Frequently saying "I love you," unexpected surprises, expressing support, a good attitude towards your partner... all build oneness in your marriage.

Intimacy in marriage cannot be maintained by sex alone. Sometimes sex is over-emphasized because this emotional connection is severely lacking. Some couples do well in bed and have it nailed down to ten minutes flat, but romantic affection is nowhere to be found. This leaves couples with an "empty" disconnected feeling over time.

The problem in today's marriage is that couples are so rushed that they neglect investing in their spouse like they should. Everything in life seems to take precedence over your marriage relationship. Sure, they may have sex a couple times a week, but they don't act like lovers outside the bedroom. Often couples suffer in silence or might not find the words to express how they feel.

Here is a formula to further communicate this thought:

Sex minus Romance = Sexual Dissatisfaction

Romance minus Sex = Emotional Disconnection

"There is a difference between temporary relief and true satisfaction."

Whenever there is a relational disconnect we may try harder to please our spouse or distance ourselves even further out of self-preservation. The mature thing to do is to civilly talk things out.

Romance and affection can look like the following:

- Hand holding.

- Back or foot massages.

- "I love you" or "You mean the world to me" are expressed throughout the day.

- Personal hygiene is emphasized with each other in mind.

- Taking a walk together.

- Discussing details of your day together.

- Playing a fun game together.

- Slowing down and smelling the "roses of life" together.

Romantic affection and tenderness will bring a greater level of connectedness in your marriage and will certainly raise the intensity of your bedroom. This is one thing during the courtship and engagement period that seems to vanish shortly after you say "I do" for so many couples. It is easy to lose sight of each other in the midst of kids, jobs, and the busyness of life. Make it a point, regardless of your busy schedules, to invest romantically in one another.

Dr. Phil candidly states that "being in love is not like falling in love." When we walk in the room our hearts don't pound uncontrollably like they once did early in the relationship. In fact, the "infatuation" stage is the easiest part of the relationship. It is in this stage that our bodies are flooded with relationship-bonding hormones that can have the same affect as being intoxicated. That's why some people who date a lot get addicted to the infatuation stage due to the rush they feel. But in reality, couples don't live in that stage. Those hormones generally stop within 3 to 9 months of the relationship. Love takes work, but the feelings of true love remain and they are stable, not flighty. Our love becomes seasoned and mature. Love is not the same as infatuation. Infatuation is shallow and me-centered; love is deep and others-centered.

The infatuation stage can easily blind couples to glaring flaws and annoying traits that seem so adorable during the time of courtship. Once the hormones are reduced in the settling stage, we are befuddled as to how we overlooked such obvious idiosyncrasies in our partner. Often, we erroneously believe somehow that they changed drastically. But the truth is, these traits were always there; you just never noticed them until reality set in.

One thing to remember is that intimacy is not just romance or sex, but a feeling of incredible closeness and unquestionable trust where no walls are present. This kind of intimacy never fears standing naked and unashamed before your mate.

"Let the husband render to his wife the affection due her, and likewise also the wife to her husband." - 1 Corinthians 7:3

CONNECTING POINTS

- What will you do today to show romantic affection to your mate?

- What seems to be an essential key to experiencing romance and affection?

- What was it like before you were married? How can you recapture that fun side of romance?

- What is romantic or affectionate to you?

TARZAN & JANE'S FUN FACT!

Women should not blame men for "not listening." It is not their fault. Since women's voices have many more frequencies than men's, the human brain must work harder to analyze sound frequencies and comprehend the meaning intended.

Source: Discovery.com

CHAPTER 20

Date Your Mate:
101 Great Date Ideas

"People rarely succeed unless they have fun in what they are doing."

~ Dale Carnegie

DATING VERSUS MARRIAGE

When you are dating...

Passing gas is never an issue.

When you are married...

You make sure there's nothing flammable near your husband at all times.

When you are dating...

He knows what the "hamper" is.

When you are married...

The floor will suffice as a dirty clothes storage area.

When you are dating…

He likes to "discuss" things.

When you are married…

He develops a "blank" stare.

When you are dating…

He calls you by name.

When you are married…

He calls you "Hey" and refers to you when speaking to others as "She."

When you are dating…

You picture the two of you together, growing old together.

When you are married…

You wonder who will die first.

You must prioritize FUN in your marriage. The following are some fun date ideas to consider. We believe it is important to "date your mate" to keep the relationship alive and vibrant. If you have any ideas you'd like to share, please email us at office@MeTarzanYouJane.com.

STAYING AT HOME

1. Candlelight dinner

2. Movie night

3. Game night

4. Karaoke night (freekaraoke.com)

5. Watch wedding videos or view wedding photos

6. Massage night

7. Make the biggest or craziest sundae ever

8. Make the biggest and wildest sub sandwich ever

9. Make your own dance floor and dance the night away

10. Have a picnic in your own living room

11. Bring home your favorite fast food and serve it on your fine china

12. Feed each other Chinese food using chop sticks

13. Build a campfire and make smores

14. A game of bocce ball in the back yard

15. Make a snowman (if you're in that part of the world that actually gets snow)

16. Fondue night followed by a bubble bath

17. Play the Wii

18. Watch home videos

19. Write a poem to each other

20. Write a silly song for each other

21. Write an acronym of each other's name

22. Go to the library and read to each other

23. Breakfast in bed

24. Home fashion show

SHORT TRIPS

1. Nearby stay at a bed and breakfast

2. Overnight at a hotel

3. Trip to Amish country (or the country if no there are no Amish communities around)

4. Go to a local farmers market or farm animal auction

5. Massage get-away

6. Rent a cabin

7. Visit a chocolate or cheese factory

FUN & FREE (OUTDOOR FUN)

32. Tennis anyone?

33. Frisbee golf at a local park

34. Walk in the park

35. Picnic in the park

36. Live concert at a park or town square

37. One-on-one basketball at a local park

38. Roller blading

39. Hiking or jogging

40. Bike riding

41. Visit a botanical garden

42. Drive to the country and park and watch the stars

43. See fireworks or have a display of your own

44. Go to an old car show

45. Tour the most expensive neighborhoods

46. Test drive a really cool sports car

47. Fly a kite

48. Bird or animal watching

49. Play air soft guns (play nice)

50. Ride quad runners or a motorcycle (helmets please)

51. Star watching on a clear night from a huge hill

52. Go fishing

53. Water skiing (know someone with a boat?)

54. Walk on the beach (if you are near an ocean or big lake)

FUN & RELATIVELY INEXPENSIVE

55. Dinner and a movie

56. City aquarium

57. County or state fair

58. Local city theatre

59. Comedy night

60. Take a one night class together

61. Take ballroom dancing lessons together

62. Go to garage sales in rich neighborhoods

63. Drive-in movie

64. Visit a museum

65. Jazz festival

66. Home and Garden Tour

67. Home and Garden Show

68. Car or Sports Show

69. Farmer's market

70. Go to the driving range

71. Go to a local arcade and play Pac Man, pinball, ski ball or whatever

72. Play paintball or laser tag

73. High school game

74. Go on a hayride

75. Go to an old pizza joint for dinner

76. Go to a local pool and swim or just hang out in the Jacuzzi

77. Petting zoo

78. Animal safari

79. Water park

80. Ice skating

81. Picture gallery

82. Workout at a local gym together

83. Go to the shooting range for some target practice

84. Visit your hometown or college town and reminisce

85. Snow skiing

86. Paint ball

87. Go hunting

88. Camping in a tent or rent a camper

89. Horseback riding

90. Ride go-karts

FUN & EXPENSIVE

91. Dinner cruise

92. Professional ballgame

93. Dinner theatre

94. Amusement park

95. Scuba diving

96. Charter a boat

97. Rent a limo or a fancy car and paint the town

98. Visit a hall of fame (football, baseball, basketball, rock-n-roll, etc.)

99. Trip to Disney World/Land

100. Go to a 5-star restaurant

101. Go to the mall and pick out a nice outfit for each other

DATE NIGHT SUGGESTIONS

HAVE A DATE NIGHT AT LEAST TWICE A MONTH

There's an old saying, "If it took dating to get her, it's going to take dating to keep her." Date Nights help keep the romance alive. Date Nights are a great way to connect with one another on a deeper level. Date Nights communicate to your partner that s/he is a high priority to you. Your actions will often speak louder than words. Ideally, a once-a-week Date Night is ideal, but sometimes can be very difficult with kids, work schedules, and sheer exhaustion.

PLAN AHEAD

If you don't schedule your Date Nights don't expect them to happen. If you fail to plan, then plan to fail. Coordinate your calendars and decide what night or days will work for both of you. You may have to plan a day when it is not the craziest day of the week at the office. If you're able, plan a year in advance. Calendars can fill up fast, so don't delay. Also, remember to plan for a babysitter. Last minute calls to a sitter may put a damper on things if they are not available. Plan your Date Nights with your spouse in mind.

BUILD EXCITEMENT

Talk about your upcoming Date Night. Tell your partner how you can't wait to spend time with him or her. Anticipation can be half the fun.

DON'T FORGET YOUR MANNERS

Do NOT answer the cell phone unless it is your kids or the babysitter. We would have to remind my kids not to call us unless it was an emergency. We'd get calls over the silliest things, but it is important for your children to know that mom and dad prioritize one another. It will build security in them. Date Nights are not a time to take business calls or calls from friends. Keep your limited time together as a couple as something sacred.

BE BALANCED AND AVOID RUTS

Spend time doing a fun blend of casual and formal times together. The formal Date Nights for many will be the exception, not the rule, often due to economic reasons. The 101 Date Night Ideas can be a help to planning ahead and saving money too. Don't get in a rut; try new things. Do things you BOTH like to do. You may also want to connect with another couple, but this should be the exception not the rule.

ONE "RULE" TO NEVER FORGET

Never talk about issues during fun times! Save the "issues" for your weekly Team Meeting. Talk about fun things and events, but never deep discussions or problematic issues. If you do, soon your brain will associate your Date Night as a chore or time of contention. Have fun! Need we say more?

REMEMBER THE GOAL OF DATE NIGHTS

The goal is to connect and have fun! Bring back the laughter. Laughter can be the best medicine. Studies have shown that laughter not only has a positive impact on our health but on our marriage as well. Children laugh more than 300 times a day and adults a meager 17.[97] Laughter can help lower your blood pressure, keep ulcers from forming, decreases strain on your heart, boosts your immune system and helps tone facial muscles and nourishes the skin. Laughter is also aerobic exercise. Never allow laughter to cease in your marriage. It has kept us afloat even during the toughest of times.

For some, your initial Date Nights are going to feel a little strange and even uncomfortable. With the absence of kids, home projects, the computer, and other distractions, it may be like learning to relate to each other like you used to. It may have been so long and you may have accumulated so much hurt that it may be initially hard to connect. But it is important to keep at it and continue to forgive each other and rekindle that flame of romance. Date Nights, if prioritized, can revolutionize a marriage. We firmly believe that love is spelled T-I-M-E. Take some time and make each other feel special. Your marriage depends on it.

CONNECTING POINTS

- What does your spouse like to do?
- Plan the next 12 months of Date Nights.
- What has been your greatest obstacle when it has come to Date Nights?
- What is the best night to have a Date Night?

TARZAN & JANE'S FUN FACT!

If men want a happier marriage, they should let the wife be the boss over household issues. A team of researchers at Iowa State University studied the relationship of 72 couples and found the following: Women, having stronger opinions regarding their home and family, tend to control household matters (housework, family times, family schedules, etc.). And husbands were the happiest if they did not disagree with these decisions regarding household matters. Husbands who had opinions about these issues were more likely to be involved in spousal arguments.

Effects Of Divorce On Men

I T IS NOT UNUSUAL FOR INDIVIDUALS to suffer from a major illness two years after a divorce due to the traumatic pain and stress associated with such a split. Divorce is often more devastating on men than on women. Here are some of the effects:[98]

- Higher error rates

- Impaired problem solving

- Narrow and rigid focus (can't see other's perspectives)

- Lower creativity

- High distractability

- Heavy foot on the gas while driving

- Hair-trigger reactivity

- Anxiety, worry, depression

- Resentment, anger, aggression

- Alcoholism

- Poor eating habits

- Isolation

- Shortened life span

- Suicide

Without a doubt, both men and women suffer from the traumatic effects of divorce. However, men seem to suffer greater psychological harm for several reasons. Due to the shame factor, men experience a significant sense of failure. Men face emotional isolation because they lack the family and social support network that women take with them after divorce. Men may wonder why no one comes around or calls. The fact is, women often maintain and nurture a strong support system that many men do not have.[99]

Jungle Commitment

~ Protecting Your Marriage ~

Steve's grandparents, Lottie & Chester Narewski,
had an amazing 60 years of marriage.

CHAPTER 21

How Committed Are You?

"There's a difference between interest and commitment. When you're interested in doing something, you do it only when circumstances permit. When you're committed to something, you accept no excuses, only results."

~ Unknown

RALPH WAS DRIVING HOME ONE EVENING when he suddenly realized that it was his daughter's birthday and he hadn't bought her a present. He drove to the mall, ran into the toy store, and said to the shop assistant, "How much is that Barbie in the window?" In a condescending manner, she said, "Which Barbie? We have Barbie Goes to the Gym for $19.95, Barbie Goes to the Ball for $19.95, Barbie Goes to the Beach for $19.95, Barbie Goes Nightclubbing for $19.95 and Divorced Barbie for $265."

Ralph asked, "Why is the Divorced Barbie $265 when all of the others are only $19.95?" "That's obvious" the sales lady said. "Divorced Barbie comes with Ken's house, Ken's boat, and Ken's furniture."

Divorce. It's everywhere. It is an epidemic at all levels of society. It is weakening the very fabric of our society – the family. From Hollywood celebrities to Christian celebrities to urban and rural America, divorce rates continues to be at an all-time high. But how can we stop this dangerous trend?

God hates divorce (Malachi 2:16). We believe God hates divorce because He hates what it does to couples, children and the credibility of the institution of marriage. Divorce creates a seething bitterness and damages one's self-esteem. Furthermore, it creates loneliness and regret. When a person says they want a divorce, what they are really saying is "yes" to a boatload of pain and suffering. Desiring a divorce often pinpoints a shallow and myopic viewpoint. It has been well documented that in children, divorce brings insecurity, lower grades, and affects their self-esteem. Children of divorced families and those who grew up in a home where the parents had a lousy marriage are far more likely to divorce than children from healthy homes with a happy marriage. Divorce damages people's lives. When so many couples divorce, it leaves many questions and little hope for the younger generation.

Many people struggle to understand the meaning of the word "commitment." Commitment is best demonstrated by one's actions and attitudes. We often say we are committed, but in reality our actions and attitudes bring that into question. The word commit, as it correlates with relationships, means to deliver for safe-keeping, entrust, consign or to make a pledge. Commitment is displayed when we deliver our hearts to another and pledge our loyalty despite the other person's shortcomings.

Here are some shocking statistics on divorce in America:

- 3,000 children will see their parents divorce every day (US Census Bureau)

- Over 50% of first-time marriages are ending (US Census Bureau)

- 67% of second and 74% of third marriages are ending (divorcerate.org)

- Over 25 million children live in a single-parent household (US Census Bureau)

- In one day you lose 50% of everything you own

- 34% of divorced moms live below the poverty level[100]

- The average age a man gets his first divorce is 31 and a woman is 29[101]

- The number one reason the guy gives: We grew apart[102]

- The number one reason women gave: Infidelity[103]

- Total cost for a divorce is $15,000[104]

- Total cost for a wedding is $19,000[105]

- The average salary of a married man $36,920[106]

- The average salary of a divorced woman $29,892[107]

Maybe one of the more surprising statistics was the fact that only 10% of those who divorce are happier and satisfied in their next marriage after ten years.[108] In other words, life and marriage doesn't get better simply because you ran from your mate and your problems. Only 25% of second marriages have a bond strong enough to avoid a second divorce.[109] A lesser known fact is that those who divorce due to infidelity rarely marry the person whom they had an affair with. Only 3% actually marry their mistress. And of those who do marry, that marriage lasts on average five years. The divorce rate among those who married their lovers is 75%.[110] We firmly believe it is because the relationship was built upon betrayal which fosters mistrust. This is not the foundation you'd want to build a marriage upon.

Marriage is a covenant that is designed to be binding "until death do us part." We are to remain committed to our covenant partner for life. People make many excuses for divorcing their partner. Here are some of them:

"I HAVE OUTGROWN THIS MAN/WOMAN."

This is another way of saying I am too small too recognize my own immaturity. Besides, if you are so much more mature than your partner, then it should be easier for you to love them where they're at.

"I'M NOT IN LOVE ANYMORE."

In other words, feelings of romance dictate my commitment.

"I NEED TO FIND MY SOUL MATE."

And how do you know when you've found that person?

"GOD DOES NOT EXPECT ME TO BE MONOGAMOUS."

Really?! What Bible are you reading? Obviously this type of person is either ignorant of biblical standards or has intentionally dismissed what God really thinks on this matter altogether.

"WE'RE JUST TOO DIFFERENT."

No, you knew that before you got married! Nice try! Besides, don't opposites attract.

"ALL MY FRIENDS TELL ME THIS IS WHAT I NEED TO DO."

Since when do your friends dictate your personal choices?

"S/HE DOESN'T LOVE ME ANYMORE."

Does that exempt you from showing your love and commitment?

"MY SPOUSE HAS AN ADDICTION."

It may be difficult and very frustrating, but you may be just the one to bring them out. Since when is divorce a reason to run from a spouse who needs help?

"WE DON'T HOLD TO THE SAME BELIEFS OR VALUES."

Didn't you check this out before you were married?

"I CAN'T STAND MY SPOUSE'S FAMILY AND THEY CAN'T STAND ME."

But you're not married to them. And besides, what if the next marriage turns out to be the same way?

"THERE IS A LACK OF COMMUNICATION."

Then seek counseling or learn to interact with one another. Start by the way you talk to your spouse. Talk to them the way you'd like to be talked to.

"It's easier to run than it is to understand your spouse's perspective. No one grows whenever they run, and if you do, you'll find your problem intensified on the other side."

"I FEEL 'LED' BY GOD TO LEAVE."

It is always annoying when people try to spiritualize their selfish intentions as if the Holy Spirit is going to lead someone to do something that totally violates God's Word.

"HE ABUSES ME EMOTIONALLY."

This is a very vague excuse people often give. Now, we do believe there can be emotional abuse, but how does that actually translate and how does that justify a divorce?

"S/HE DOESN'T MAKE ME HAPPY."

Since when is personal happiness the prerequisite for staying married? We have discovered that if an unhappy person marries they end up even more unhappier than before. Start taking responsibility for your own emotional state and quit blaming your spouse. If you help make others happy (starting with your spouse), you'll find that happiness awaits you.

"I DON'T FIND HIM OR HER ATTRACTIVE ANYMORE."

Maybe s/he doesn't find you attractive anymore either. Should s/he walk out on you? The point is, people age and won't look like they once did – that's life and we all must get over it.

"MY SPOUSE IS SICK OR DISABLED."

This is more of a reason to stick together. If marriage was solely for your personal fulfillment then you'll be tempted to run. Remember, marriage is a commitment that must be kept "in sickness and in health, till death do us part."

These common "reasons" people use are nothing more than excuses for refusing to push through problems that are normal in marriage. It's easier to run than it is to understand your spouse's perspective. No one grows whenever they run, and if you do, you'll find your problem intensified on the other side. That you can bank on.

The relationship between commitment and doubt is by no means an antagonistic one.

"Commitment is healthiest when it is not without doubt but in spite of doubt."

- Rollo May

CONNECTING POINTS

- Are there any excuses you have held to even secretly to justify a divorce?

- Why does God hate divorce?

- What does the word covenant imply?

- What are some consequences for breaking a marriage covenant?

- When is it ever appropriate to justify a divorce?

TARZAN & JANE'S FUN FACT!

The left and right hemispheres of women's brains have a stonger connection than men's brains due to a thicker corpus collasum and more densely packed neurons. This makes women better at multi-tasking and expressing emotion, where men physiologically have a harder time applying words to their emotions due to this weak connection between the brain's hemispheres.

Source: Discovery Channel's "Science of the Sexes".

CHAPTER 22

Strength of Commitment

"A faithful man who can find?"

~ Proverbs 20:6

"Do you," THE MINISTER ASKED THE GROOM, "take this woman for better or for worse, through sickness and in health, in good times and in bad, whether she be…" "Confound it. Preacher," broke in the bride, "you're gonna talk him right out of it!"

So how committed are you really? How can you tell? Well, Steven Stosny & Patricia Love developed a quiz to test your strength of commitment.[111] This is a quiz every couple needs to take to locate not only their commitment to their partner, but to discover their overall emotional health.

The following items represent beliefs and practices related to the strength of your commitment to your partner and your relationship. Read each statement and answer "true" or "false."

1. I focus more on my partner's faults than on his/her strengths.

2. I have habits of great concern to my partner (for example, drinking, spending, overworking, flirting, displaying anger).

3. I am in a better mood at work than I am at home.

4. I am difficult to live with.

5. I prefer sharing exciting events with someone other than my partner.

6. I put my own needs before my spouse's.

7. I put my own needs before the relationship.

8. I wouldn't want my partner to know about all the activities I engage in on the computer.

9. I have romantic fantasies about a person in my life other than my partner.

10. I dress to attract the attention of someone other than my partner.

11. I talk negatively about my partner to others.

12. I would rather spend time with my friends/colleagues than my partner.

13. I have romantic feelings for someone other than my partner.

14. I have sent e-mails I would not want my partner to read.

15. I get more pleasure from work than from my relationship.

16. I have more than one friend that I am closer to than my partner.

17. I put far more energy into work than into my relationship.

18. I'm nicer to other people than I am to my partner.

19. There is someone who brightens my mood far more than my partner.

20. It feels like my partner and I are growing apart.

21. I am frequently in a bad mood.

22. I get more pleasure from e-mail relationships than from my relationship with my partner.

23. Much of the time I spend with my partner I am stressed out or exhausted.

24. I am continually multitasking.

25. It's difficult for my partner to get my undivided attention.

26. I give my hobbies/pastimes more attention than I give my partner.

27. My favorite activities do not include my partner.

28. I leave it up to my partner to keep the excitement going.

29. My life has few high points.

30. Even "God-events" don't make me as happy as I think they should.

Total of "true" answers _____

Love and Stosny add:

"The purpose of this quiz is to give you an objective look at your commitment to your relationship – as well as your general well-being. It is important to re-member that your overall attitude reflects the strength of your commitment to a happy, healthy relationship. Generally, the more "true" answers you gave, the weaker your commitment." [112]

10 SIGNIFICANT FACTORS THAT INFLUENCE DIVORCE

- Young age at time of marriage
- Premarital sex with your mate
- Cohabitation prior to marriage with your mate or any other person
- The number of sex partners you have had
- Previous marriage
- Family interference
- Parents divorced
- Parents had a lousy marriage
- If you or your spouse works third shift on a regular basis
- Abusive father or a poor relationship with your father (esp. for women)

SO WHAT CAN YOU DO TO STRENGTHEN YOUR COMMITMENT?

FEED THE RELATIONSHIP, QUIT STARVING IT

If you starve something long enough it's going to die. When I (Steve) was young I caught a snake but I failed to feed it (Although I am not fond of snakes, I am an animal lover). Honestly, I am amazed how long it took for it to die. But I re-member how it first lost its color and then became very lethargic until it keeled over. Relationships are the same way. They first lose their luster until they become lethargic and apathetic. Eventually they lose all hunger before they die.

"Prayer is powerful.
It should never be the last resort but our first step."

We can starve our relationship through silence, prolonged anger, lack of sexual and emotional intimacy, just to name a few. But we can feed the relationship through humility, teachability, desire, initiative, passion, and a willingness to serve the other partner.

Husbands are admonished to nourish and cherish their wives (Ephesians 5:29). The word nourish means to rear up to maturity, i.e. to cherish, train, and bring up. The word cherish means to brood, i.e. to foster or cherish. Both words carry the idea of creating an environment where the wife can grow. Like a tender young plant in a garden, we must weed around it, gently water it and give it plenty of sunshine and air to breathe. It is a picture of a husband who cultivates an atmosphere in which his wife can flourish.

MAKE A CONSCIOUS DECISION TO COMMIT DESPITE HOW YOU FEEL

This can be a toughie for most. Faith, like love, is not a feeling but something you do. The problem today is that we confuse feelings with commitment. Commitment is a choice you make regardless of how you feel, even if your spouse refuses to take responsibility for their actions.

BE AWARE OF THE FACTORS OF YOUR BACKGROUND

Your upbringing has fashioned you more than you realize. For example, if a woman has a poor relationship with her father, it can affect a marriage dramatically. According to Time Magazine, "Women with poor relationships with their fathers are more likely to get divorced from their husband. That's not the case for the the groom - the quality of his relationship to his father does not impact the odds."

Also, consider how your past relationships may have impacted or skewed your thinking towards men or women. Past relationships can also strain a marriage when unrealistic expectations are placed on your partner. All of these factors can negatively influence our strength of commitment in marriage.

ASK FOR GOD'S INTERVENTION

Prayer is powerful. It should never be the last resort but our first step. If God can turn the heart of kings, he can change you or your partner. Psalms 56:9 declares, "The moment I call to you in prayer, the tide of the battle changes." Prayer changes things.

ASK FOR THE COUNSEL OF MATURE LEADERS AND QUALIFIED COUNSELORS

Godly counsel can catapult a marriage almost instantly to a new level. Be very careful who you go to for advice. Some people will only go to those who will tell them what they want to hear. In a multitude of counselors there is safety (Proverbs 11:14). Going to the right person in a time of trial can save you from further defeat.

NEVER SHAME YOUR PARTNER

Ladies, each time you reject your husband's advances it has a way of shaming him. Men, each time you belittle your wife's opinion and disregard her feelings, it has a way of shaming her. Shame will always cause your partner to drift from you until the relationship suffers damage so great that it will take a miracle to resuscitate it. Shame always denotes lack of commitment.

COMMIT TO UNSELFISHLY SERVING YOUR SPOUSE

We love the admonition from Henry Cloud and John Townsend:

"No relationship is going to survive if all the members are not getting some desires met; vice versa, no relationship is going to thrive if the members get their individual needs met and the relationship always suffers. It is good for a relationship at times to 'serve' its members." [113]

KEEP GOD IN THE CENTER OF YOUR MARRIAGE

We saw this stat in a church in South Carolina that showed a one-in-ten chance of divorce if the couple was married in a church. A one in a hundred chance of divorce if the couple attended church together; and a one-in-a-thousand chance of divorcing if the couple prayed and read their Bible together. Wow! We like those chances. Praying together, reading the Bible together, going to church together; these have a lasting impact on a marriage. When God is the central focal point of your marriage, you will experience an oneness with your mate too few people will ever know.

UNDERSTAND WHAT "COVENANT" MEANS

Marriage is a covenant NOT a contract. A marriage covenant is a binding agreement between a man and a woman that is not supposed to be broken except by death. Possessing a "covenant mindset" is vital to a strong marriage. A covenant means that we remain faithful even when our spouse isn't what we expected him or her to be. We don't bolt just because things are diffilcult.

CONNECTING POINTS

- How did you score on the Strength of Commitment Test?

- What areas can you work on to communicate commitment to your partner?

- What is meant by "starving" the relationship?

- What is something you can do right now to improve your strength of commitment to your partner?

- Would you be willing to implement times of prayer and Bible reading with your mate? When will you begin? What time of day? Will you initiate?

TARZAN & JANE'S FUN FACT!

The typical U.S. Congregation draws an adult crowd that's 61% female, 39% male. This gender gap shows up in all age categories.

Source: "U.S. Congregational Life Survey – Key Findings," 29 October 2003, <www.uscongregations.org/key.htm>

IS THERE EVER A TIME TO LEAVE A MARRIAGE?

In some instances, yes. Although God hates divorce, at times it may be the only viable option. Here is a quick breakdown:

Adultery: We've successfully helped couples work through the pain of infidelity. However, if a partner strays through a physical adulterous act and/or refuses to change, you have the choice to stay or leave (Matthew 19:1-10).

Abandonment: When a spouse desserts you without any intention of returning, then it can be grounds for a divorce (1 Corinthians 7:10-16).

Abuse: You are not expected to live in fear for your physical well-being at the hands of an abuser. If the abuser persists and refuses to get help, leaving may be your only healthy choice (1 Corinthians 7:10-16).

Fight for your marriage fervently, but never rush into a divorce.

CHAPTER 23

Dealing With Temptation

"There are several good protections against temptation, but the surest is cowardice."

~ Mark Twain

A MINISTER PARKED HIS CAR IN A NO-PARKING ZONE in a large city because he was short of time and couldn't find a space with a meter. So he put a note under the windshield wiper that read: "I have circled the block 100 times. If I don't park here, I'll miss my appointment. FORGIVE US OUR TRESPASSES." When he returned, he found a citation from a police officer along with this note. "I've circled this block for 10 years. If I don't give you a ticket, I'll lose my job. LEAD US NOT INTO TEMPTATION."

Temptation is all around us. We face it every day. It may mean being tempted to eat too much, drive over the speed limit or go to a bar and drown our sorrows by downing a bunch of beer or wine. But there is one temptation that faces all of us and that is the temptation to become unfaithful to our spouse. This unfaithfulness may start off as a gazing stare towards a voluptuous co-ed, to flirtatious behavior that feeds our ego and excessive need for attention, to developing a close friendship with a member of the opposite sex, to an all out affair.

Shockingly, studies have found that anywhere from 30 to 60% of all married individuals will have an extramarital affair in the United States.[114] One man, who knows the pain of straying through adultery admits, "Because the straying partner has been so disconnected from their spouses for so long, it doesn't seem wrong anymore in their mind." [115] With this in mind, no one plans on having an affair, but how many plan on taking steps to prevent it? I believe many cases of infidelity come simply because obvious traps are ignored.

Here's the step by step scenario of infidelity:[116]

First... there is **ATTRACTION**. It's quite normal to notice an attractive person, but it is another thing to feed that attraction. We must learn to guard our eyes and mind.

Second... there is **FLIRTATION**. Flirtation is a common way to let another person know that you are toying with the idea of going to the next level. This escalates if the flirtation is reciprocated.

Third... there is **SEDUCTION**. This is where there is a bold (even subtle) steps toward overstepping relational boundaries and violating your marriage covenant. Boundaries are discarded at this point. To seduce means to lure and entice to sexual intercourse.

Fourth... there is **ADULTERY**. At this point the couple is infatuated with one another and the downward spiral begins.

And finally... there is **DECEPTION**. At this point, the fallen no longer see clearly nor feel the illicit relationship is wrong. They attack the innocent and side with the guilty. It is extremely difficult to rationalize with someone in this stage, if at all.

FIGHTING TEMPTATION

BE AWARE

We all are vulnerable. Never think it couldn't happen to you. *He who thinks he stands take heed, lest he fall (1 Corinthians 10:12).*

DON'T BE OBLIVIOUS TO THE OBVIOUS

Beware of obvious pitfalls such as magazines, risque videos, the seductress or smooth-talking casanova, or frequenting certain places of entertainment.

ESTABLISH BOUNDARIES

There are some people you should keep at a distance and there are certain places you should never go. There are certain conversations you should never engage in with a member of the opposite sex.

RECOGNIZE WHEN BOUNDARIES ARE THREATENED OR COMPROMISED

Never give someone the benefit of the doubt when you feel you are in a compromising situation. If someone touches you inappropriately, don't dismiss it or explain it away. Actions always speak louder.

GET DEFENSIVE

Communicate boldly and firmly when lines are crossed. Never give sympathy to someone who is trying to destroy your marriage and family life.

GET YOUR SHOES ON AND RUN

When temptation arises RUN! Sometimes the best remedy is your quick exit.

Facing temptation is not wrong, but feeding the temptation is.

KEEP THE HOME FRONT IN TACT

Keep the fire of romance alive with your spouse. Why would anyone stray when there is a heart-to-heart connection with your mate and a peaceful home life?

"Sexual rejection from your mate will empower temptation and weaponize lust."

CONNECTING POINTS

- What are common temptations you face?
- What can you do to deal with temptation?
- Do you think your spouse would understand your temptations?
- Is there anyone you need to be guarded against at work, school, etc.?

TARZAN & JANE'S FUN FACT!

Sometimes Aging Stinks...

After 40, both men and women need 120 calories less per day.

The capacity of the lungs decrease by up to 40% after age 40.

Source: Discovery Channel's, "Science of the Sexes".

Love Vs. Infatuation

"Never criticize your spouse's faults; if it weren't for them, your mate might have found someone better than you."

~ Unknown

PEOPLE WE HAVE COUNSELED who were involved in a full-blown affair can be likened to talking to a brick wall... it doesn't move! Counsel goes in one ear and right out the other. When a person enters a new romantic relationship, the initial phase is the infatuation stage. This is the season where hormones are released in your body at an alarming rate. This was God's way of binding couples together in the covenant of marriage.

The infatuation stage causes couples to get giddy around each other and can have the effect of being intoxicated. The chemicals cause the reasoning aspect of the brain to be "deadened" for a time. This is a time when you are blinded by not only your new partner's glaring flaws, but by your own insidious behavior. No amount of reason or counsel can get the new "love birds" to see straight.

The infatuation stage usually lasts no longer than a year; that is when the body stops this rush of bonding chemicals. It is interesting to note that when King David had the affair with Bathsheba, God did not send the Prophet Nathan to confront him until a year later. It was probably only then that David was able to "come to his senses" and receive logical, wise counsel.

Unfortunately, many people get addicted to the infatuation stage of relationships. Once the rush is over, they get a dose of reality and see things they've never been able to see before. That's why we counsel singles to refrain from the physicality of the new relationship as long as possible. Otherwise, individual's perception is skewed and they end up bonding with someone who truly is incompatible with them. Some are so addicted to this infatuation rush that they become a "serial" dater. They go from relationship to relationship and remain in an immature emotional state. Real love is developed and seasoned when we see the glaring faults of our mate and still love them deeply and sincerely; something that is impossible to do in the infatuation stage.

Once a person strays and enters the infatuation stage, they must act on what they know, not on what they feel. With God's grace, they can escape such folly and possibly save their marriage.

CHAPTER 24

Professional Boundaries

"Marriage is only as strong as what it costs to protect it."

~ Henry Cloud & John Townsend

"Guard your heart with all diligence."

~ Proverbs 4:23

A MAN-ABOUT-TOWN WAS SITTING IN A BARBER'S CHAIR having a shave and manicure when he looked at the pretty young manicurist and said, "You're cute, how about a date tonight?" The manicurist smiled and said, "I'm sorry, but you see, I'm married!" "Big deal," said the man-from-out-of-town. "Phone the bum and tell him you'll be home late tonight." "You tell him," said the manicurist sweetly, "He's shaving you!"

Many times people don't deliberately fall into an inappropriate relationship, they simply ignore common sense boundaries. Men and women will naturally be attracted to one another without any help. Therefore, we need to be proactive in order to protect the most important human relationship we have... our marriage. Dr. Shirley Glass, a marriage and family therapist in her practice over the past two decades found that 46% of unfaithful wives and 62% of unfaithful husbands had an affair with another co-worker.[117] In light of this alarming statistic, we must be proactive at protecting our marriage, avoid naivete and compromising situations.

ESTABLISHING PROFESSIONAL BOUNDARIES: REMOVING THE GRAY AREAS OUT OF PROFESSIONAL RELATIONSHIPS WITH THE OPPOSITE SEX

OVER-FAMILIARITY

Endearing names should be kept confidential. A co-worker may learn of your "pet" name. We have one for each other. Although we have others, we will spare you the details (mainly out of embarrassment!).

Honey, Sweet Cheeks, Dearie, Cutie Pie, Sweetheart, et cetera are not acceptable names coworkers and strangers should use when addressing you. Let the person know that nicknames make you feel uncomfortable and let them know how you want to be addressed. Maintain professionalism. Nicknames indicate a personal connection.

PHYSICAL BOUNDARIES

Personal space and touching are a no, no. Hands on the shoulder, back rubs, pats on the back, frontal "bear" hugs, et cetera are not acceptable; an arms length posture is healthy and by all means keep your hands to yourself.

ROMANTIC BOUNDARIES

Gifts can be a huge red flag. One gift may be a nice gesture (depending on what it is). Two smells like romance. And three, he or she probably wants more than a "thank you" in return. Be very careful what gift you receive from a boss or co-worker. As a matter of protocol, Jane pick out something for one of our female staff members and Steve pick out one for the men.

"Be wise as serpents and gentle as doves." ~ Jesus Christ

SOCIAL BOUNDARIES

Alcohol and associates just don't mix. This is where many people put themselves in a compromising situation. This is where many scandals start: during happy hour. The question is who is trying to get happy? Don't be naive. It is better to deny an offer to hang out over a drink even if it is to discuss business. It simply doesn't look appropriate and will undoubtedly lead to a marital conundrum. Incidentally, studies have shown that it may take only two drinks before a man is legally drunk and only one for a woman. Once again, alcohol and associates just don't mix.

CONVERSATIONAL BOUNDARIES

Do not disclose marriage issues with others. This is often the number one way the door gets opened for inappropriate relationships. No one but your spouse or professional counselor needs to know about your marriage problems and intimacy issues. Never discuss your sex life with others. Communicate your discomfort immediately if someone begins to share their personal details. Your silence may be taken to mean tacit agreement.

PERSONAL APPEARANCE BOUNDARIES

Dress for success, not for a date. Do you look attractive or seductive? Do you look like, smell like, and act like you are ready to go out and paint the town? Check your motives. If you're not sure about an outfit, ask your husband what he thinks. Generally speaking, if you have to ask if your skirt is too high or your blouse is too low, then it probably is. Remember to dress professionally for work, not like you are ready for date night. If you're not selling something, then you shouldn't be advertising.

Men don't really have to worry about dress since women are not visually stimulated. However, men need to guard their eyes from gawking over attractive women. Noticing an attractive woman is one thing; taking that premeditated double-take is another.

SOCIAL NETWORKING

Texting and facebooking is the new "lipstick on the collar." Be careful not only who you connect with via social networking, but be vigilant when it comes to the "what" and the "how" of your banter. You just may be sending the wrong signals. What purpose would you have befriending or possessing the cell number of an ex-boyfriend or girlfriend? That is unless you are you're looking to rekindle an old flame. By the way, we have full access including all logins and passwords to any account. Unless you have something to hide, full disclosure says "I am willing to live 'above board' and protect my marriage." This brings accountability and makes your mate feel secure. Defensiveness is the first sign you may be straying.

"Rehashed" relationships are ex-lovers you have reconnected with. Shockingly, 82% of married people who reunited with an ex via social networking or socially have entered into affairs.[118] It may be due to reminiscing that brings up old feelings and longing for the good ole days.

FAMILY BOUNDARIES

Do not allow family to interfere with or undermine your marriage or family. This includes parents, siblings, or even children. Your marriage must be protected regardless of who came in the picture first.

GENERAL BOUNDARY TIP

Avoid even the appearance of impropriety (1 Thessalonians 5:22). Alone in a dark restaurant, driving alone with another, lodging with a co-ed colleague in order to "save" money, spending long conversations on the phone, foolish jesting, flirting, etc. are inappropriate and you are setting yourself up for a fall.

Quit hitting the snooze button every time the professional alarm goes off. It just may save you a whole bunch of unnecessary heartache. Truthfully, our idea of commitment is often fairly shallow. Commitment is demonstrated on the steps we take and the price pay in order to protect our marriage.

When it comes to relational boundaries, we love what Gina Cameneti, says: "Error on the side of the ridiculous." Some of these boundaries may seem ridiculous to those who haven't established the healthy boundaries, but we believe it is essential to wisely and proactively protect the most important relationship you have on earth - your marriage!

Signs That You Have Crossed the Line

SEXUAL DESIRE

If there is an intense battle to go to the next level, the best thing to do is to avoid this temptation altogether and get your mind under control.

SECRECY

Lunch meetings with a member of the opposite sex is hidden from your spouse. Emails, text and phone messages are hidden from your mate.

SOUL CONNECTION

At this point there is a level of emotional intimacy that is flat-out dangerous to you rmarriage covenant. You share more with this person of interest than your own spouse.

"Boundaries are not something you 'set on' another person. Boundaries are about yourself... A boundary that is not communicated, is a boundary that is not working... Our notion of faithfulness in marriage is often too shallow... A marriage is only as strong as what it costs to protect it." - John Townsend & Henry Cloud

SOME PRACTICAL SUGGESTIONS

1. Speak highly of your spouse in public.

2. Push back immediately when someone crosses the line.

3. Politely but firmly draw boundary lines in the sand and don't deviate.

4. Punch it! Run when faced with sexual temptation.

5. Pray when facing temptation.

CONNECTING POINTS

- Is there someone you need to clearly establish or communicate boundaries with at work, school, family, church, or the club?

- What safeguards do you have in place to protect your marriage covenant?

- What danger signs have you noticed (or have been oblivious to in the past) that immediately send you "red flags?"

TARZAN & JANE'S FUN FACT!

Men are Good for Church!

A study from Hartford Seminary found that the presence of involved men was statistically correlated with church growth, health, and harmony. Meanwhile, a lack of male participation is strongly associated with congregational decline.

Source: C. Kirk Hadaway, FACTs on Growth: A new look at the dynamics of growth and decline in American congregations based on the Faith Communities Today 2005 national survey of Congregations. Hartford Institute for Religion Research, http://hirr.hartsem.edu.

CHAPTER 25

Establishing Healthy Marital Boundaries

"Above all else, guard your heart, for it affects everything you do."

~ Proverbs 4:23

I T WAS A CROWDED DAY AT THE OFFICE. It was noisy and a bit chaotic since the new offices weren't completed yet. The CEO, Rick had an important meeting with one of his department leaders Judy, but found it difficult to focus on the issues at hand. Rick and Judy thought it might be better to go to a Starbucks and meet.

The dilemma was that Rick was a Christian along with his wife Susan. Together they had established an unwritten policy that as a married couple they would never dine, drive, meet, or be alone in another person's home of the opposite sex. Rick immediately called Susan and asked her if she thought it would be okay if he and Judy met for coffee and business matters just this one time. Susan did not like the idea, but since it was only a one-shot deal due to the office situation, she agreed.

Several weeks later, Susan again got a phone call from Rick basically with the same scenario about meeting with Judy alone at Starbucks. This time Susan had a real gut feeling about this but dismissed it... after all, Judy had been here close friend for years. This was the first time in their over 20 years of marriage that she ever questioned Rick's motives regarding another woman. However, Susan quickly rejected her suspicions and acquiesced to Rick's request to meet with Judy alone for the second time.

Well, needless to say these "meetings" Rick had with his staff member Judy continued outside the office and he no longer made phone calls to his wife since she seemed okay with it. Rick and Judy continued to meet for "business" and the relationship grew closer and closer and deeper and deeper. Rick would tell his wife that he was going on a business trip in another state but was actually several towns away at a hotel with Judy.

Do not be deceived: "Bad company ruins good morals."
~ 1 Corinthians 15:33 (NRSV)

The extramarital affair went on for about nine months before Rick and Judy were caught. Judy had a troubled marriage already, so it was easy for her to stray. She was the controlling type who used manipulation and personal charm along with her good looks to get her way. It was Judy's husband Lance who realized what was happening. It was during an argument between Lance and Judy where Judy threatened to leave Lance. Lance had observed Judy around Rick several times before but he quickly dismissed his jealous thoughts thinking, "My wife would never do such a thing." However, Lance, without even thinking said, "You'd leave for Rick, wouldn't you?" Judy's cover was blown.

Rick and Judy were finally exposed; their secret rendezvous was over. Now Rick and Susan and Lance and Judy had some major decisions to make. Would they try to reconcile their marriage? Do they divorce and marry their new lovers? To make things more difficult, both parties had several children and both were confessed Christians. To top things off neither Susan nor Lance had any idea their spouses were being unfaithful.

"There are real predators out there waiting for you
to let down your guard."

Rick and Judy ended up separating from their spouses and family and moved in together. But it wasn't long and Rick and Judy started having problems. So Rick moved back home and both couples tried to reconcile with their spouses. Rick and Susan went to counseling and part of Rick's restoration process was that he was to sever all ties with Judy 100%. This lasted for a few days but Rick and

Judy were so infatuated with each other they moved back in together and both couples divorced.

Rick was the CEO and Judy was one of his staffers. Stories of infidelity are being written everyday. But what can we do to affair-proof our marriage?

The average first-time marriage in the United States, according to the U.S. Census Bureau, lasts only 8 years. One study concluded that 98% of all adulterous relationships that marry will end in divorce in 5 years. So, if you think your second marriage will be better, think again. Second time marriages fail 75% of the time.

Stories like Rick are so typical, and yet we can glean some very important boundary issues from this tragic incident. These boundary issues are dealt with candidly from biblical writers thousands of years ago and are still applicable to us today. People are people who have the same needs but also face the same temptations and tendencies just like King David did with Bathsheba.

After I asked Susan how the affair started with her ex-husband Rick and his mistress Judy, this is what she said, "I think it all started very innocently." We are warned in Scripture to be "wise as a serpent but harmless as a dove" (Mark 10:16). In others words, we cannot afford to allow life to take us by surprise. We have to be wise, discerning and proactive.

As we are writing this we are counseling several couples for infidelity. It is devastating to all of those involved. In each case, it has to do with sex in the workplace. Although most of the affairs started off pretty innocently, there are often clear-cut boundaries that have been violated.

So What Can We Learn From This Tragic Story?

DEVELOP AND HOLD ONTO PERSONAL BOUNDARIES

Boundaries are meant to protect. Like a fence, fireplace, speed limits, etc. If you are married, it is never a good idea to meet all alone for an extended period with those of the opposite sex under any circumstances, even for business purposes. Don't try to rationalize and justify your position. The fact is Rick and Judy could have still met in the office despite the noise. If they really needed to go outside the office then Rick could have taken another staff member with them for accountability purposes.

DON'T DISMISS THE "GUT CHECKS"

Rick and Judy no doubt violated their consciences. People can get excited about the new possibility of a new relationship especially when their current one is stale, unpredictable and downright boring. At some point every straying spouse has willingly dismissed the warning signs and justified their behavior or thoughts.

DON'T WEAR TOO MANY RELATIONAL HATS WITH PEOPLE

Rick's mistress Judy was Susan's (Rick's wife) best friend. Rick and Susan along with Lance and Judy would go on family vacations together. They hung out together. They knew each other and their families well. Rick was also Judy's supervisor and friend. It is important for a boss to keep a healthy relational distance from employees of the opposite sex. It is equally important for spouses to carefully choose their friends as well. Over-familiarity can be dangerous, especially with those of the opposite sex.

SURROUND YOURSELF WITH PEOPLE OF CHARACTER

Even people with good character can fall miserably. However, it is less likely when you are in the company of people who really live what they believe. Here are a few words of wisdom:

"Do not be deceived: Bad company ruins good morals." ~ *1 Corinthians 15:33 (NRSV)*

"He who walks with the wise grows wise, but a companion of fools suffers harm." ~ *Proverbs 13:20 (NIV)*

BENEFITS OF ESTABLISHED BOUNDARIES

BOUNDARIES PROVIDE SECURITY FOR YOUR PARTNER

Knowing that you took forethought and preventative measures to guard the most sacred relationship above every other human on the face of this planet, your marriage, will send a clear signal to your partner's value. The security each of you will sense is priceless.

BOUNDARIES PROVIDE SAFEGUARDS TO PROTECT YOUR MARRIAGE

People fall more out of ignorance and lack of preparation than anything else. Boundaries protect everything valuable in life. The value you place upon your marriage is determined by the steps you take to protect it.

BOUNDARIES PROVIDE FORETHOUGHT SO YOU OWN'T BE TAKEN BY SURPRISE

The old saying, "To be forewarned is to be forearmed" is more than just a cute colloquialism. Life can be immensely enjoyable but everyday there are battles we must fight, and purity is one of them.

BOUNDARIES PROVIDE A GUARD AGAINST NAIVETÉ

There are real predators out there waiting for you to let down your guard. It doesn't mean we have to go around suspicious and suspecting of every nice person we come across. But it does give us the awareness to be "wise as serpents and harmless as doves."

CONNECTING POINTS

- What areas have I been known to be naive?

- How does wearing too many relational hats with people affect you?

- Have you established any safeguards to protect your marriage?

TARZAN & JANE'S FUN FACT!

Men and women who go shopping together as a couple can usually do so for 72 minutes before they start to quarrel, a "retail psychologist" has calculated. The man will have had enough by then, whereas the woman will happily shop for another 28 minutes before shopping fatigue sets in.

Source: Iowa State University Study

Tarzan & Jane Must Live in "Cleave" Land

"Therefore a man shall leave his father and mother and be joined to his wife, and they shall become one flesh."

~ Genesis 2:24

GOD SANCTIONS MARRIED COUPLES to be joined or literally to "cleave" to one another. The word *cleave* is a Hebrew word that literally means:

To cling, adhere, to stick, pursue closely, catch by pursuit, abide, fast, cleave, fasten together, follow close or hard after, be joined, overtake, keep, pursue hard, overtake, join.

In other words, when God tells us to cleave to our spouse, it means to pursue him or her with great energy and intensity. This is not meant to be a one-time occurrence but a way of life.

Remember the beginning stages of your relationship when you were dating or engaged? Do you recall the incredible amount of time and forethought you took for your new found love? You may recall the long, long phone calls that lasted two, three, even four hours - the conversation to you seemed like 30 minutes tops. Then there were the dates that were carefully and creatively planned. There was the goodbye kiss that was full of passion and you hoped would never end. You brought flowers, wrote love letters, gave surprise gifts, spoke with encouragement and sensitivity, laughed at each other's jokes, and had great optimism for the future.

So, what happened?

Life happened!

The infatuation hormones ran out. They normally do within the first year. Familiarity set in. Flaws became more and more visible and it left you wondering how you've failed to see these glaring problems before marriage. The stress of kids, job, finances, in-laws, and disappointments left us heartbroken, hurt and with diminishing hope.

Marriage is spelled W-O-R-K. The only place where success comes before work is in the dictionary. Notice the word cleave is anything but a passive, lazy approach to marriage. We must pursue our mate with great energy and quit making excuses. We realize that work and kids consume most of couples' time and energy. Some days we are so beat as a couple that being intimately close sounds like a chore... how sad is that?

So, what can we do as a couple? The following are some practical tips.

ORGANIZE YOUR LIFE

Take an inventory of your life. Assess what needs to be tweaked, adjusted, scaled back, or simply eliminated from your life. Assess where you are investing your time and see if it is something that is truly producing fruit in your life. A cluttered and disorganized life will inevitably bring distraction and cause us to deviate from our priorities.

PRIORITIZE EACH OTHER

Here's how the order of your priorities should look:

GOD

Your time with God which includes time for prayer, reading the Bible and church attendance. We need to pursue God first with great energy and zeal.

MATE

Our mate should have no earthly rivals regardless of how busy you are and how many responsibilities you have, there is no greater human responsibility you have than your spouse - no excuses! Love is spelled T-I-M-E.

KIDS

Depending on which stage of parenting you are in will determine how much "freedom" you will have as a couple. The younger the children, the more responsibility you will have as a parent. Parenting may reduce but shouldn't drown out all of the time and energy couples spend on each other.

JOB

When priorities are out of whack it is often because we have made our J-O-B our G-O-D.

SERVICE

Studies have shown that volunteerism is good for your health. We need to be available to serve in our place of worship, be a little league coach, or serve on the PTA or city board. Service to your church or community is important, but not at the expense of your family.

To prioritize, according to Websters Dictionary, means *to arrange the proper order of importance*. Prioritizing your mate means you will not allow anything to take precedence over them. This includes: children, parents, in-laws, job, hobbies, school, and friendships. The list can be endless.

"Never ever lose the 'chase' in marriage."

Prioritizing your spouse does not always mean spending equal time with them, but it does mean giving them the attention and care they need. In other words, I spend more time at work than I do praying or reading my Bible. But God is more important than my job. I spend more time doing chores around the house than I do being romantic with my wife. But my wife is more important.

To keep things in perspective we must be careful not to compartmentalize our lives. In other words, I work and bring home an income because I prioritize my wife and kids. I do chores around the house because I prioritize my wife and kids. And yet I do all of these things to bring honor to God, to be a good steward of what is entrusted to me, and fulfill God's purpose for my life which includes wife, kids, and career.

STOKE PASSION'S FIRE!

Never ever lose the "chase" in marriage. Flirt with each other. Date each other. Mate with each other. Speak sweet to each other. Keep things fun! Passion never stays alive on its own... it is intentionally stoked like a log on the fire.

When the Lord tells us to cleave to our spouse— He means to pursue him or her with great energy and zeal—it means making it a way of life.

CONNECTING POINTS

- What can you do today to pursue your mate with great energy?
- What are some things you can scale back, modify or eliminate in order to free up more time or money with the distinct purpose of investing in your marriage?
- What can you do to help keep your priorities straight?

The Heart Of The Jungle

~ Connecting Emotionally ~

Jane has has a passion for helping people
with special needs.

CHAPTER 26

Compassion & Sensitivity

"... I sat where they sat."

> ~ Ezekiel 3:15 (NKJV)

"But when He [Jesus] saw the multitudes, He was moved with compassion for them..."

> ~ Matthew 9:36 (NKJV)

ONE EVENING WHILE A HUSBAND AND WIFE were getting ready for bed, the husband noticed his wife standing in front of a full-length mirror taking a hard look at herself. "You know, dear," she says, "I look in the mirror, and I see an old woman. My face is all wrinkled, my boobs are barely above my waist, and my butt is hanging out a mile. I've got fat legs, and my arms are all flabby." She turns to her husband and says, "Tell me something positive to make me feel better about myself." He studies hard for a moment thinking about it and then says in a soft, thoughtful voice, "Well, there's nothing wrong with your eyesight." Services for the husband will be held Saturday morning at 10:30 at St. Anselm's Memorial Chapel!

We must learn to be sensitive to our spouse. Sensitivity will connect you emotionally to your spouse, particularly when we learn how to be sensitive to our partner's fear and shame. We must not forget that early in your relationship you once had that sensitivity. As a matter of fact, it was that sensitivity that drew you to one another emotionally or else you never would have married in the first place.

This emotional connection raises the level of compassion and passion for one another. It really does. Whenever we quit responding to each other's fear and shame we connect at a deeper level. We are continually learning how to be sensitive and in tune with each other. In other words, we must be at our best when your partner is at his or her worst. When we connect with our partner instead of reacting in a negative fashion, our partner will eventually reciprocate. Compassionate sensitivity will disarm your partner and they will warm up to your soft gestures. Don't expect them to right away. Consistency is the key.

> *"The happiest couples in the world are the ones who have compassion for each other."*

If you don't feel emotionally healthy, your remedy may be as simple as re-connecting with your partner. I believe in many instances your partner can be a significant factor to your emotional health. Many people are facing depression and discouragement simply because they are living life in an emotional vacuum disconnected from their spouse. The key to your healing may be tied to your mate. Obviously this is going to take two willing parties. Note: Some are married to someone who is emotionally unstable irrespective of their mate. In no wise are we trying to shift blame for someone else's emotional problems. However, each one of us has a direct impact on our spouse's emotional well-being.

· It is imperative to connect emotionally with your partner even when you disagree. And yes, it is possible. Whenever you try to work through a problem without an emotional connection, it only seems to get worse. That is why most couples who go to counseling are worse off a year later. Why? Because trying to simply talk through problems without an emotional connection is like trying to drive a car with very little gasoline; you'll go but not very far. Talking, especially about issues, without any emotional connection will only cause further relational escalation. Compassion is the fuel that connects us and keeps us going to new levels with our partner.

So the lingering question is, "How can I emotionally connect with someone who is ticking me off, and at the same time, can't agree on a big issue?" The answer is this: You can connect with your mate by your approachable spirit, soft tone, agreeable disposition, humility and attitudes that say "I care about you." When you allow an issue or your emotions to control you, you've lost the ability to connect and bring hope to a difficult situation. If you come across with an impervious attitude, then don't expect things to change until you do. William James is apropos when he puts it this way:

"Whenever you're in conflict with someone there is one factor that can make a difference between damaging your relationship or deepening it. That factor is attitude." [119]

As you mature in the relationship, you will discover how to connect even when you disagree. This is known as the ability to disagree agreeably. Early on in our marriage me it seemed like our world was upside down until we came into 100% agreement on everything. I (Steve) felt as if she had to agree with me on everything or else I felt disrespected. Obviously this was nothing more than immature insecurity on my part. However, it was the shame I was feeling that was the underlying problem of why I "needed" her to agree with me.

Please don't miss this: Your emotional connection to your partner is more important than any issue you are facing. However, immature people do not know how to do this. Compassion will make us sensitive to our partner in every way even when we disagree. The happiest couples in the world are the ones who have compassion for each other. Empathy is always more powerful than sympathy; to be sympathetic means to understand where the other person is coming from (which is an excellent quality), but to be empathetic means to actually feel their pain. It is having the compassionate ability to walk in their shoes.

Seeing and feeling things from your partner's point of view is known as empathy. This may be one of the most important skills in developing true, heartfelt intimacy with your spouse.

*"A fool takes no pleasure in understanding,
but only in expressing his opinion." ~ Proverbs 18:2*

Compassion is the ability to feel the other person's pain. The only way you can do that is to connect on a heart-to-heart level. It was the prophet Ezekiel who "sat where they sat" and felt the pain of the people (Ezekiel 3:15). The best marriages that maintain a deep connection with their mate have kept this sense of compassion and empathy for one another.

Today, I am happy to report that Jane and I can disagree agreeably (more than ever), even when it comes to issues we are passionate about. And we can now do this even if we are on opposite ends of the spectrum. Sensitivity to the other person's feelings is more important than the issue itself regardless of what it is.

Consider this passage of Scripture:

"Finally, all of you should be of one mind, full of sympathy toward each other, loving one another with tender hearts and humble minds. Don't repay evil for evil. Don't retaliate when people say unkind things about you. Instead pay them back with a blessing. That is what God wants you to do, and He will bless you for it. For the Scriptures say, 'If you want a happy life and good days, keep your tongue from speaking evil, and keep your lips from telling lies. Turn away from evil and do good. Work hard at living in peace with others. The eyes of the Lord watch over those who do right, and His ears are open to their prayers. But the Lord is against those who do evil'." ~ 1 Peter 3:8-12

Compassion builds unity (agreement), sympathy (sensitivity), a tender heart (tenderness), and humility (attitude). Can you imagine a marriage that resembles this?

What robs us of compassion for each other? The Bible makes it very clear in Proverbs 18:2, "A fool takes no pleasure in understanding, but only in expressing his opinion."

A fool literally means a rebel. A rebellious heart is a hardened heart that is inconsiderate, rude, defiant, and looks out for number one. A foolish heart can become callus because of past hurts and disappointments that were not handled properly. Instead of dealing with traumas of life we have learned to bury them and end up learning to function in our dysfunction.

An understanding heart will build compassion towards your partner despite all of the pain and hurt you have experienced from them. Most of the time, no one sets out to hurt their mate. It often happens accidentally and not intentionally (that usually comes later once the hurt has accumulated over time). Fools (rebels) only want to express themselves but they have no desire in connecting with or understanding the other person. In other words, a fool refuses to see past their pain or their views, they live in a rather small world.

Consider more passages on understanding:

"Husbands... treat her with understanding as you live together." ~ 1 Peter 3:7 (NLT)

"...Only the Lord can give an understanding wife." ~ Proverbs 19:14 (NLT)

"...Understanding will keep you safe." ~ Proverbs 2:11 (NLT)

"Wisdom is the principal thing; therefore, get wisdom. And with all your getting, get understanding." - Proverbs 4:7 (NKJV)

"...A man of understanding holds his peace." - Proverbs 11:!2 (NKJV)

"Good understanding gains favor..." - Proverbs 13:15 (NKJV)

"Those who control their anger have great understanding..." - Proverbs 14:29 (NLT)

"Understanding is a wellspring of life to him who has it..." - Proverbs 16:22 (NKJV)

"...A man of understanding is of a calm spirit" - Proverbs 17:27 (NKJV)

"He who keeps understanding will find good" - Proverbs 19:8 (NKJV)

"Counsel in the heart of man is like deep water, but a man of understanding will draw it out" - Proverbs 20:5 (NKJV)

"...A man of understanding and knowledge right will be prolonged" - Proverbs 28:2 (NKJV)

Even King Solomon asked for an understanding heart and that request greatly pleased the Lord. Without an understanding heart we can sabotage relationships and opportunities that God has set before us. The word understanding simply means "to put two and two together." A person of understanding can often recognize (not excuse) the source of the pain which has become the other person's modus operandi. Once we see and share in another person's pain, we can quickly connect and remain calm when we would normally go ballistic.

To illustrate this point, one morning Jane was in a tizzy about every little thing. It was as if she was just aching for a fight. At first, I simply tried to ignore it, but she kept on. I would go into another room just to avoid her but soon she followed with another comment coupled with an attitude. Then it dawned on me and my understanding was quickly enlightened - it was her time of the month. When she tried to bait me again this time I just laughed and slowly shook my head. I went up to her and put my arms around her and calmly said, "Honey, everything is going to be okay. And I also know that things look a little bleaker at this time of the month." She took a deep breath, smiled and said (my favorite words to hear), "You're right, Steve. Thanks for helping me put things into perspective."

Now I obviously haven't always handled situations in this manner, but the more understanding I gain, the calmer I respond instead of reacting in anger. If I didn't understand what was going on I swear I would have thought she was just trying to be difficult and acting crazy. As men, we have no idea what it is like for women each month, but we can have an understanding heart which leads to a compassionate response.

Compassionate understanding allows us to 100% unconditionally accept our spouse but not necessarily 100% approve of what they are doing. Acceptance is much different than approval. Acceptance, however, must come first.

WHEN MEN EMOTIONALLY DISCONNECT

Ladies here are a few things you need to know about men.

MEN DISCONNECT WHEN YOU ARE ABRUPT

Whether it is positively or negatively, whenever you increase emotional intensity it releases a jolt of adrenaline for him that makes it hard for him to connect. Abruptness automatically sends men into protect mode instead of connect mode.

MEN DISCONNECT WHEN YOU SHOW DIMINISHED INTEREST

For instance, if you don't enjoy sex, he doesn't either. If he bares his soul to you, don't answer the phone or interrupt him. If you absolutely have to break away make sure you touch him and speak soft to him.

MEN DISCONNECT WHEN YOU SHAME THEM IN ANY WAY

Harshness, belittling, dismissing him, bringing up past failures are all forms of shaming that cause men to close up and go back into their shell or sometimes, even attack back. There are many times well-intentioned wives don't even realize they are shaming their husband. When a woman stimulates shame in a man, she is wrong even if she is right.[120] Here are some great examples:

- Comparison: "I wish you could be as handy as Lucy's husband." Or, "Why can't you treat me like Larry treats his wife?"

- Not measuring up: "You work so hard and get paid so little, when will you ever make what you deserve."

- Excluding him: "I decided to enroll the kids in a six week summer camp. I figured you wouldn't mind."

- Condescending: "Why did you ever pick out this color... it looks stupid."

- Harshness: "You know I just can't take this any longer."

- Showing no interest in his interests: "Football is such a stupid sport, how can you stand watching it?"

- Belittling his work: "Just what is it you do all day?"

- Globalizing: "All men are pigs." Or, "Men are incapable of understanding women stuff."

- Justifying: "If you didn't act that way I would have never said what I said."

- Disrespecting: "Why do you waste your time with that job? You're bigger than that."

- Dismissing: "Sex again? We just did it yesterday."

MEN DISCONNECT WHEN YOU DISRESPECT HIM

It's been said that men would rather be rejected than disrespected. Men will tune out and even become combative with those who show disrespect. For example, rolling your eyes when he is speaking to you is considered disrespectful. Since honor is a man's number one need, it is imperative that wives demonstrate proper respect.

WHEN WOMEN EMOTIONALLY DISCONNECT

WOMEN DISCONNECT WHEN YOU INSTILL FEAR

Men can instill fear quickly in a woman without even realizing it. Since men are usually larger then women, and their voices are deeper... it can translate into intimidation. When a man arouses fear in a woman, he is wrong even if he is right.[121] A man instills fear and anxiety in a woman in the following ways:

- Whenever he lacks direction for his life.

- Whenever he can't hold down a job and significantly support her and the children.

- Whenever he gawks at another woman.

- Whenever he chooses his mother, the kids, or work over her.

- Whenever he is passive and abdicates his place of leadership.

- Whenever he lacks backbone and is easily influenced by the wrong people.

- Whenever he is irresponsible and wasteful with money.

- Whenever he is verbally harsh or physically rough.

- Whenever he goes behind her back.

- Whenever he makes major decisions without first consulting her.

WOMEN DISCONNECT WHEN YOU ARE ANGRY

As men we are normally more emotionally modest than women, but yet we have no problem showing an emotion called anger. When we are angry we become harsh, curt and insensitive. This harshness will automatically disconnect your wife from you emotionally at some level and she may not be so responsive to your advances later in the evening (if you know what I mean).

WOMEN DISCONNECT WHEN YOU AREN'T GIVING HER YOUR FULL ATTENTION

When a woman doesn't feel she is important to you she immediately senses feelings of insecurity. Sometimes we need to put the remote down (after we turn off the TV) and give complete attention with full eye contact, engaging in your wife's conversation. At times she is not looking for you to fix a problem but simply to listen intently and show that you care. It is amazing how focused we are on sports, work, employees at the office and home projects, but neglect the most important person in our life, our wife.

How to Be a Great Lover

Men, if you want to be a great lover, here's some advice from Stosny and Love that rings true:

"Well, here's some free advice on how to be a great lover: Make an emotional connection with her. The sexiest thing you can do is the most healing to your relationship: Cultivate a high level of compassion for your partner."[122]

We couldn't agree more!

SOME MORE THOUGHTS ON THE FEAR & SHAME DYNAMIC

Because men struggle with shame, they also struggle with confidence and makes them vulnerable to passivity. Shame to men is like kryptonite is to Superman - it has a crippling effect. It is vital that a wife help build her husband's confidence by her words and by the way she responds to him. By the way, according to many surveys, confidence is the number one quality women are attracted to. The Bible reminds us not to cast away our confidence (Hebrews 10:35).

Because women struggle with fear, they also struggle with seeking to control. Control, in the negative sense, is rooted in fear due to the fact that when fear is present trust is absent. The Bible tells us one result of original sin, that a woman's "desire shall be towards her husband" (Genesis 3:16). The word *desire* literally means "*to run after or **run over**.*" This is a picture of dominance. Incidently, men are attracted to women that have positive outlooks, cheery dispositions, and beautiful smiles; the polar opposite of what fear produces. Fear may cause a wife not to trust her husband's leadership.

It is essential that a husband learns to calm his wife's natural propensity towards fear in how he treats her and supports her.

We can trace the beginnings of this fear and shame dynamic back to the first married couple - Adam and Eve. The Bible records:

*6 So she took some of the fruit and ate it. Then she gave some to her husband, who was with her, and he ate it, too. 7 At that moment their eyes were opened, and they **suddenly felt shame** at their nakedness. So they sewed fig leaves together to cover themselves. 8 When the cool evening breezes were blowing, the man and his wife heard the LORD God walking about in the garden. So they hid from the LORD God among the trees. 9 Then the LORD God called to the man, "Where are you?" 10 He replied, "I heard you walking in the garden, so I hid. **I was afraid** because I was naked. 11 "Who told you that you were naked?" the LORD God asked. "Have you eaten from the tree whose fruit I commanded you not to eat?" ~ Genesis 3:6-11 (NLT) [Emphasis Ours]*

Notice that the battle with shame and fear has continued since early in human existence. Sexual shame and unexplained fear were the first signs of sin.

As couples, it is imperative that we are sensitive to this fear and shame dynamic and how powerfully and negatively this can impact our marriage if we are negligent. Learn to calm each others sense of shame and fear. When this occurs, your marriage will take a quantum leap to the next level!

CONNECTING POINTS

- What can you do to promote an emotional connection with your spouse? If you are not sure, then ask your mate.

- Wives: Of the three things listed for reasons men disconnect, which one do you need to work on the most?

- Husbands: Of the three things listed for reasons women disconnect, which one do you need to work on the most?

- How can you calm your spouse's sense of fear or shame?

TARZAN & JANE'S FUN FACT!

Research has shown that women talk almost three times as much as men, with females talking on average 20,000 words a day and males just 7,000.

Source: http://www.guardian.co.uk/lifeandstyle/2006/nov/27/familyandrelationships

CHAPTER 27

Building Unity & Togetherness

"Marriage is a team sport. You either win together or lose together."

~ Jeff McElory

A SEVEN YEAR-OLD SON ASKED HIS MOM where people came from. The mother responded, "God made them from the dust of the ground." Later the little boy wanted his dad's perspective so he asked, "Dad, where did people come from?" His dad replied, "We all came from monkeys." So the confused boy went back to his mom and said, "You said we came from the dust of the ground, but Dad said we came from monkeys. What is true?" The mother replied, "Your Dad was just talking about his side of the family and I was talking about mine."

So there we were in our basement office, Jane and I along with our two year-old son, Caleb. I had just released our financial secretary; something I didn't want to do but had to do. I had warned Jane for months that this is where things were going and I needed her to learn the bookkeeping system. Well, she didn't. So, once I dismissed our bookkeeper, Jane was trying to catch up quickly. Unfortunately, I kept giving Jane a constant reminder that she should have listened to me and things would have never come down to this. Maybe it would have been no big deal with one or two "I told you so's" but I just wouldn't quit.

Finally, Jane had enough.

She pushed the chair away and turned around and punched me with all her might. Then pointed at me and said, "I didn't marry you to be your secretary" and marched upstairs. I stood there glaring at my two year-old and said, "Caleb, I think your Daddy is in big trouble. Would you go upstairs first and try to smooth things over for me?"

Well, needless to say, I was a jerk that day. No one likes "I told you so's." The fact was, even though Jane didn't follow through with my earlier request, she was still willing to do the job; after all, she is a quick learner. Insensitivity and harsh attitudes will destroy the marriage connection. Jane and I did apologize to each other. I learned to watch my words and attitudes and Jane learned to quit "man handling" me! Martin Luther said, "To have peace and love in marriage is a gift which is next to the knowledge of the Gospel." We totally agree!

In order for a marriage to survive, let alone thrive, we must pay particular attention to the words in which we speak. Toxic words will destroy any relationship. Words can produce life or death in any situation. Have you ever walked into someone's home and instantly you knew you were walking in a toxic environment where the husband and wife were in a heated battle? You could almost cut the air with a knife it's so thick. Guard your words! Keep your words sweet, some day you might have to eat them.

Remember that catchy song by Huey Lewis called "Happy to be Stuck with You." So many married couples feel "stuck" because their life and marriage seem to be going nowhere. We have a great marriage, but we can also tell you that it hasn't always been that way. We've had to commit to putting forth our best effort and implement these following marriage builders on a consistent basis.

GIVE GRACE

Grace is not something we earn or deserve. Grace is to be given generously and freely. One thing we've learned is that grace makes you gracious. Couples need to give grace consistently for their marriage to succeed. Ask yourself: Are you irritated by trivial things? Do you allow your mate to make mistakes without getting all bent out of shape? Do you continually remind your spouse of their past mistakes? Do you have a hard time forgiving your spouse? Love will cover a multitude of sins and mercy triumphs over judgment.

WORK AS A TEAM

Marriage is a partnership and partnership requires teamwork. Jesus said "A house divided will not stand" (Luke 11:14). There is no teamwork without order and responsibility. Define certain roles and be responsible with them. Learn to be interdependent and work toward a common goal. Never allow your children or extended family to disrupt the teamwork between you and your mate.

HAVE A REGULAR DATE NIGHT

Get a baby-sitter and have a blast. Find time to converse on a deeper level over dinner or by taking a long walk in the park. Do something fun together and get home early enough so you and your spouse can have more fun. Be sure to plan these out at LEAST twice a month.

BE COURTEOUS

Don't forget your manners. Unfortunately at times we treat strangers with more courtesy than our own mate. Love is courteous. The word courteous means "of court-like manners, polite."[123] Have you forgotten the little things? Often the little things send a stronger message of courtesy than the expected "big" things.

PRAISE EACH OTHER

Words are so powerful that a day may be ruined or memorable based on one comment. Encouragement is something we all need especially from our spouse. When was the last time you complimented your mate without any ulterior motive? It has been said that encouragement is the oxygen in the soul. Learn to praise your spouse in front of other people too. Criticizing your spouse or putting them down, especially in front of others, can be devastating to a marriage. Start building up your partner with your words.

AFFIRM EACH OTHER

Let your partner know when they got it right! For example, you could say something like, "Thanks for setting aside the time to listen to me and the struggles I've been going through... It means more than you'll ever know" or "Thanks for bringing that situation to my attention. I realized that my attitude was sour... I am sorry." Regardless of what it may be, proactively affirming your spouse will provide a safe atmosphere and will build confidence in you and your relationship together.

PRAY TOGETHER

Couples that pray together will most likely stay together. Prayer acknowledges God is their ultimate source of strength. Prayer will not only strengthen your marriage, it creates an atmosphere of praise in your home. If Jesus prayed often, don't you think we should as well?

A strong marriage is one of the greatest testimonies you can have and brings great honor to God. Together, marshal your efforts and commit to applying these marriage tips. It's just a matter of time until your marriage blossoms into all God designed it to be.

CONNECTING POINTS

- How can you give more grace?

- How can you foster teamwork?

- What is holding you back from having at least a biweekly date night?

- Will you commit to praising and encouraging your spouse?

- Will you schedule a time to pray with your spouse this week? If not, why?

TARZAN & JANE'S FUN FACT!

Men grasp a situation as a whole and think globally, while women think locally, relying on details and nuances.

Source: http://peoplerelationships.syl.com/battleof-sexes/differences

CHAPTER 28

It's A Matter Of The Heart

"The heart is deceitful above all things and beyond cure. Who can understand it?"

~ Jeremiah 17:9 NIV

FOR TWO YEARS A MAN WAS HAVING AN AFFAIR with an Italian woman. One night, she confided in him that she was pregnant. Not wanting to ruin his reputation or his marriage, he paid her a large sum of money if she would go to Italy to secretly have the child. If she stayed in Italy to raise the child, he would also provide child support until the child turned 18.

She agreed, but asked how he would know when the baby was born. To keep it discreet, he told her to simply mail him a post card, and write 'Spaghetti' on the back. He would then arrange for the child support payments to begin.

One day, about 9 months later, he came home to his confused wife. "Honey," she said, "you received a very strange post card today." "Oh, just give it to me and I'll explain it later," he said. The wife agreed and watched as her husband read the card, turned white, and then fainted.

On the card was written:

Spaghetti. Spaghetti. Spaghetti. Spaghetti. Spaghetti. Three with meatballs, two without. Send extra sauce.

Although this may be a humorous joke, adultery is no laughing matter. Many couples have been deeply bruised and traumatized by infidelity and divorce (not to mention what it does to the kids). Adultery begins with a callus.

Have you ever had calluses on your hand? I (Steve) grew up in a home where my parents were not afraid to work us hard. I do appreciate the work ethic my parents instilled in me and I have the calluses to prove it. I can still remember the first set of calluses I developed on my hands. I was shoveling a ditch and my hands were screaming with pain! I had blisters on my hands and they filled with water. I made sure I wore gloves but that provided no relief. As the blisters popped, my hands remained sore. Once my hands healed up, I'd be back shoveling away. My hands once again became sore and blisters formed and the cycle repeated itself. In time, however, the blisters turned to calluses. Once calluses are formed, it is an indication that all feeling is deadened in that area. Calluses are hard, thick and often discolored places on the skin.

"Guard and protect your heart... keep it tender before your mate. Jesus reminds us that divorce is a result of a hardened, callused heart... A hardened heart is the biggest killer of marriage."

When calluses form upon the fabric of our heart they have the same result. We lose feeling towards the one who hurt us as a protective measure to ensure we won't be hurt in the same way again. When we have been hurt in the same place repeatedly, calluses can form easily unless we purposely keep our heart tender. However, if we choose to be unforgiving, bitter, offended and numb to our spouse, these calluses will affect every area of our life eventually.

In the Bible, Jesus reveals the number one reason for divorce and infidelity. Let's look at this closer:

Some Pharisees came to him to test him. They asked, "Is it lawful for a man to divorce his wife for any and every reason?" "Haven't you read," he replied, "that at the beginning the Creator 'made them male and female,' and said, 'For this reason a man will leave his father and mother and be united to his wife, and the two will become one flesh'? So they are no longer two, but one. Therefore what God has joined together, let man not separate." "Why then," they asked, "did Moses command that a man give his wife a certificate of divorce and send her away?" Jesus replied, "Moses permitted you to divorce your wives because your hearts were hard. But it was not this way from the beginning. I tell you that anyone who divorces his wife, except for marital unfaithfulness, and marries another woman commits adultery." - Mark 10:3-9

Jesus made it very clear the main reason for divorce and infidelity: it was hardness of heart. Very few things can penetrate a hardened heart. A hard heart can be seen in the way we treat each other, in our attitudes, in what we say, and in what we don't say. It is revealed by our feelings or the emotions we withhold.

WHAT ARE THE SIGNS OF A HARDENED HEART?

First of all, a hard heart is often harsh. Harshness is a sure sign that there are some things that are left undone.

Secondly, a hardened heart is one that has become stoic and unresponsive. If you have little feeling or refuse to respond to your spouse, you can be sure that your heart is hard.

Thirdly, your fuse is short but your memory is long. You may remember dates and times of specific hurts and you bring them up over and over again. This is a clear sign that your heart has grown callus.

So how does our heart grow hard?

As we mentioned earlier, our heart grows hardened through refusing to let go of the hurt caused by our spouse. You can no longer see past your pain. Maybe your spouse forgot your birthday or your anniversary. Maybe they have been harsh towards you or did something insesnsitive. Maybe they never communicate their love and commitment to you or seem to be interested in other people or things more than you. Whatever the reason, your heart may have become hard along the way. You may not notice, but believe me, other people will besides your spouse.

HOW CAN OUR HEART BE HEALED?

REMEMBER WHERE YOU HAVE FALLEN

Awareness precedes change. Until you are aware of a problem it is impossible for you to fix it. Soul searching and self-awareness is vital if you ever seek to change. Maybe you feel so mad right now that you could care less if you ever change. But let us remind you of the commitment you made on your wedding day: "for better or for worse." We know it can be easier to run than it is to face a problem, but unfortunately whenever we run from our problems, we have a way of bringing all of them with us. If you are uncertain if your heart is hard or not, we dare you to ask what your spouse thinks without getting mad as a hornet if s/he tells you what they honestly feel.

REPENT

To repent means to change your mind and your ways. We need to repent to God and our spouse for our bad spirit, harsh words, and irresponsible behavior. Repentance has a way of softening our heart.

DO THE FIRST WORKS

Begins to do the things that initially drew the two of you together. You preferred one another, you sacrificed, you were sweet, and you aggressively demonstrated your love for one another. Faith is an action! Do what you know to do even if you don't feel like it. Your act of kindness can soften a hardened heart.

CHOOSE TO FORGIVE EVEN IF YOU CAN'T FORGET

Forgiveness isn't amnesia. Like love, forgiveness is a clear-cut choice, not a feeling. Forgiveness is truly an act of faith despite how you feel. It is doing the right thing even when your spouse isn't. Joyce Meyer asserts, "Forgiveness is the core ingredient in every successful relationship."[124] Forgiveness is always the right choice and will keep a marriage from stagnancy and will heal deep wounds. Extending this grace to your spouse will not only inspire their heart to soften towards you, but it will soften yours as well.

INVEST YOUR HEART AGAIN

John Townsend and Henry Cloud attest,

"Some do not leave physically, but they leave emotionally. They forsake the relationship by taking their heart out of it." [125]

When you face disappointments and ongoing hurt, it is tempting to slowly withdraw your heart and disconnect emotionally. Keep your heart open.

Two Things Will Happen

SWEETNESS RETURNS AGAIN

Something happens when you choose to lay aside your offense, bitterness and unforgiveness. Peace and joy is the fruit of a compassionate heart. People will notice something about you. You will look different, think different, speak different and your attitude will radiate once again with sweetness. Whenever we carry around toxic emotions we poison ourselves and those around us by our bad spirit (Hebrews 12:15).

IN TIME YOUR SPOUSE RESPONDS TO THE NEW YOU

Just as your spouse responded to you when you first met, don't be surprised if you get the same reaction! The reason the two of you ever got married is because you fell in love with each other's kindness. You put your best foot forward, at least initially. But over time, we get comfortable and over-familiar with each other and seriously take each other for granted.

How Can I Know I Have Really Been Healed Of A Callused Heart?

The problem in trying to reconcile our broken marriage is that we want a secret, quick-fix formula for success. I have heard people say, "But Steve and Jane, I am doing all of this stuff to change my marriage. I'm doing the date nights like you suggested, I am leaving notes around the house, and I even bought some gifts, and to top it off I have been using kinder words... but nothing has changed! I don't understand!" It's may be because your heart hasn't really changed yet. You can do a lot of good things, but if your heart remains unchanged, it will come out and your spouse will sense it. Your spouse may also be testing you to see if you are being genuine.

The litmus test for knowing the condition of your heart can be summed up in two ways:

1. You feel lighter on the inside. You don't have this "heaviness" that plagues you day after day.

2. You spouse notices that you really changed (in a good way).

Guard and protect your heart... keep it tender before your mate. Jesus reminds us that divorce is a result of a hardened, callused heart (Mark 10:1-9).

Connecting Points

- What areas of your heart do you feel is in jeopardy of becoming hard?
- What causes your heart and love to turn cold towards your spouse?
- What can you practically do to guard your heart in today's world?
- How is unforgiveness destructive to your heart?

TARZAN & JANE'S FUN FACT!

Although men's brains are bigger, women have more neurons densely packed within the brain, making men and women equally as smart.

The right side of the brain is more developed in men, making them better at visual and spatial skills (ex: directions), while the high functioning left side of women's brains make them better at both written and verbal language.

Source: Discovery Channel's, "Science of the Sexes".

CHAPTER 29

Bringing Back Value

"What we obtain too cheaply, we esteem too lightly."

~ Thomas Paine

BERNICE GALLEGO, AN ELDERLY LADY who found an 1869 Cincinnati Red Stockings card in her attic, put it up for sale on eBay with a starting price of $10 and then pulled it down after realizing it might be worth much more. As it turns out, Gallego's hunch was right. After a three-week online auction, the Fresno resident sold what is believed to be one of history's first baseball cards for $75,285.78. Not bad for doing a little spring cleaning.

Another true story I once heard was about a woman had a neat looking rock she put in her garage sale and sold it for $10. This attractive rock ended up being one of the largest diamonds in the world. Talk about not knowing what you have!

In each case, these individuals failed to recognize what they had in their possession. The same holds true for you and your partner. Your partner is more valuable than you've ever realized. The hidden talents, perspective, beauty, intelligence, uniqueness, and so on... it's all there.

The problem is we haven't been able to access it much because we failed to value our partner which puts a demand on that hidden treasure. As a result, that treasure remains latently dormant and unrealized in your relationship. Sure, you could have married from a choice of a dozen other people, but the fact is you didn't... you married the one you have... warts and all. Now is the time to value and appreciate the wonder your partner really is instead of focusing on all he or she is not. When the focus becomes on how you can change your spouse, you automatically devalue them.

Enough is enough! You deserve so much more! Not with another person, but with the one you pledged your life to. There are so many unrealized memories and dreams you have yet to tap into because of a critical spirit. Instead, be one that values, esteems and honors your mate despite the hurts you have encountered.

"Honor is directly linked to what level you live a blessed life!"

Thomas Paine said, "What we get cheaply, we esteem lightly." In other words, what we fail to invest in, we will show little value towards. We've learned as leaders that if we offer a free seminar, fewer people will show up. However, if we charge a small fee, it is amazing the value placed on that same seminar with a lot fewer no-shows.

What if our Western culture went back to the days of having a dowry that a young man had to give to his prospective in-laws before he had permission to marry their daughter? A dowry meant that a young man had to be disciplined enough to work and save in order to have a wife. By the way, it had to be something significant. A dowry also places added value to his future "investment." What man will easily walk away from something he had to work so hard for?

"Your words, attitudes, and overall behavior can create an environment for your partner not only to grow, but to flourish!"

Jimmy Evans tells a story that truly communicates value. In a poverty-stricken island, men bought their wife with a dowry. Since no money was used in their culture, they used produce or animals as a medium of exchange, even for a dowry. The ultimate dowry was a cow and three cows was a record. A cow used in dowry was reserved for the most beautiful of women.

There was a wicked man who had a daughter. She was worn down, quiet, her hair was all matted down, and very homely. She was verbally abused by her father and her spirit was crushed and left feeling unworthy, tired and she had no self-esteem. A young suitor came along and wanted to purchase this man's daughter. Initially the father thought the young man was joking.

Then, the father was stunned that he offered to pay five cows as a dowry for her. The father gladly accepted his offer and off the two went to their new life and village.

This whole incident really ate at the father for the next two years. Finally he couldn't take it and went over to their house on the other side of the island. So the father goes and knocks on the door and a gorgeous, radiant woman answers the door. It was his daughter.

"My daughter looks good," the father said to his son-in-law. "I know, she always did!" said the son-in-law. Then the father proceeded, "I need to ask you a question that has plagued me for a long time. You knew you could have bought my daughter with a few chickens or a pig. Why did you pay 5 cows for my daughter?" To his amazement the young man said, "It's simple! I made a decision long ago that I will only have a five-cow wife."

Make a decision today that you will have a "five-cow" mate! You cannot change your spouse, but you can certainly inspire them to greatness. Your words, attitudes, and overall behavior can create an environment for your partner not only to grow, but to flourish!

THE PRINCIPLE OF HONOR

For my last birthday (Steve), which falls in December, I had many birthday wishes and I truly felt honored. But there are times I wish every day were my birthday. Nobody talks harshly or critically of you on your birthday. People go out of their way to communicate how they feel about you on your special day. It is a day of honor.

There was a time when Jane and I decided that we were not going to do much for each other in the name of frugality. You see, our goal was to be debt-free and we thought of nearly every area in our lives that we could cut back on. Our birthdays and anniversary was no exception. This proved to be a bad idea. The result was failing to demonstrate much needed honor to each other. We didn't need to spend lots of money in order to give honor.

I think we'd all agree that we live in a very dishonoring society. We dishonor our President, parents, the police, pastors and spiritual leaders, bosses, our spouse, the elderly; the list is endless.

Honor is directly linked to what level you live a blessed life! Showing honor is directly linked to the type of marriage you now have or will have. When we dated our mate it is amazing how we'd go out of our way to give honor and preference to our potential mate. Now, through time and an accumulation of hurt, honor is often thrown out the window.

How We Dishonor

Keith Moore, a pastor and teacher, points out five areas we show dishonor to others. We are going to use these five points in the context of marriage.

IGNORING

Whenever you choose to ignore your spouse's needs, you are dishonoring them. The needs of a husband and wife are critical to marital harmony and you ought to do everything in your power to meet them.

Here are other areas we ignore our mate:

- We fail to give undivided attention or eye contact.

- Ignore their opinion.

- Ignore spending quality time with them.

INTERRUPTING

Allow your partner to speak without continually interrupting them. Steve admits was the master at interrupting Jane. When you listen intently honor is given.

INTRUDING

This means to push or force yourself upon others. Whenever you push your agenda, opinion or idea, you begin to dominate your mate. Freedom of speech and freedom to think independently is critical to showing honor. You can still show honor even if you disagree. Being pushy, demanding, or nagging will eventually lead to a dead-end road.

INTERFERING

This means to meddle or hinder another. Do you interfere with your partner's dreams? Do you try to hinder them from doing what is in their heart to do? Support your spouse and be their biggest cheerleader. Your support brings great encouragement and honor. Remember when you married your husband or wife, you also married their dream.

INSULTING

An insult is something intended to hurt another. You dishonor your partner anytime you use profanity, sarcasm, hurl accusations (especially false ones), gossip or slander, publicly contradict, revert to name calling, or threaten divorce. Sometimes we can insult without intending to do so, but the majority of the time it is premeditated with the motivation to injure. Use your words wisely. Wise words bring healing.

HONOR DEFINED

Honor means to prize, value, highly esteem or respect, to revere, to fix value upon, to give preference to, to regard, to esteem to a high degree of dignity, and costly. Do you view your spouse in this light? If you do, I would guarantee your marriage is strong and full of happiness.

"Love each other with genuine affection, and take delight in honoring each other." ~ Romans 12:10

This is a powerful passage for couples because it reveals how to keep the flames of love beaming.

SHOW GENUINE AFFECTION

This means to be authentic in showing affection. It's not just being affectionate but putting your heart into it. Do this even if you don't feel like it. We believe that feelings follow action. Putting your heart into to something is independent of feelings anyway.

TAKE DELIGHT IN HONORING EACH OTHER

Most of us were never taught to honor. If kids are dishonorable it is usually because they grew up in a home where the parents frequently dishonored one another. We need to take delight and plan to honor our mate and watch it spill over onto our children. We honor through word, action, and thought. Here are some practical things you can do:

- Let your mate choose the movie or the restaurant.

- Without asking, give a back or foot massage or other acts of affection.

- Give your mate the night off and do their share of the housework,

- Make your spouse's favorite dinner (or buy it if you're not a good cook).

- Speak incredibly kind to them.

The bottom line is this: no marriage will survive when there is an atmosphere of continual dishonor. We limit God's power in our life when dishonor is present. Take great delight in honoring your mate today!

CONNECTING POINTS

- What areas can you work on that will add value to your partner and your marriage?

- How is a marriage depreciated?

- How does adding value inspire your spouse?

- When you feel devalued, how do you react?

- How does honor release God's power in your life (Matthew 13:53-58)?

TARZAN & JANE'S FUN FACT!

Men tend to be more independent in their thoughts and actions, while women are more willing to follow the ideas suggested by others.

Source: http://peoplerelationships.syl.com/battleof-sexes/differences

Creating A Safe Environment

L ADIES... WHAT IF YOU SAID TO YOUR HUSBAND, "I think we need to talk!" Do you think he'd respond with... "Gee, I thought you'd never ask!" Or, better yet, "Honey, that is a great idea. There are so many things I have been carrying on my heart and I need to share the depths of my soul with you. And I am dying to know how you've been feeling." Ah, well... neither, right? He'd probably respond with silence, withdrawal or something to the affect of "I think things are going well. No need to talk here!" You see, all men hear when you say "we need to talk" is how much he has failed you and cannot please you. The shame men naturally sense will often drive him farther away from you. Men will go to great lengths in order to avoid this sense of shame and inadequacy. That's why men are known to hide in their caves. They would rather isolate themselves than feel inadequate or like a loser.

Guys... what if you said to your wife, "You know I sense we have drifted in our relationship and would love to connect with you." After picking herself off the floor from disbelief and utter shock, she'd probably wonder what you have been drinking.

Ladies, the more connected your husband feels towards you the more likely he will be vulnerable and transparent with you. That's why creating a safe atmosphere for your husband will do wonders for your marriage. Men and boys are easily aroused to anger, shame, and of course, sex. Atmosphere is key. It is imperative that you are not too direct with him conversationally and with your attitude. If you are, it will naturally release cortisol in men and quickly arouse him to anger and/or shame. Men can quickly go into protect and attack mode. That is how God wired men. Nonetheless, men still need to harness this natural reaction and bring it under control thus developing the fruit of the Spirit such as gentleness and kindness.

Guys, when you control your temper and calm her fears, as much as depends upon you, your wife will trust you more. Whenever you put her on edge with your intimidating language or posture, you can potentially further the emotional disconnection. Having an approachable spirit that is safe will draw your wife towards you.

Women view relationships as a place to interact in order to connect. Men view relationships as a safe place, as a means of connection rather than interaction. Women feel secure when they are connected. Men feel secure when they have a safe place to dwell.

Rumble In The Jungle

~ Connecting Relationally ~

Good lovers fight once in a while.
Fight fair. Then have fun making up!

CHAPTER 30

The Pain Of The Jungle: Overcoming Hurts

"Keep your eyes wide open before marriage and half shut afterwards."

~ Benjamin Franklin

"LOVE LIKE YOU'VE NEVER BEEN HURT." That was posted on Facebook recently. Wow! What a statement! We tend to become more cautious and reserved the more we have been hurt. Life can have a way of wearing out our natural love pretty quickly. The truth is, love will pay the price, take the risk and become vulnerable despite life's disappointments, even when it comes to our spouse. I (Steve) was sharing recently with someone that you'll probably never feel more pain and hurt than you will from your spouse. Why is it that? It's not that we intentionally try to hurt our spouse, and yet we do more often than we'd like to admit. We also use a different measuring stick when it comes to our mate than anyone else. What we tolerate with a friend or co-worker, we'd never tolerate with our mate.

I remember the first big hurt I felt from Jane was when we had our first child, Caleb. Jane didn't want me to leave her side in the birthing room. She held my hand ever so tightly and was sweet as Grandma's apple pie. Then all of a sudden, like a storm rolling in from out of nowhere, she insisted that I was "smothering" her by my presence. She even asked the nurse, "Would you do something with him? He's driving me up the wall!" I was crushed. I should've known better than to take it personally at that moment during labor, but I did nonetheless. I never felt so hurt by her. Once the labor was over, I was back in her good graces. But man, did that hurt!

One thing is certain; those closest to us will always hurt us the most. Pastor David Pratt of W. 58th St. Church in Cleveland makes this point clear when he says, "Pain is in proportion to love. The more we love someone, the greater we are hurt when that person disappoints us." If a stranger is rude to us, we can be a bit miffed and go our merry way. But not so with your spouse, we live with them 24/7. We shouldn't run away from them just because we got hurt. I think all married people have said to themselves on at least one occasion, "For God's sake, if my spouse loved me so much then why does s/he insist on being so doggone hurtful?" The old song immediately comes to my mind... "Love Stinks." Well, sometimes I guess it does.

"As a partner, we are either inspiring our mates to live at a higher level or frustrating them and causing more pain and hurt."

The greater the expectation, the greater the chance of becoming hurt and even worse, offended. The expectations we place on our partners are at times, God-like. We unconsciously carry the mindset that anything less than perfection is unacceptable. In the meantime we are good at overlooking and justifying our chronic shortfalls, coarse behaviors and sour attitudes. God help us be more understanding.

Handling hurts in marriage will be an ongoing art to be learned. It's not what happened one time, but what happened over time that causes an accumulation of hurt to mount. When our spouse repeatedly does the same old thing it can stockpile hurt over time. King Solomon reminds us that repeating a matter can separate the best of friends (Proverbs 17:9). Therefore an accumulation of hurt will separate you more and more over time unless it is dealt with properly. Being hurt is quite different than staying hurt. Here are a few things we have implemented to avoid staying hurt in marriage.

FORGIVE IMMEDIATELY DESPITE HOW YOU FEEL

Once again, forgiveness remains a hot topic. Real forgiveness, like real love has nothing to do with feelings and emotions. They are an act of will, a choice to be made. Feelings are always secondary when it comes to principle. Feelings change; truth does not.

DEFY THE URGE TO SPLURGE

Watch your mouth! Guard it! Put a muzzle on it and make no excuses for slip-ups! Words will destroy or give life, but it's up to you, not your spouse. There was a time when my eldest son, Caleb, accidentally shot our family cat (yes, it really was an accident). He was testing out his air soft rifle by blindly shooting it at a box under his bed. The problem was little kitty was sleeping near the box he was hoping to hit. Our rule when the guns were first purchased was "There are NO accidents... ever!" Air Soft guns can take out an eye and cause life-altering problems.

The same holds true with our words. We need to view them in the same light we do with bullets - with GREAT caution. The problem is that we are so flippant with our words we simply dismiss the harm we cause by rationalizing to ourselves, "Oh, they're just words. I didn't mean anything by them." We are warned that we will be judged by God for every idle word we speak (Matthew 12:36). Not some, but EVERY SINGLE ONE.

NEVER GO TO BED UPSET - EVER!

You may not be able to get in a huge discussion but you can find an emotional connection until you are able to work through the details. The key is having an agreeable spirit even when hurts are present. If you sense your spouse is distant or hurt, then come to them with a gentle spirit that seeks connection. And if your partner entreats you in this matter, respond with kindness. After all, they took a risk by opening their heart to you. Don't allow an "issue" to keep you from emotionally connecting.

HAVE AN APPROACHABLE SPIRIT

Your attitude is one that communicates either "I want to connect with you" or "I don't give a rip about you." We have devoted a whole section on approachability. As mentioned in a previous chapter, there are generally three modes people typically walk in:

- **Avoid Mode**: This is characterized by deliberately excluding your spouse and often comes in the form of quiet pouting.

- **Attack Mode**: This is characterized by turning negative energy against someone. It can simply be a poor attitude.

- **Approach Mode**: This is characterized by going towards someone with positive energy. In this mode you desire to appreciate more, understand more, learn more and be more for your partner. In this type of atmosphere your spouse will inevitably warm up to your approachable spirit. Create a safe atmosphere that fosters dialogue and acceptance.

ASK GOD TO SHOW YOU WHERE YOU'VE CONTRIBUTED TO THE PROBLEM AT HAND

As a partner, we are either inspiring our mates to live at a higher level or frustrating them and causing more pain and hurt. Marriage needs large doses of wisdom that comes from God and God alone.

Maybe you've carried a contemptuous attitude. It could be that you are a difficult person to live with. Or it may be that you have a few blind spots and have no idea how you come across but others see it clearly. Either way, none of us have obtained to perfection and have need for improvement.

"[God] heals the brokenhearted, binding up their wounds." ~ Psalm 147:3 (NLT)

CONNECTING POINTS

- How agreeable are you?
- Do you find yourself harboring bitterness and resentment over long periods of time?
- Do you keep bringing up past disappointments to your partner?
- How can you be more approachable towards your partner?
- Is there anything you need to forgive your partner for once and for all?

TARZAN & JANE'S FUN FACT!

Humans consume approximately 85,000 lbs. (the equivalent to a humpback whale) of food in their lifetime.

Humans spend 5 years of their lives eating.

Source: Discovery Channel's, "Science of the Sexes".

CHAPTER 31

Wedlock Or Deadlock

"Never go to bed mad. Stay up and fight."

~ Phyllis Diller

A COUPLE DROVE DOWN A COUNTRY ROAD for several miles, not saying a word. An earlier discussion had led to an argument and neither of them wanted to concede their position. As they passed a barnyard of mules, goats, and pigs, the husband asked sarcastically, "Relatives of yours?" "Yep," the wife replied, "in-laws."

It's been said that marriage is made in heaven but so is thunder and lighting. Every married person knows that no one can make you more infuriated than your spouse can. Forgiveness and wise conflict resolution are relationship staples and a marriage won't survive without them.

One disparaging, thoughtless remark can spoil a whole day of marital connection. If there is a relational impasse that isn't dealt with quickly and gingerly, your pristine marital wedlock can quickly turn into a stifling marital deadlock. One relational gaffe can disrupt a perfectly peaceful day. Martin Luther once said, "Nothing is more sweet than harmony in marriage, and nothing more distressing than dissension." When a wife doesn't sense love from her husband, she reacts. And similarly, when a husband doesn't sense respect from his wife, he reacts.[126]

Stosny & Love attest:

"One reason that talking about your relationship has not helped is that fear and shame keep you from hearing each other, regardless of how much 'active listening' or 'mirroring' you try to do. The prerequisite for listening is feeling safe, and you cannot feel safe when the threat of fear or shame hangs over your head. The threat is so dreadful that the limibic system, the part of your brain in charge of your safety, overrides any form of rational thinking. Almost everything you hear invokes fear or shame."[127]

A marriage study completed by John Gottman at the University of Washington concluded that you can predict, according to statistics and research, with 93% accuracy, the likelihood of a divorce if these four things happen:

CONSTANT CRITICISM

This is defined as fault finding. It is possessing a chronic negative and cynical attitude. A victim of this attitude feels that they can never do anything right. Jesus was constantly criticized by the Pharisees who watched Jesus closely to find fault (Mark 7:2). Nit-picky people are hard to please and demand standards that they themselves have no intention of keeping.

King Solomon wrote, "He who has a deceitful [crooked] heart finds no good..." (Proverbs 17:20 NKJV). In other words, a critical spirit is a problem of the heart. It is overlooking one's own shortcomings while over-emphasizing the faults or perceived faults of others. It is a deceived and crooked heart.

DEFENSIVENESS

This is defined as a state or posture of defense, ready to attack, or a protective mode. It is not allowing your spouse the right to complain or voice their opinion; it is a form of censuring. Many times a chronically defensive person immediately turns the table on the other person whenever there is a disagreement. They often accuse the other person for exactly the behavior they are exhibiting.

"...A wise person will calm anger." ~ Proverbs 29:8 (NLT)

A defensive person is easily annoyed and will not let you vocalize your concerns; in fact, they don't want to hear it. What they are really saying is that they have no interest in pleasing you and everything is basically "your fault."

Defensive people make it nearly impossible to have a peaceful relationship with them. They are in a perpetual state of self-deception and holding to an unteachable spirit while making excuses for their unreasonable behavior. Eventually this will lead to relational suicide if it's not dealt with correctly.

CONTEMPT

This is defined as aged anger, to despise, disrespect, or shame. A contemptible person is notorious for condescending remarks. They will quickly disparage any idea or suggestion by a perfunctory remarks like, "Oh, that's so stupid, why would you suggest that?" Or, "You're such an idiot for feeling that way." A contemptible person will judge your feelings and intentions of your heart. This attitude will certainly take a relationship down a path of destruction if not rectified quickly. Ill-advised words can be very painful and destructive to a marriage.

STONE WALL

This is defined as to exclude, confine, to close oneself off, or to be closed. At this stage the person has shut themselves off and refuses to dialogue civilly. Relationally speaking, they are done! This is often the last stage before divorce and they have lost all hope for a better tomorrow. They are holding onto an offense and refuse to be consoled at this point.

The ancient wisdom tells us:

"It is harder to make amends with an offended friend than to capture a fortified city. Arguments separate friends like a gate locked with iron bars" ~ Proverbs 18:19 (NLT)

An offended, stonewalled person is unresponsive to the gestures of another. It is a state of extreme harshness and a hardened heart.

How To Fight Your Battles Fairly

"Cash, check or charge?" I asked, after folding items the woman wished to purchase. As she fumbled for her wallet I noticed a remote control for a television set in her purse. "So, do you always carry your TV remote?" I asked. "No," she replied, "but my husband refused to come shopping with me, and I figured this was the most evil thing I could do to him legally."

Arguing isn't all bad. We'd rarely go to new relational heights without some form of conflict. The goal of conflict resolution is to connect with your spouse on a deeper level. Let me share some great ways on how to have a good fight where both of you win and a new connection is established. According to Ephesians 4:25-32, these practical tips will help you fight fair.

BE HONEST (V.25)

Sometimes arguments are mere smoke screens for other issues that you are afraid to talk about. Learn to speak the truth in love (Ephesians 4:15).

BE CONTROLLED (V.26)

An out-of-control temper can cause great hurt and ruin in a short period of time. "Be angry and sin not" means to control yourself.

BE RECONCILABLE (V.26)

Your anger has a time limit on it: by the time the sun goes down. That suggests being amendable and vulnerable enough to deal with the issue at hand. Don't procrastinate or delay in any way. The longer you wait the worse off it gets and the more time calluses have to form on your heart.

Note: Some disagreements will NOT be resolved right away. Staying up all night will only make you more irritable and can build resentment especially if you have to work in the morning. A suggestion here would be to connect at some level before going to bed. The key is NOT resolving the issue as much as connecting and seeking a spirit of agreement even when tempers have become heated.

BEWARE (V.27)

Warning: falling asleep with unresolved anger issues awakens an opportunity for the enemy of your soul to take a place of leverage in your life.

BE GRACEFUL (V.29)

·Your words will either build up or destroy. Words have the ability to connect or disconnect. Your level of intimacy and the ability to overcome conflict will be directly linked to the words you use. Life or death: you choose! Your sour spirit or gracious spirit may alone determine the outcome of your conflict.

BE TENDERHEARTED (V.31-32)

A tender heart will always plow through difficult times. Removing bitterness, a contentious attitude, and disrespectful words keeps our hearts tender towards our mate. Choosing to be kind and forgiving will create an environment for your spouse to open his or her heart to you and allow restoration to occur.

"...a wise person will calm anger" - *Proverbs 29:8 (NLT)*

"Blessed are those who have a tender conscience, but the stubborn are headed for serious trouble" - *Proverbs 28:14 (NLT)*

"Don't wait for your spouse to take the first step. Assume the first move is always yours." ~ John Townsend & Henry Cloud

CONNECTING POINTS

- Do you display any of the four behaviors of the John Gottman study? If so, which one(s)?

- What can your spouse do to help be a calming agent when you're angry?

- What behavior angers you the most about your spouse?

- How do you handle your anger?

- What practical step can you take to ensure that you never go to bed angry?

TARZAN & JANE'S FUN FACT!

If women have a disagreement with each other it affects all aspects of their relationship. Men can have a disagreement, move on to another subject and socialize together; it rarely affects the relationship.

Source: Simma Lieberman Associates

CHAPTER 32

Conflict Resolution

"Live in harmony with each other... and don't think you know it all! Never pay back evil for evil to anyone. Do things in such a way that everyone can see you are honorable. Do your part to live in peace with everyone, as much as possible."

~ Romans 12:15-18 NLT

ONE MAN RECALLS THE STORY when he bought his wife a new car. She called her husband and said, "There's water in the carburetor." "Really," the husband replied. "And just where is the car?" She said, "In the lake."

Socrates once said, "By all means marry; if you get a good wife you'll be happy. If you get a bad one, you'll become a philosopher." Sounds like Socrates had some unresolved marital conflict.

In this section, we want to help you overcome conflict strategically and peacefully. Let's face it, problems are going to occur in every stage of marriage. Problems never go away, but the types of problems and how you resolve them as a couple will change over time, or at least they should. For example when you were engaged, the major sources of conflict were most likely your fiancee's family and jealousy. Early in marriage it would be sex and communication. Then it turned to conflict over money (which seems to happen at every stage).

What we have experienced is what we often hear in counseling... "I don't feel respected or heard by my partner." Sometimes people confuse "hearing" with "agreeing." Maybe your partner really does hear you but doesn't agree with your conclusion. How do you handle that? In this chapter we hope to help you communicate and listen effectively. At the same time we hope to "arm you" with practical tools to help you "disarm" your partner as you work together in overcoming conflict.

Work on problems as a team; that means you have to be willing to participate, cooperate and be harmonious. So many times we see our spouse as "the enemy" who needs to be defeated. When in conflict, often we see our spouse as the primary source of our problem and believe he or she alone is standing between you and your happiness. This approach is flawed because it reeks with an air of superiority and is only trying to put your spouse in his or her place - down. Be honest with yourself without trying to mask any hidden pride. When pride is present, conflict never goes away... it only grows. "Only by pride comes contention" (Proverbs 13:10). Pride is also deceptive, enabling you to believe you are exempt from taking any responsibility in the problem.

"Trust in the Lord with all your heart; do not depend upon your own understanding. Seek His will in all you do, and He will direct your paths." - Proverbs 3:5-6 (NLT)

Some couples hate conflict so much that they actually avoid it. They rush into a quick solution but never get to the root of the problem, often out of fear. The problem with this poor form of "conflict resolution" is that the real issues are never truly addressed or even brought up. Over the long haul, this couple is mounting up some serious problems they must deal with in the future. Unfortunately many couples lack the resolve or conflict resolution skills to overcome such a relational tsunami and a permanent disconnection occurs. That's why it is imperative to address problems honestly, timely, respectfully and successfully.

4 STEPS TO HANDLING CONFLICT PEACEABLY

STEP ONE: TALK ABOUT IT TOGETHER!

Address ONE issue at a time and be specific as possible. If you are arguing about money (which is usually the case), what aspect do you want to discuss? Is it the use of credit cards? Budgeting? Out-of-control spending? Lack of agreement?

DO NOT try to solve the problem without first understanding and really hearing what your partner has to say. Too often we try to solve a problem without really understanding our partner's point of view.

When addressing the problem, one person has the floor. One technique is to have the person speaking hold something like a baton, remote control or some knickknack that demonstrates they have the floor. When someone has the floor, it is only for a short time. Speak within one minute or only two or three sentences. This keeps the conversation focused and gives your partner time to mirror back what you said and speak themselves. When someone is speaking, you are NOT allowed to interrupt, make faces, or walk away.

When speaking, it is vital that you use a harmonious tone, respectful body language and uplifting words. The listener needs to validate their spouse and be respectful of their opinions and feelings even if you disagree with them. Being "agreeable" is more important than agreeing on everything.

"Confess your sins to each other and pray for each other so that you may be healed. The earnest prayer of a righteous person has great power and wonderful results" - James 5:16

During times of "intense fellowship" be sure to show how the actions of your spouse directly affected you. Do not use harsh tones, accusatory or subjective comments. If you're going to "fight," then fight fair. Even in the sport of boxing there are grounds rules in which to fight. One rule is universal: no hitting below the belt.

If your partner does not want to talk at the moment you desire to talk, then respect their decision not to talk about the problem at that time. However, it is up to your partner then to reschedule with you immediately to connect within 24 hours. It is equally important not to allow a problem to linger without addressing it.

Sometimes just having a heart-to-heart discussion about a source of conflict is all you need. You may not need to solve anything. What is important is that you both feel respected and heard by each other. What seemed so insurmountable now seems minute simply because you talked through some important issues respectfully. In our marriage, this was a biggie that resulted in so many needless problems. If we just slowed down and took the time to really listen, we would have eliminated days of frustration. Thankfully we have greatly improved over the years.

STEP TWO: PRAY ABOUT IT TOGETHER!

Bring God into your situation. God will give you the grace to walk through problems together and He will also give you the wisdom to solve your problems. Prayer is extremely powerful and has a way of uniting couples.

"Don't worry about anything; instead pray about everything. Tell God what you need, and thank Him for what He has done. If you do this, you will experience God's peace, which is far more wonderful than the human mind can understand". ~ Philippians 4:6 (NLT)

"Trust in the Lord with all your heart; do not depend upon your own understanding. Seek His will in all you do, and He will direct your paths." ~ Proverbs 3:5-6 (NLT)

"Confess your sins to each other and pray for each other so that you may be healed. The earnest prayer of a righteous person has great power and wonderful results." ~ James 5:16

As you can see from these scriptures that prayer is powerful and can change your circumstances. We believe that nothing of lasting significance will happen apart from prayer. The most powerful prayer partner you'll ever have in life will be your mate. There is great power released when couples are unified in prayer.

Fasting may be an option as well. Prayer and fasting is a time to be set apart in order to develop a sensitivity to what God may be leading you to do. Never diminish this powerful step in conflict resolution.

STEP THREE: SOLVE IT TOGETHER!

We cannot emphasize enough the importance of working as a team. John Maxwell has said, "Teamwork will make the dream work." In marriage you will win together or lose together; there is no in between.

Breakdown your problem area into a specific, more manageable piece and deal with them one at a time. No matter what the issue is, break it down into smaller pieces. As the old saying goes, "Yard by yard, it's hard; but inch by inch, it's a cinch."

Once you've narrowed your focus, then begin to brainstorm together to come up with possible solutions. Here are the ground rules for brainstorming:[128]

- Any idea can be suggested.

- Write them down.

- Don't evaluate ideas during brainstorming, verbally or non-verbally. This includes making faces.

- Be creative. Suggest whatever comes to mind, no matter how ridiculous it might seem.

- Have fun with it.

Once you have several viable options then agree together on the solution. DO NOT agree with a solution unless you are not in agreement with it. Don't agree then later blame your spouse because it was their stupid idea. Be honest. When it comes to a solution make sure you do two things: Agree on it and be specific about it. The more specific you are about the solution, the better chance you will implement it.[129]

In marriage you cannot have what you want all the time. If you think you can then marriage will be a "bear" for you. Since we cannot have what we want all of the time, then we need to learn to compromise and find the overlap which is common ground you can agree on together.

STEP FOUR: FOLLOW-THROUGH TOGETHER!

You may have a great plan to solving the problem but without follow-through, nothing ever changes. Some good ways of following through include:

- Set goals and deadlines.

- You may need to make some adjustments in your solution along the way.

- Hold each other accountable through weekly meetings at home or Star-Bucks.

- Divide responsibilities between the two of you. In other words, who is going to handle what?

- Be as structured as you need to be in order to find the resolution to your problem.

In time you will discover that your solution was nothing more than a series of small steps you agreed upon. If you feel you have "hit a wall" during this follow-through process, then ask yourself:

- "Did we really thoroughly discuss the main components of the issue?"

- "Am I feeling accepted and respected by my spouse along the way?"

- "Am I fulfilling my part of the solution or have I slacked off?"

- "Am I taking this conflict resolution seriously or do I think it is rather juvenile?"

The Key Point... Together!

Notice that each step requires doing things together. Once again, marriage is a team sport. Both of you must be willing to participate equally. Going through each of these steps without real agreement will only lead to hopelessness and frustration. Talk, pray, solve and follow though together... then watch amazing things happen!

Connecting Points

- Will you plan a time to speak with your spouse about a problem or potential problem this week?

- Will you commit to praying together regularly? If not, please explain why.

- What is the importance of follow through? How can you effectively follow through as a couple once a solution is determined?

TARZAN & JANE'S FUN FACT!

Women get things done at work by building relationships. Men build relationships while they are working on tasks with each other.

Source: Simma Lieberman Associates

CHAPTER 33

Jungle Warfare

"A fool gives full vent to his anger, but a wise person quietly holds it back."

~ Proverbs 29:11 NLT

"Speak when you are angry and you will make the best speech you will ever regret."

~ Ambrose Bierce

WHEN THE JONES FAMILY MOVED into their new house, a relative asked five-year-old Sammy how he liked the new place. "It's terrific," he said. "I have my own room. Mike has his own room, and Jamie has her own room, but poor Mom is still in with Dad."

Conflict is inevitable, so learning to manage our emotions during conflict will determine a good outcome. Many have learned to function in such dysfunction, that they often have become comfortable with destructive habits that have caused serious hurt and damage to their marriage. These negative patterns must stop!

Plain and simple, doing the right thing will produce the right results. Doing the right thing does not always involve feeling like doing the right thing. We must practice self-control. Handling conflict properly may boil down to whether or not you are going to do the right thing or act defiantly. Successful conflict resolution requires humility.

"Pride leads to arguments; those who take advice are wise." ~ Proverbs 13:10

Rules Of Engagement

Believe it or not, marriages can learn a lot from sports. If only we demonstrated the same commitment sports teams demonstrate, we believe marriages wouldn't be suffering so much. The following is a step by step guideline for engaging in "jungle warfare" in marriage.

DESIRE TO WIN: THE MARRIAGE CONNECTION

To keep things in the proper context, winning is not referring to winning an argument or getting your way, but rather working together and staying connected. In relationships, generally one of you is a "Pursuer" and the other is a "Withdrawer." This means when conflict comes, one of you is anxious to deal with it directly and quickly while the other hopes it goes away by sweeping it under the rug or delaying the inevitable. The Withdrawer may shut down, avoid altogether and is afraid it'll turn into an all-out fight. Sometimes the Pursuer needs to back off and wait for better timing and the Withdrawer needs to come out of the silence and deal with reality. The main point is to desire to win in marriage by handling conflict constructively instead of disrespectfully.

KNOW YOUR WEAKNESS: RECOGNIZE WARNING SIGNS

Conflict is hard to resolve when the conditions are not right. For example, we need to learn to recognize when we are most vulnerable and unreasonable. Whenever you are hungry, angry, lonely or tired (the acronym: HALT),[130] you are going to be on edge. It doesn't necessarily mean you shouldn't talk during these times, but understand what may be triggering negative emotions in you or your spouse.

THE GAME PLAN: TALK THROUGH BEFORE SOLVING

Come up with a plan first. Game plans aren't done on a fly. They require discussing issues thoroughly enough that each person feels understood, respected and heard. Rushing to a solution rarely accomplishes much. Sometimes couples rush to a solution in order to quickly end a conflict or disagreement. Even apologies can be ways of quickly acquiescing and ending an argument externally, but internally you are still angry and frustrated.

Discussing the problem is about understanding your partner's perspective, while solving a problem is about taking action together.[131] Never rush to a solution until you truly understand your partner and the problem itself.

Talking through a problem will keep you from feeling like you are always walking on eggshells not knowing when the next eruption will occur. We've all felt that way at some point.

WHEN TO CALL A TIME-OUT: STOPPING A FIGHT IN ITS TRACKS

In sports, many coaches will call a time-out when the team is losing focus or allowing their emotions to get out of hand. Time-outs are called when they are experiencing negative momentum. Players are often pulled from a game until they settle down. One personal foul or technical foul can cost a team dearly. Time-outs are an important technique for protecting your relationship. Time-outs are vital. Here's how it works in marriage.

A time-out helps us get a grip on our emotions (specifically our temper). It is a relationally destructive practice to spew forth destructive words and hurtful attitudes. Time-outs allow us time to get ourselves under control. It also gives time to correctly see the main points of the argument and hopefully view things from your partner's perspective.

"Your marriage should be characterized as fun.
If you don't take life by the horns it will take you for a ride."

In relationships, a time-out must be respected immediately. Once a time out is called in sports, the team cannot run another play. You don't call a time out and just walk away either. You can simply and gently say to your spouse, "Things are getting heated right now, let's cool off a bit and talk a little later, would you mind?" This humble approach isn't acting independently but includes your spouse and respects him or her as a fellow team member.

A time-out is not a way of avoiding important subjects. The time-out should not last days or weeks. A cooling off period may be an hour or longer, but the discussion should continue within 24 hours. Use your time-out to think, pray and calm down. Time-outs give each other a little extra space for a brief period of time in order to connect at a deeper level.

TIMING: WHEN TO TALK

In sports, timing can be everything. Calling the right play at the right time can mean the difference between winning and losing. In marriage, timing is extremely important. Couples should be able to talk about anything. But at what time is the question. So here are some important rules of engagement when it comes to timing. Never discuss important matters or topics that have been explosive in the past during the following times:

- Meal times
- Bedtime
- Getting ready for work or church
- Getting kids off to school
- Getting ready to walk out the door for work
- As soon as you walk in the door
- Date nights or fun times
- Prayer times
- Family fun times

Fun times need to be just that... fun! Transition times are hurried and will lack focus and attention. Timing is crucial to relational success.

AUDIBLES: LISTENING AND SPEAKING SKILLS

One of the biggest lessons couples can learn is how to converse without tempers flaring and things getting out of control. One way to combat this is to take turns speaking and listening. One major rule is this: the who has the floor can only share two or three sentences at a time. This prevents one person from dominating the conversation and allows communication in "bite-size" chunks that are easier to swallow. The speaker is the one who has the floor and holds a remote control or anything as a sign that the "floor is taken." Permission must be granted to have the floor. The key is to be respectful and validating. Once the speaker is done, the listener must mirror back or rephrase what was spoken in a brief sentence or two. This will give the speaker the security that they are being heard. Taking turns and sharing tactfully but honestly can stop an implosion and enable each other to understand the other person's point of view. This may seem a bit mechanical, but believe me, it's much better than the alternative.

WEEKLY TEAM MEETINGS: STAYING CONNECTED AND BEING PROACTIVE

Each couple needs to schedule (yes schedule) a weekly couple's meeting. We can be so busy that we continually put off important things. A weekly couple's meeting helps you accomplish several goals:

- It helps keep your marriage on track.

- It is a great way of proactively dealing with things before they turn into a big issue.

- It is an excellent way to keep relationally connected by communicating the week's events, potential problems or escalating problems.

We need to learn to be proactive in our communication rather than reactive when conflict arises. Then issues become "radioactive" and become topics couples avoid. This weekly couple's meeting should be a time to talk about the week's events, plan for upcoming events, voice any concerns, talk about any issue, or evaluate your marriage. Some meetings are more structured than others, but the key is to have them consistently, even when things are going great. The meeting can last from 15 minutes to one hour, just make sure you don't skip them.

TEAM TOGETHERNESS: BUILD UNITY AND DEEP CONNECTION

As a couple, you'll never have a great marriage if all you do is focus on "business" or serious issues. It's time to have fun! Unfortunately, since we're all so busy we need to schedule most of our fun times. What's also unfortunate is that some are so busy that they have neglected the fun side of marriage and you may be stagnating as a couple. Good news, you can turn that around starting today!

Some Suggestions

Date Nights: This is a scheduled time (at times spontaneous) where you invest and prioritize your relationship. Remember this rule: no kids! It is a time just for the two of you. It is NOT a time to discuss hot topics or issues.

Fun Times: Your marriage should be characterized as fun. If you don't take life by the horns it will take you for a ride. Sure, there are many things we cannot control in life, but we ought to prioritize fun times with your mate. It may be a weekly or nightly card game, computer game, checkers, chess, or whatever. It may involve taking a walk, a workout, a game of tennis, a bike ride or simply watching your favorite TV show.

Love Making: In many marriages, one is a high desire "horny toad" and the other is a low desire "cold as ice" person when it comes to sex. If you have to schedule this, then do it. The key is to be there for one another. Is it unrealistic to have sex every day? Yes. But that doesn't mean you can't try. As Christians, we believe we are involved in a spiritual war of light versus darkness. Prayer is a way we do spiritual warfare; however, we also believe physical intimacy is spiritual warfare too. The more connected you are sexually as a couple, the less likely you will be vulnerable to intruders of your marriage.

"But the wisdom that comes from heaven is first of all pure. It is also peace loving, gentle at all times, and willing to yield to others." ~ James 3:18

CONNECTING POINTS

- When it comes to conflict, which one of you tends to be the Pursuer and which one is the Withdrawer?

- What inflames you whenever a conflict occurs? (e.g., bringing up past mistakes, using privy information against you, name calling, disrespectful body language, sarcasm, etc.)

- What "rule of engagement" do you believe will help your spouse the most when dealing with conflict?

- What is your plan to have that "team togetherness?"?

TARZAN & JANE'S FUN FACT!

What women say is attractive in men? Here are some qualities: Confidence, personality, leadership, one who makes her feel special, and a man who can socialize well with others.

Source: http://whatdowomenfindattractive.blogspot.com/ & http://www.whatattractswomentomen.com/what-do-women-find-attractive-in-men/

CHAPTER 34

Great Expectations

"Anger always comes from frustrated expectations."

~ Elliot Larson

"Marriage means expectations and expectations means conflict."

~ Paxton Blair

EXPECTATIONS. WE ALL HAVE THEM. Expectations of our spouse are the reason we walked down that aisle and said "I do." We were convinced that this man and this woman would treat us like royalty all the days of our life. Never did we imagine there would be times where they would treat us so harshly and so indifferently. For most couples, their expectations come crashing down and reality sets in after a short time of being married.

On a scale of one to ten, our expectations of a total stranger are about a two or a three. We expect people to treat us cordially and with decency. We do not expect them to cater to us or give us anything outside of simple common courtesy. So if a stranger does something unusually nice such as allow us to cut in front of them in a busy supermarket checkout line or gives us their extra movie ticket, we think they are the best because they have exceeded our expectations. Instead of being a three on the expectation scale they have jumped to a five.

However, on a scale of one to ten, our expectations of our spouse are clearly a ten for most people. That means if our spouse treat us any less than what is expected, we fume at being so ill-treated. If our partner's treatment may be a seven or an eight, yet they have fallen short of our expectation level, we think we are being treated like chopped liver and deserve better from them.

Expectation defined means a strong belief that something will happen or be the case in the future. It is a belief that someone will or should achieve something. Things have a way of changing after marriage. Women marry men they hope to change, but men marry women they hope will never change.

Dating is a time of collecting your expectations; it is a time of assessment of a prospective mate. Jeff McElroy has humorously said, "Dating is the practice of looking good and the art of lying."[132] Unfortunately, some expectations we have are hidden and we don't even realize we have the until we are married. Most couples fail to discuss their expectations with one another prior to marriage and even after. Things like:

- Are we in agreement with having children?

- How many kids are we going to have?

- How often are we going to have sex each week?

- Are both of you going to work outside of the home? How will we discipline our kids?

- Whose parent's house are we going to visit during the holidays?

- What type of lifestyle will we have?

- Where are we going to live? What kind of a house? What kind of neighborhood? (Jane is a city girl and Tarzan is a country guy)

- Will we go to church together? Which one?

- How will we spend money? Will we be big savers?

- What roles will we have in marriage?

The Truth About Expectations

Expectations drive us and mess with our thought processes. Expectations that go unmet can rapidly skew how we perceive our mate, and consequently we can view them in a bad light.

UNCONSCIOUS EXPECTATIONS

Most of us are unaware of our expectations. Unfortunately, we don't discover these unconscious expectations until long after we are married. A dose of self-awareness can go a long way. Unconscious expectations cause us to act or react the way we do. When our mate does not match your expectations, often we feel unloved and uncared for. We reason, "If s/he loved me so much then why wouldn't they know what I expect?"

These unconscious expectations are the "fine print" of our marriage covenant. Disappointment, anger, and sadness are key indicators that your expectations have been shattered. We assumed that our mate would automatically do certain things once we were married. When expectations go unmet, we convince ourselves that our spouse really doesn't care for us. Men assumed their wife would watch football with them just like they did when they were dating. Women assumed their husband would patiently endure hours of shopping with them like they did when they were engaged. Men also assumed their wife would be sex-crazed like they were on the honeymoon. Women also assumed their husbands would continue to be a "romantic stud" year after year. Our expectations soon shatter and we feel trapped thinking, "I guess this is my lot in life."

> *"Your expectations get you to the altar.*
> *Once there, you must alter your expectations."*
> *~ Jeff McElroy*

UNSPOKEN EXPECTATIONS

Couples fail to discuss their expectations with one another both before and after marriage. When an expectation isn't voiced, it is sometimes and foolishly assumed that, "He or she ought to know this... why should I have to say anything? If s/he loved me they would automatically know this and follow through. It goes without saying that your partner is not a mind reader. Even some of the simplest things must be spelled out. Men and women think differently (not wrongly) on multiple issues and their needs differ significantly. That means your partner may not "get it" right away. Be honest and graceful and share your expectations with them.

UNMET EXPECTATIONS

Unmet expectations cause great frustration and a huge source of conflict in marriage. Needs can also be used synonymously with expectations. Consider the needs men and women have.

Deep-seated Needs She Expects To Be Met By Her Husband

RELATIONAL & FINANCIAL SECURITY

A wife expects her husband to be faithfully dedicated to her and hold down a decent job. A husband needs to consistently demonstrate his loyalty to his wife by refraining from viewing pornography or gawking at other women. This helps a wife feel relationally secure. A husband who works hard and seeks the best employment possible makes his wife feel financially secure.

ROMANCE AND TENDERNESS

A wife expects her husband to make her feel special through periodic surprises and demonstrate his love though gentle non-sexual contact outside the bedroom. A wife believes her husband will continue to show her tenderness and affection like he did early in the relationship. This tenderness will often cause a wife to feel more secure and even more sexual towards her husband.

MEANINGFUL CONVERSATION

A wife expects her husband to take an interest in her and connect emotionally through daily communication and transparency. The strong "silent" type might have a certain mysterious appeal initially, but that doesn't last long before it becomes extremely annoying.

"Be open to God's expectations for you and your marriage."

PROTECTIVE LEADERSHIP

A wife expects her husband to take the initiative and be proactive with her and the children. It means influencing decisions that relate to the family as well as working as a team. This includes areas like spirituality, finances, education, entertainment, friendships, and so forth. A husband who demonstrates protective leadership is a polar opposite of the stereotypical passive husband who is so laid back that he abdicates all form of backbone and simply says, "Yes, Dear" in a whiny voice. A passive husband is one who regulates important matters for his wife to handle alone. A protective leader does not imply a controlling, dominating husband who does what he wants when he wants without any input from his wife. Men must learn to initiate and develop leadership skills. Incidentally, men have a strong propensity to protect their wife and children. Be cautious that you do not confuse his desire to protect as control.

A FAMILY MAN

A wife expects her husband to be committed and make time for the family and participate in his fair share of caring for the home. A wife is expecting her husband to prioritize the home above hobbies, friends, and even career.

DEEP-SEATED NEEDS HE EXPECTS TO BE MET BY HIS WIFE

HONOR, APPRECIATION & RESPECT

A husband expects his wife to show proper respect and gratitude for what he does. This includes "bragging" on him in front of the children, your parents, and friends. He wants to feel like more than a paycheck... he wants to be your hero – that knight in shining armor. Remember how special you made him feel early in the relationship? Men may act tough and not get too excited, but don't let that fool you. They love it!

When I (Jane) was preoccupied over what Steve didn't do instead of what he did do, it only frustrated him and he felt underappreciated. When I began to focus on all he did do, not only did he feel appreciated and respected, but it made it easier for him to go the "extra mile" for me. Honor, appreciation and respect go a long way. No man is going to cheat on a woman who honors and respects him.

AN EXCITING SEXUAL PARTNER

A husband expects his wife to be available for him sexually and with a great attitude. Shopping at Victoria Secret is also a plus. Remember how sexual you were early in marriage? A sexually satisfied husband will be energized towards you. Conversely, a sexually deprived husband will show extreme frustration and face unnecessary temptation.

PHYSICAL ATTRACTION & CHEMISTRY

A husband expects his wife to take care of herself recognizing that he is visually stimulated. A woman who takes care of herself physically has confidence but also communicates her desire to meet her husband's needs. Men feel hurt when a wife gets all "dolled up" for work or when she goes out with her friends, but rarely if ever gets all decked out for him. A husband is not expecting his wife to be a centerfold or have a large bust, but one who cares for herself. There is an old Anglican wedding vow that a bride says to her groom:

> *With my body I will love you,*
> *With my body I will adore you,*
> *With my body I will declare your worth.*

A "PLAY" MATE (A RECREATIONAL COMPANION)[133]

A husband expects his wife to connect with him on a recreational level. This can include active sports like mountain climbing, biking, hunting to something more laid back such as a playing cards or a board game or watching football. What you do isn't as important as your willingness to connect with him recreationally.

Men love it when their wife takes interest in his hobby. Many men think it's rather sexy when his wife is interested in guy stuff, like football. Seek to understand his world and watch him become more vulnerable with you.

DOMESTIC SUPPORT (HOMEMAKER)[134]

A husband expects his wife to prioritize the home front even if she has a career. Although responsibilities must be shared, a man needs his wife to give the home a "woman's touch." He'll feel lost without her.

Each one of these expectations plays an important role in marital satisfaction. Proactively meet your partner's needs without being asked. This willing attitude just might be the spark your marriage has been waiting for.

CONNECTING POINTS

- What unreasonable expectation did you have coming into your marriage?
- How have you altered some of your expectations?
- How has your family and cultural background affected your level of expectation in marriage?

TARZAN & JANE'S FUN FACT!

Women are more relationship oriented, and look for commonalities and ways to connect with other women. Men tend to relate to other men on a one-up, one-down basis. Status and dominance is important.

Source: Simma Lieberman Associates

Expectations Continued

L ET'S TAKE A CLOSER LOOK at how expectations can affect our marriage.

UNREASONABLE EXPECTATIONS

The more unreasonable expectations you have, the harder your marriage is going to be. Jeff McElroy sums it up: "Your expectations get you to the altar. Once there, you must alter your expectations."[135] You cannot expect your spouse to love you the same way your parents did or show love to you the way your ex did. Whenever you begin to compare, instead of appreciate, you devalue your mate. Unrealistic expectations places unnecessary pressure on your partner to do what isn't humanly possible.

Unrealistic expectations look something like this:

- My partner and I should never disagree.

- Christian couples should never have conflict.

- Christian men don't get tempted.

- My spouse ought to heal my deepest wounds.

- My partner needs to do things the way my momma did.

- We must spend every Sunday over at my parents.

- My husband makes all of the decisions independently.

- My partner should insist we live at the same socio-economic level my parents did.

This list can be endless. For example, if your husband had a blue-collar job, don't expect him to be the CEO of Microsoft. This expectation is unrealistic and will create resentment and marital dissatisfaction. Likewise, if your wife desires children and now decide that you never do, it is unreasonable to expect her to alter her desire for this important aspect of marriage.

Here are some realistic/reasonable expectations:

- You can expect your spouse to be faithful.

- You can expect your spouse to meet your basic marital needs.

- You can expect your partner to demonstrate their love and commitment for you.

- You can expect your partner to establish proper boundaries with the opposite sex.

- You can expect your partner to be available for you as much as possible.

- You can expect your partner to prioritize you above all human relationships.

- You can expect your partner to work as a team.

- You can expect your partner to treat you with dignity and respect.

There are some deep needs we all have that only God can meet. When you expect your partner to be the "be-all, end all" for you, then you are going to be greatly disappointed. Truth be told, our partners make lousy substitutes for God.[136]

Understand God's Expectations

Be open to God's expectations for you and your marriage. God expects us to serve Him and obey His principles regarding marriage. This point needs to be emphasized because God's blessings will flow upon a couple that honors Him and walks in His ways.

God has clear expectations for you and your marriage. If so, what are they? God expects the following:

- Be loyal and stay committed to each other (Malachi 2:14-16).

- Meet each other's needs (1 Corinthians 7:1-6).

- Leave your parents and cleave to your spouse (Ephesians 5:31).

- Wives must accept the leadership of their husband (1 Peter 3:5).

- Husbands must honor their wife (1 Peter 3:7).

- Wives must respect their husband (Ephesians 5:33).

- Husbands must love their wife (Ephesians 5:25).

- Wives must possess a submissive posture towards their husband (Ephesians 5:22).

- Husbands must dwell with their wife with understanding (1 Peter 3:7).

- Wives must possess a gentle spirit (1 Peter 3:4).

Following God's ways and meeting His expectations is a recipe for marital success.

The Basis Of Our Expectations

Expectations come from many things. Frustration begins when what is happening doesn't match what we expect. Our level of satisfaction is directly determined by whether or not our expectations are being met. Expectations can affect every aspect of marriage. The more unmet expectations you have in marriage the more frustrated you will become.

FAMILY BACKGROUND

This includes things such as:

- How your parents interacted with one another.

- How your parents demonstrated their love for you.

- How your parents showed you affection (if they did at all).

- How involved they were in your life.

- How they disciplined you.

Family background can determine if your marriage is going to function as a team or if will be matriarchal or patriarchal in nature. It will influence you on how or if you discipline your children. Make no mistake, your upbringing has tremendous influence on who you are today whether you realize it or not. Trust me, your partner most likely sees this clearer than you do. Our upbringing creates expectations we may not even realize early on.

CULTURAL BACKGROUND

This includes things like:

- What country you grew up in.

- What part of the country you grew up in.

- What nationality you are and the cultural expectations attached to that.

Some families make it clear that they expect you to marry within your culture. But what if your mate has a unique cultural background? Your cultural background can create strong expectations in marriage.

PREVIOUS RELATIONSHIPS

Previous dating relationships or a previous marriage has also formed our expectations. Expectations formed on how to show love, make love, what you consider romantic, how to interact with one another, how to handle conflict, communication, who apologizes first, et cetera.

Parental relationships can form our expectations. Sometimes we "read into" things because of how we were treated by our parents. Minor things can quickly turn into major problems if we don't realize the source of our expectations. You expect your partner to do the same things your parents did and may feel unloved if they fail to do fulfill that expectation. For example, growing up, my mom alway put our clothes in our drawers whenever she did our laundry. So when Jane and I were married, initially I felt she didn't care as much when she plopped my clothes on the dresser or bed. We need to be aware that some of the expectations we have of our partner is a direct result of our experiences with others.[135]

"Expectations must be evaluated, communicated, and altered."

Chivalry, things like opening doors for your wife, often stem from how your father treated your mother. And conversely, if your father didn't treat your mother well, that can affect how a wife sets her expectations... whether they are too high or too low. If we look carefully, we'll discover that many of our expectations we have for our mate are based on previous relationships.

CULTURAL INFLUENCES

TV has shaped America more than we'd like to acknowledge. Cultural mind-sets are the collective thinking among the populous and determines what we think is normal or expected.

For example, many believe you are expected to sleep with your boyfriend or girlfriend before marriage even though God's expectations differ greatly. What is viewed as normal becomes an expectation.

Another example of how TV has shaped our thinking is the aggressiveness of women. If the average husband believes his wife is going to act as sexual like the woman on the TV show, he has another thing coming. These women in the TV shows are being paid to act that way. They aren't real. Besides, men are probably the ones writing the scripts. They are paid actors to act the way they do when the camera is rolling. If they really were that sexual, then why did her real-life husband run off with another woman? Cultural influences shape our level of expectation in marriage.

CORE BELIEFS: RELIGIOUS, SPIRITUAL, AND OTHERWISE

We all have a core belief system even if you're not a religious person. The greater this difference is, the greater risk your marriage has of disconnecting.

Just because you have a Christian background does not mean you will instantly be on the same page when it comes to spiritual matters. Consider the following areas:

Bible reading: Some strongly feel Bible reading/study ought to be done daily while others are content do so on a "as-needed" basis. Some feel couples ought to read the Bible together while others don't see the need for a joint Bible study.

Prayer: Some believe prayer is a daily essential while others don't. Some feel couples ought to pray together while others think it's a deeply personal matter.

Church Attendance: Do we go to church together as a couple or do we attend separately? If we attend together, what church should we go to, traditional or contemporary?

Service: How much time should we devote to serving others?

Giving: Maybe you believe in tithing (giving 10% of your income to church). Your partner believes in giving too, but a whole lot less than you think is acceptable.

In the book, *A Lasting Promise*, the authors put it this way:

"Sometimes, young couples from different spiritual backgrounds marry, believing that the differences will not matter. But people tend to return to their roots when they have children or as they age. What does not seem too important now may become much more important later."[138]

That's why it is so important that engaged couples learn to be "equally yoked" in marriage. Due to the enormous amount of heartache, the Bible instructs us in Second Corinthians 6:14 to marry with believers of like precious faith:

"Don't be unequally yoked together with unbelievers..."

Now, if you're a Christian and your spouse is not, the Bible instructs you to stay married and serve your spouse. It is through your love that s/he may come to Christ. Since you knew on the front-end that your partner was not a person of faith or similar faith, then don't use that as an excuse to get out of your marriage.

Once again, expectations must be evaluated, communicated, and altered. If you have unrealistic ones, then alter them. If you believe you have healthy ones, then communicate them. But, by all means, evaluate your expectations, that way you can determine the healthy ones from the unrealistic ones. It is incumbent upon each spouse to do whatever is necessary to meet the healthy expectations of our partner. Your marital success depends upon it.

ME TARZAN, you JANE!

JUST IN CASE...

Selecting A Good Marriage Counselor

"Counsel in the heart of man is like deep water. But a man of understanding will draw it out."

~ Proverbs 20:5 NKJV

MY FRIEND "EDDY" AND HIS WIFE "SUSAN" were suffering from serious marital problems so they decided to go to a marriage counselor. They entered the room and sat down. Eddy decided to break the ice and asked the counselor, "So, how long have you been married?" He said, "To my current wife, three years." "Really," Eddy asked. "How many times have you been married?" "Three!" the 63 year-old counselor replied. So that was the last time they went to that counselor figuring he had enough marital problems of his own.

They searched for a new counselor and made an appointment. When Eddy and Susan walked into the room, they couldn't help but notice how young he looked. "Out of curiosity," Eddy inquired, "How old are you and are you married?" The young counselor responded, "I am 23 years-old and truthfully I have never had a serious relationship." Surprised Eddy said, "Wow! So how can you help me?" The young lad said, "Because I have a counseling degree." They never went back.

Eddy and Susan tried for the third time and stumbled across what seemed to be a reputable counseling center. This time it was a woman who seemed very educated, distinguished and wise. Once again, Eddy and Susan were very curious now to ask about the marital status of this new counselor. Eddy, now a pro, asked the counselor, "So how long have you been married?" To their utter shock and amazement, the counselor said, "I have never been married in my life, but I have been living with a man now for over 20 years." Then to make matters worse she added, "It's just like being married." Unfortunately this discouraged couple gave up on counseling all together and at the time of this writing they are separated.

One of the biggest gaffe couples make is choosing the wrong counselor. We did. One counselor we went to made it very clear to me (Steve) in private that there was no hope for our marriage. I was stunned! There was no affair, pornography or anything like that, just normal marital problems and we hit a wall, an impasse like every couple does at some point... we needed some objective intervention! Instead, he tried to steal my hope. Needless to say, we never went back to him.

At some point in our marriage we will need some input from an objective third party whenever we reach a marital impasse. These individuals must be seasoned, possess wisdom, have a good marriage themselves, and prize confidentiality with sensitive and very personal information. Above all, they need to give you hope!

Here are some thoughts on selecting a good marriage counselor.

PRAY FOR DIRECTION

We believe every couple's first reaction should be to pray for God's direction.

GET A RECOMMENDATION

Are there any couples you know who have gone through successful marriage counseling?

ASK THEM QUESTIONS

Don't be intimidated to ask them direct questions like Eddy did. Questions such as:

- What is their view of the Bible or biblical principles on marriage and divorce?

- What reasons do you believe a couple should divorce?

- Have they had a good track record helping couples reconcile?

- Do they have any references?

TRY THEM OUT

Afterwards ask each other what your impressions were. Don't expect them to be perfect or have all the answers. Ask yourself, "Do I have more hope or less hope since our visit?" "Was the advice given solid and practical or just theoretical and trite?" If things aren't adding up, move on.

BE IN AGREEMENT

Agreement is very important for couples. If one person is feeling uncomfortable or coerced then there is a greater chance that person will close up. If you cannot agree 100% on which counselor to use then at least reach some kind of a consensus.

COMMIT TO ONE

For progress, accountability and even to be a good steward of finances, try to stick to one that is working. However, you may also want to seek out a mature couple you can glean and model from without the counseling fees. Just be sure to find a way to bless them for their time and wisdom. Once you commit to one, be sure to follow through with assignments you are given. And please remember this, especially for men: There is absolutely no shame in seeing a counselor. Everyone, even the most successful couples, needs intervention from time to time.

Traditional counseling often does not work. For many couples, it is often an indication of a marriage that is on life support. Some couples won't even consider counseling until one of them is serious about leaving. With this in mind, it is even more critical that you are wise in selecting a marriage counselor.

One final point: No amount of counseling can overcome an unforgiving spirit. Humble yourself, take responsibility and commit to personal maturity. A humble spirit of forgiveness might not only save your marriage, but it just might revolutionize it.

Connecting Points

- What makes a good counselor?

- What specific non-negotiables must you see in a prospective counselor?

- How long do you think you ought to stick with a particular counselor?

- What are the warning signs of a poor marriage counselor?

- Do you know of a mature Christian couple you can receive marriage mentoring from? If so, will you ask them to come alongside you and your spouse?

Jungle Economics

~ Connecting Financially ~

The 4 Monkeys:
Caleb, Faith Victorya, Luke & Christianna

CHAPTER 35

My Money, My Honey, & Me

"Too many people spend money they haven't earned, to buy things they don't want, to impress people they don't like."

~ Will Rogers

THERE IS A STORY OF A COUPLE named Henry and Henrietta. They were well off financially due to Henrietta's income and inheritance. Henrietta would frequently remind Henry where their fortunes came from. She would flamboyantly tell Henry as they drove in their nice Cadillac Escalade, "You know, if it weren't for me and my money, we wouldn't have this luxurious vehicle."

"I know, I know," lamented Henry. Later Henrietta boasted as they walked through their plush living room, "You know, Henry if it wasn't for me and my money none of this imported furniture would be here." Finally, Henry had enough and said, "Well, Henrietta, the truth is, if it wasn't for your money, I wouldn't be here either."

Did you know that money problems equal marriage problems? According to many researchers, the number one problem in marriage is money! Some say communication and that may be true, but communication over what? Money! We all have different views and philosophies when it comes to the mucho denarii. It's been said that, "When poverty enters the front door, love goes out the back door." Don't let that be the case.

The most common source of disagreement in families in the United States is money. In fact, 37% of all married couples indicate that the number one problem in their marriage is finances. Happily married couples, however, agree on how to handle money 48% more than do unhappy couples.[139]

Whenever we address singles, we remind them of the importance of being financially solvent due to the overwhelming stress that is associated with financial struggles in a marriage. So to the singles we say, "If there is no finance, then there is no romance." If the man can't hold done a job, then she shouldn't even consider the possibility of marrying him.

Nonetheless, you ARE married and divorce should not be an option just because you are struggling financially. Chances are you didn't get in this mess by yourself and it will take some teamwork to get out it. It has been said that "Money in marriage is oceans of emotions surrounded by expanses of expenses." Ambrose Bierce said that the word budgeting is defined as "The art or science of managing revenues and resources for the best advantage of the manager."

Marriage Financial Dangers to Avoid[140]

DISREGARDING YOUR PARTNER'S INPUT

In marriage usually one of you is more of a spender and the other is more of a saver; this usually depends on your personality or background. One thing we have learning is listen to each other's perspective.

We all come with different perspectives. Some believe that providing security for their spouse is by shopping and showering gifts upon them. Others display love by saving money and showing what they have accumulated for them. We all have strengths and weaknesses when it comes to finances. We must learn to utilize our strengths and recognize our weakness.

It is equally imperative to remember that your spouse, regardless of their spiritual condition, serves as God's mouthpiece to you. God gave you a mate to work hand-in-hand with for life. They can clearly see your flaws and blind spots. Accept their input, even if it is not packaged in the most tactful way, as God's mouthpiece to you.

"Husbands, likewise, dwell with them [your wife] with understanding."
~ 1 Peter 3:7 (NKJV).

CONTROLLING THE FINANCES

Marriage is a partnership not a dictatorship. Dominance means disproportionate control. We may have differing functions but equal value. Dominance is not about who carries the checkbook and pays the bills, it's about control and carries with it an attitude of superiority. There is a danger in marriage when one person controls the values, decisions and priorities related to money.

Remember this important lesson in marriage: Just because you brought home the paycheck does NOT mean it is ALL yours. Your spouse doesn't have to have an income to provide input when it comes to the finances. When you said "I do," what you were saying was that 100% of what I have belongs to my mate and 100% of what my mate owns belongs to me. Marriage is not a 50/50 proposition, but a 100/100 effort.

"...Be humble, thinking of others as better than yourself." ~ Philippians 2:3 (NLT)

DISAGREEMENT OVER SPENDING

Spousal agreement is huge and should never be underestimated. You may be in agreement with your office manager, business partner, best friend, parents, but if you lack agreement with your mate - buyer beware!

Several years ago a friend and I (Steve) had an idea of investing in real estate out West where the property values were skyrocketing. My wife was in agreement. Several other couples asked if they could join us in this new and exciting venture that looked to be very promising financially. There were two one acre parcels that sold for $200,000 each and was $80,000 under the going rate.

"Accumulating debt is a huge danger to any marriage. It's supposed to be until death do us part not until debt do us part."

We each put our $20,000 down as a group then something amazing happened... before closing on the deal, we had an offer come in that would give us somewhere between $275,000 and $300,000 for each parcel guaranteeing each investor at least $25,000 a piece net profit. I consulted with my business friend, the listing realtor (also a friend), other investors and they all recommend that I hold the land since the market was booming. Everyone I spoke with told me to hold EXCEPT Jane. I totally disregarded her words because she wasn't an "expert" in this field. Well, needless to say, that was unbelievably stupid, not only relationally, but financially as well.

We held onto the properties and in one year sold one and made $100,000 as a group. We all received our $20,000 initial investment back. The property then shot up to $350,000 and suddenly the market crashed... and did it crash hard! One of the hardest hit areas during a recession was undeveloped land like ours. Pricing plummeted to under $30,000 per acre. We were stunned. Jane had the "I-told-you-so" look on her face and from time to time would remind me that we wouldn't be in this mess if I had just listened to her.

But the fact was she was right!

Never discount your spouse's perspective. He or she is there as God's safeguard for both of you. We all have blind spots that can be ignored through excitement and zeal.

Men are typically greater risk takers than women when it comes to finances. There were two major things God revealed to me through this whole real estate debacle. First of all, there was greed in my heart that I didn't realize was there. And secondly, unity with a spouse is absolutely essential.

When we are not in agreement financially or otherwise, our policy is to take the safest route. That may mean holding back instead of investing. That may mean not moving instead of relocating.

There are two basic rules for investing according to my good friend, Ralph Criswell, that I violated. They are...

- Do not invest with money you cannot afford to lose.

- Never loan money for investments.

To my chagrin, I did both, but thank God for a forgiving wife and God's mercy. Just remember that agreement is vital for a happy marriage.

"...A home divided is also doomed." ~ Luke 11:17

"Can two people walk together without agreeing on the direction." ~ Amos 3:3 (NLT)

A MOUNTAIN OF DEBT

Accumulating debt is a huge danger to any marriage. It's supposed to be until death do us part not until debt do us part! I've met couples who are in a crisis mode year after year. No matter what their income is, they are still at the same level when it comes to their debt to income ratio. I saw an article online that read, "How I Thrived Off of $15,000 in One Year" and another article next to it that read, "How We Scraped by on $350,000 Income." You see, it's not about how much you make, but your philosophy of how you are going to spend it.

Some people have this mentality: the more I make the more I can borrow. Get rid of that stinking thinking. Unnecessary debt creates incredible pressure in a marriage. You'll never get out of debt just wishing it will go away. Quit waiting for that check to arrive in the mail and do something about it. Go to a financial counselor and by all means attend something like Dave Ramsey's Financial Peace University which is a 13-week course for married couples (www.daveramsey.com).

Boats, motorcycles, clothes, and food are lousy debt. "Good" debt are things like homes and sometimes cars. I recommend no debt, but it may take some years before a couple can pay cash for a car, let alone a home.

Years ago Jane and I came up with a two-year plan to get out of debt. At that time we were making $40,000 dollars a year. We had $16,000 plus in debt and we agreed that we would not make any purchase over $20 without first consulting and agreeing with the other. I remember calling her when I was at Wal Mart to get some cheesy things and I'd have a well-scripted, prepared statement for Jane. Sometimes she would just laugh at my compulsiveness. I'd say, "Oh, we have to have this for our home gym." "Really," Jane asked, "Just how did we survive without it?" Then Jane would take a "low blow" approach and say, "Look, you're the leader of the home and I trust that you will make the right decisions as the Lord leads you." I'd feel so convicted I'd put whatever it was back on the shelf.

"Can two people walk together without agreeing on the direction?" ~ Amos 3:3 (NLT)

The good news is that we were out of debt in 16 months (how ironic). The very last payment we owed was $1,000. Someone from out of state, who had no idea what we were doing, said they felt the Holy Spirit lead them to give us $1,000. The final payment was paid in full. Then we saved up to purchase our first home. Isn't God good? You see faith without works is dead. Couples who are implementing a wise plan and are unified will see good results over time.

It was said of the Prodigal,

"...he wasted all of his money on wild living." ~ Luke 15:13 (NLT)

Connecting Points

- Do you have a plan to get out of debt? If so, what is it?

- How do you handle disagreements over spending?

- How can you become more financially unified?

TARZAN & JANE'S FUN FACT!

When entering a room, men look for exits, estimating a possible threat, and ways of escape, while women pay attention to the guests faces to find out who they are and how they feel.

Source: http://peoplerelationships.syl.com/battleof-sexes/differences

CHAPTER 36

"My Money" Attitudes

"With money in your pocket you are intelligent, talented and good looking, too."

~ Yiddish Proverb

A SUNDAY SCHOOL TEACHER WAS TEACHING HER CLASS about the difference between right and wrong. "All right children, let's take another example," she said. "If I were to get into a man's pocket and take his billfold with all his money, what would I be?" Little Johnny raises his hand and with a confident smile blurts out, "You'd be his wife!"

When a spouse says, "I earned the money, therefore I have the right to control it," they are essentially saying that they have disconnected with their spouse financially. That is not the attitude of a covenant partner.

In marriage, two become one – meaning, all that is yours is now theirs and all that was theirs is now yours. His debts are her debts. His wealth is now her wealth. Every single thing you have in life is now surrendered to your spouse including your body.

At a wedding one couple put in their vows, "And with all my worldly goods I thee endow." In other words, they are saying, "I am giving you everything I have." That's how covenant works. The lesser is blessed by the greater.

Guys, it's no longer "my toolbox" or "my truck." It now becomes equally her toolbox and her truck too. Seriously. Of course that goes with bank accounts too.

The kitchen is no longer "her" domain but "our" domain. Attitudes we have towards money and possessions are attitudes that are often carried toward our spouse.

INHERITANCE ISSUES

There is a couple whose wife received $50,000 and she spent it all on herself and her start-up business. She told her husband, "It's my money from my parents and I can do whatever I want with it." Needless to say, this couple has a lousy marriage.

With another couple, the wife also received over $60,000 in inheritance and he spent it all on himself. He bought himself a new $30,000 truck and built a standalone garage. Talk about pure selfishness! He wouldn't even consider his wife's request of remodeling the kitchen. These attitudes have the potential to destroy a relationship. Note: We believe whoever directly inherits the money ought to have "veto" power in spending of the inherited funds.

OUT-OF-CONTROL SPOUSES – NOW WHAT?

If your spouse is out-of-control then you may need to go to another extreme in order to gain control. If your husband or wife is a gambler, alcoholic, drug user, or wasting significant amounts of money, you need to stop giving them money.

One addict was using his kid's savings for his out-of-control habit. Therefore, a spouse may have to temporarily take control of the finances until the other person is delivered from his or her addiction. Do not enable bad behavior. But generally speaking, couples need to work together on their financial decisions; but there are some cases where tough love needs to be demonstrated and monies must be secured. Yes, we have counseled such couples.

CONTROLLING SPOUSES

Controlling spouses seek to use money to control their spouse. Some men are chauvinistic about finances and feel it is their birthright to control the money. I know of husbands that went out and bought a new vehicle and never even consulted with their wife. When you begin to operate in Christ-like authority, it means becoming a sacrificial servant and including your spouse in major decisions. It means putting the needs of your spouse and family ahead of yours; just as Jesus commanded us to love our wife as Christ loved the church and gave Himself for it (Ephesians 5:25).

One wealthy man would give his wife a meager allowance to live on while he feasted on the best of the best. She drove a beater and he's in a fancy luxury car. He dressed in the most luxurious of clothing but he wouldn't think twice of buying her some decent clothes.

PRENUPTIAL AGREEMENTS

According to Jimmy Evans, "Prenups are essentially a death sentence on a marriage."[141] This is not only an issue of control, but it is very selfish. It is basically saying, "I am not committed enough to you to give all of myself and what I own." Marriage is a covenant which essentially means, "Everything I own, you now own. And everything you own, I now own." The only area I believe a prenuptial agreement may be acceptable is when it comes to blended families protecting a biological child's inheritance or savings. Otherwise, I believe prenuptial agreements should be avoided because of what it communicates on the front-end of your marriage covenant.

The bottom line is that we must guard against worldly mindsets and attitudes when it comes to money. Learn to communicate and literally "share the wealth." Realize that everything you own... you really don't own. God owns it all! The Bible tells us that, "The earth is the Lord's and the fullness thereof."

"The love of money is the root of all evil." ~ 1 Timothy 6:10

CONNECTING POINTS

- Do you hold any "my money" attitudes? If so, do you feel they are justified and why?

- Do you believe what's mine is hers and what's hers is mine?

- What would you do if you inherited one million dollars? Write it out.

TARZAN & JANE'S FUN FACT!

Men are able to sort out information and archive it in their head. Women tend to rewind the information over and over again. The only way to stop thinking of the problems is to talk it over. When a woman shares her problems with a man, she is not always looking for solutions, she needs someone to listen to her.

Source: http://peoplerelationships.syl.com

Your Job: Asset or Liability?

"I'm no miracle worker. I'm just a guy who rolls up his sleeve and goes to work."

~ Don Shula

CAREERS CAN BE DEMANDING no matter what field you are in. Some professions can present special challenges and demands. Work hours, work conditions, work expectations, and work schedules can have a grueling effect on a person and on a marriage.

Ideally the best time to discuss these things is before marriage. However, since most couples haven't received adequate pre-marriage counseling, you'll have to work things out harmoniously.

Here are some interesting work-related statistics:

- Men who work nights increase their chances for divorce 6 times.

- Women who work nights have a 3 times likelier chance of divorce.

- 56% of dual career/income couples say they lack any time for each other during the week.

A recent study found that the top 5 most stressful jobs in America are:

1. Enlisted Military Soldier

2. Fire Fighter

3.   Airline Pilot

4.   Military General

5.   Police Officer

Source: http://www.cnbc.com/id/45859025/America_s_Most_Stressful_Jobs_2012?slide=4

Other stressful jobs include: The President of the United States, Astronaut, Hospital Administrator, President of a College or University, Senior Pastor, and Senior Corporate Executive.

Examine your career, schedules, expectations, and see how it may be negatively affecting your marriage. Incidentally, every occupation will have some type of negative affect on our life and marriage, but it is up to us to manage them.

If you feel a certain calling in a particular area, then seek to gain your spouse's support. Do what you can not to project on your spouse the unrealistic expectations and demands of your career. Some couples feel called together like in areas of ministry and business, but many do not.

Agreement Versus Consensus

To be in agreement means to have unity, consent and to be like-minded. To have a consensus means a general agreement. In other words, a consensus does not mean you are sold 100%, but you can live with the decision. It may mean relocating, changing a career, maybe going back to school, to working more hours or taking a second job. Regardless of what you choose, be sure to be in agreement as a couple as much as possible. There is nothing worse than marital disunity when it comes to bigger issues.

Connecting Points

- Is your job a downright hazard to your marriage?

- Do you believe your spouse's job is a downright hazard to your marriage?

- Would you be willing to change jobs (not necessarily occupations) in order to preserve your marriage?

- How can you balance marriage and work better?

- Do you believe you need to find a new place of employment? What does your partner think?

CHAPTER 37

Your Financial Plan

"A budget is a way of telling money where you want it to go instead of wondering where it went."

~ Dave Ramsey

THE AVERAGE AMERICAN has 8 credit cards and over $8,000 in credit card debt alone.[140] Compulsive spending is often an indication of a rebellious heart. What was the first thing the prodigal son did once he received his inheritance? He wasted his wealth (Luke 15:13-14).

According to Jimmy Evans:

"If you are not in agreement as a couple, there is no way for you to experience true prosperity. You can have money but it will be a source of contention if you are not unified. If you don't value your relationship with your spouse more than you value money, you will never have a successful marriage."[143]

Stop judging each other and learn each other's financial perspective and come into agreement. Have a vision retreat at the beginning of each year. Go over financial goals and goals for each of your children. Plan your year and put your faith out there for what you are expecting God to do. Do a budget. Talk about how you plan on spending your money. How much will we save? How much will we give away?

Budget is a way of agreeing on spending beforehand. We agree in advance. It is the best way to take the emotion out of it. With a budget we can tell if we can go on that vacation and take the kids to private school. But can you imagine not having a budget and doing both?

"Strive to keep the unity of the spirit in the bond of peace." ~ Ephesians 4:3

Without a budget, there's a potential for every financial decision to result in a tug of war. Conflict management is better done proactively than reactively. Your spouse doesn't have to have an income to provide input when it comes to the finances.

> *"Your outgo cannot exceed your income,*
> *or your upkeep will become your downfall."*
> *~ Unknown*

CONNECTING POINTS

- What plan do you have for getting out of debt?

- How can the topic of finances not be such a volatile issue in your marriage?

- How can you improve your financial condition?

- What do you believe are the areas in the past you can learn from that caused financial hardships? How will you change that from this point forward?

TARZAN & JANE'S FUN FACT!

Men prefer strident noises, hard handshakes, and red color. They are better at solving technical problems. Women have a sharper ear, they use more words while talking, and are better at completing tasks independently.

Source: http://peoplerelationships.syl.com/battleof-sexes/differences

Prospective Household Budget

Monthly Revenue

INCOME: _____

- Salary - Husband
- Salary - Wife
- Less Payroll Taxes
- Less Giving

NET SPENDING: _____

Monthly Expenditures

HOUSING: _____

- Mortgage
- Equity Loan
- Property Taxes
- Homeowners
- Repairs / Maintenance
- Household Supplies
- Association Fees

UTILITIES: _____

- Cable TV
- Phone / Internet
- Electric
- Gas
- Trash

FOOD: _____

- Groceries
- Restaurant
- School Lunches

TRANSPORTATION: _____

- Car Payment

- Gas & Oil

- Car Insurance

- Repairs, Tires, & Car Wash

- License & Taxes

SAVINGS: _____

- Emergency Fund

- Retirement Fund

- College Fund

- Christmas Fund

CLOTHING: _____

- Children

- Adults

- Cleaning / Laundry

MEDICAL/HEALTH: _____

- Disability Insurance

- Health Insurance

- Doctor Bills

- Dentist

- Drugs / Supplements

- Optometrist

- Dermatologist

- Chiropractor / Nutritionist

PERSONAL: _____

- Life insurance

- Childcare / Babysitter

Allowance for Kids

Toiletries / Cosmetics

Hair Care

School Loan / Adult Education

Kids School Tuition

School Supplies & School Fees

Sports / Lessons

Gifts (Excluding Christmas)

Blow Money

TOTAL EXPENSES: _____

DIFFERENCE: _____

Jesus In The Jungle

~ Connecting Spiritually ~

Fun goes a long way!

CHAPTER 38

Spiritual Unity In Marriage

"How can two walk together unless they be agreed?"

~ Amos 3:3

CONNECTING SPIRITUALLY can be difficult for some people because it involves a transparency and vulnerability that could be quite uncomfortable, especially if a couple isn't connected on other levels. For example, if a couple isn't connected physically or emotionally, then spiritual intimacy will be painstakingly hard. To experience spiritual connectivity, it requires a safe and secure atmosphere where trust and acceptance flow.

If you have lingering arguments, bitterness, or unresolved issues, this spiritual connection will certainly be difficult, if not impossible. If your spouse is not a person of faith or vastly believes something contrary to you, this will also be difficult. But I believe it is still possible, though limited.

God designed marriage in such a way that it works incredibly well when unity is present. Consequently, it is quite awful when unity is missing. Spiritual unity can unlock God's supernatural power, provision and joy in a marriage where two come together as one. One of the last prayers Jesus prayed before He was to face an awful execution was for unity and oneness (John 17:20-23). It is not until a couple is unified, especially spiritually, that they will realize the awesome potential their marriage was designed to have by God Himself.

Connecting spiritually means to share your spiritual life together. This involves several things. Some of these things may be a little redundant from an earlier chapter, but we believe this is worth repeating in light of this section.

READ AND TALK ABOUT BIBLICAL PASSAGES

Reading a passage of Scripture together or even a daily devotional can spark a closeness with your mate. This is not a time to debate theology but to share how a particular passage or devotional speaks to you. The main point is to communicate together.

TALK TO GOD TOGETHER

Prayer is extremely powerful especially among married couples. Praying together can be difficult for some for various reasons. One woman refused to pray with her husband because she felt it was too personal. One man refused to pray with his wife because he felt spiritually inferior to his wife. Prayer is a time to unite, be real, and seek God together as a couple. It is not a time to judge each other's prayer or show off your spirituality. Once again, this will be very difficult if you have underlying anger or conflict.

Here is a simple way couples can begin to pray together by implementing the "6 Minute Prayer." Each person does each segment for 60 seconds.

- **Thanksgiving:** Look into your partner's eyes and thank God for some of the good traits your spouse has and all the good things they do.

- **Repentance:** Vocalize to God and your partner for the things you need to change and demonstrating remorse for the hurts you have caused.

- **Speak Life:** Declare the blessings and promises of God over his or her life.

ATTEND CHURCH TOGETHER

Worshipping God together is more powerful than you can imagine. Whenever you share the same spiritual experiences such as singing praises together, hearing the same sermon, and fellowshipping with others of like precious faith; it has a way of unifying a couple. The Bible reminds us not to forsake the assembling of ourselves together as some have (Hebrews 10:24-25).

SERVE IN MINISTRY TOGETHER

Serving others together feels good as a couple. There is a sense of fulfillment and purpose that accompanies ministry involvement. When couples share these experiences together, there is a deeper spiritual connection. You may serve in the children's ministry of your church or a food shelter in the city. The main thing is doing something together.

FAST TOGETHER ON OCCASIONS

Fasting is not a favorite subject for many but it is a Christian practice with a significant and powerful purpose. Fasting is designed to deny the body in order to gain a deeper spiritual hunger and overcome sin, discover healing and for personal breakthrough. Fasting doesn't change God, it changes us. There are times when a couple will mutually agree to refrain from sexual relations for the purpose of fasting (1 Corinthians 7:5). It is mutual, never one-sided. It is for spiritual purposes, not selfish ones. And it is for a limited time frame that is AGREED upon.

TAKE COMMUNION TOGETHER

This was something we did on our wedding day and still make it our practice. Communion is not only a memorial of what Christ has done in our lives, but it is a symbol of unity and a declaration of your commitment to God and each other.

TALK ABOUT YOUR SPIRITUAL EXPERIENCES

Simply sharing your spiritual experiences is a simple way of becoming more connected. Share what you believe God is speaking to you, how a biblical passage really moved you, or what you gleaned from the pastor's sermon. When you feel spiritually connected you feel at ease to share deeper parts of your soul, thus deepening your level of intimacy with each other.

DON'T PUT UNDUE PRESSURE ON EACH OTHER

Spiritual connectedness must be prioritized, but it must come natural, too. Like anything else that is new, it may seem uncomfortable. But the idea is to share openly and without fear of criticism or rejection. When praying or reading together, don't start off by taking huge chunks of time. This can be an immediate turn-off for future times together. Keep things fun and light-hearted, but do it together. Spiritual intimacy can launch your marriage into new levels you haven't even witnessed yet.

Connecting Points

- What has held you back from spiritual unity with your partner?

- What plan do you have for developing spiritual unity with your mate?

- What potential barriers will you have to overcome as a couple to maintain spiritual oneness?

TARZAN & JANE'S FUN FACT!

Men have a pronounced need to fulfill their goals, and women rank relationships with others first.

Source: http://peoplerelationships.syl.com/battleof-sexes/differences

THE MORE YOU AND YOUR PARTNER DRAW NEAR TO GOD,

ULTIMATELY, THE CLOSER YOU WILL BECOME TO EACH OTHER.

THIS IS DEMONSTRATED IN THE RELATIONAL TRIANGLE BELOW:

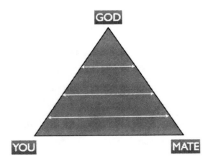

CHAPTER 39

Setting The Right Foundation

"We are not human beings having a spiritual experience; we are spiritual beings having a human experience."

~ Pierre Teilhard de Chardin

THE SECRET OF OUR SUCCESS

NO ONE GOES INTO MARRIAGE with the thought that their union won't make it across the finish line. No amount of self-determination or will power can help a person stay true to their partner as God intended all on their own. Sure, we will let our partner down and hurt them deeply at times, but what keeps marriages together?

We can assure you of this, if it wasn't for Christ's influence in our lives, we would most likely have walked out on each other a long time ago. Human love alone will never hold a marriage together. Only Christ's love in us, when no feelings are present, will help us till the end.

BELIEFS & CONVICTIONS

Nothing influences people's lives more than their beliefs. Couples with strong agreement in spiritual beliefs and practices say their faith provides a foundation that deepens their love and helps them grow together and fulfill their dreams.

What is your faith? Everyone has one. Even if you don't consider yourself as a religious person you still have faith in something. There is no shame placing your complete trust in the One who created you, your partner and marriage itself. Faith in Jesus Christ will transform your life and marriage; He is the strongest glue we know. Not only did God keep Jane and I together, He kept me together too.

How does your faith help you? Real faith is one that helps us in the here and now. False religion is one that doesn't ever affect the day-to-day living on earth. True spirituality is one of the most practical things in life because spirituality affects not just the spiritual aspects of life, but our emotional and physical well-being too. In short, I believe if it's not practical, it's not spiritual either.

CHRISTIANS & MARRIAGE

You can still be a spiritual person and struggle in your marriage. Moses, Abraham and David all struggled in their marriages. Unfortunately, statistics have shown that 1 in 2 marriages among Christians ends in divorce. Why? I believe it is due to having a faulty foundation. Even people of faith have struggled and even failed in marriage. King David is a good example of this. Your beliefs can be accurate, but if your practices don't line up with God's standards, the results can be devastating.

I was shocked when I heard a seasoned pastor of forty plus years make a startling comment when asked, "What is the most noticeable difference you see among the church of today compared to 40 years ago?" His reply got my attention when he said, "The most noticeable difference I see is that the unbeliever [non-Christian] of forty years ago was more stable than the believer of today." It's time to get back to the basics of our faith in God.

WHAT FOUNDATION DO YOU HAVE?

In order to succeed in marriage you must have a foundation that can withstand the storms of life. A spouse that mistreats his partner, mismanages money, commits an affair, prioritizes their kids or parents above their spouse, is unforgiving, addicted to pornography (including romance novels), and harsh, indicates a deeper issue – an unstable foundation.

The Bible has a great story of two men who built a house. One man built on the sand while the other built his on the rock. The story is told by Jesus in Matthew 7:24-29:

"'Therefore everyone who hears these words of mine and puts them into practice is like a wise man who built his house on the rock. The rain came down, the streams rose, and the winds blew and beat against that house; yet it did not fall, because it had its foundation on the rock. But everyone who hears these words of mine and does not put them into practice is like a foolish man who built his house on sand. The rain came down, the streams rose, and the winds blew and beat against that house, and it fell with a great crash.' When Jesus had finished saying these things, the crowds were amazed at his teaching, because he taught as one who had authority, and not as their teachers of the law."

SCENARIO NUMBER ONE: SKIMPING ON YOUR FOUNDATION

The foundation is not seen outwardly, but it is the most important part of any structure. Once we looked at a gorgeous home in a beautiful neighborhood. We couldn't understand when we first looked at the real estate ad why it was selling so inexpensively. So we went. The home was unbelievable and it was in our price range. But there was one "little" glitch – the home had sunk. The foundation was never laid correctly and as far as we were concerned, that home was worthless to us. You could place a marble at one end of the hallway and it would roll without help across the length of the house.

You see, the foundation is the most important thing of all. God is the creator and designer of marriage. He knows how it will work and He knows how to fix any problems. Marriage was the first institution He established on earth.

So if you hear God's Word and refuse to apply its principles to your life, you are doomed for failure. Marriage will NEVER reach its full potential for people who lack a spiritual foundation.

SCENARIO NUMBER TWO: SETTING THE FOUNDATION

When construction of a building begins about 80 to 90% of the work is complete. Before you see anything erected, the plans were drawn and modified, the city board of zoning and appeals meetings were held, the construction team was selected, the land was purchased, the utilities were put in, and the list goes on and on. Then once the foundation is poured and set, the building shoots up like a mushroom almost overnight. But most of the work was really complete before anything was ever viewed with the naked eye. The foundation is critical.

So what does it mean to be spiritually strong? How can a couple build a healthy, strong foundation that can cause them to withstand the storms of life? Remember, storms come to everyone, they don't discriminate. But the question remains, who will go through these storms successfully?

Here are some scriptural, but very practical ways of establishing your spiritual foundation upon which to build your marriage.

REPENT FREQUENTLY

Unless you haven't done so, confess your sins to God and one another. Turn to Jesus Christ and ask him into your heart. Scriptural Support: 1 John 1:9, Psalm 51, Psalm 66:18, James 5:14.

READ THE BIBLE DAILY

The Bible is a powerful book that will change the way you think and as a result will change the way you act. Scriptural Support: Joshua 1:8, John 6:63, Hebrews 4:12.

TALK TO GOD DAILY

No relationship will excel when there is a communication problem. Not only does God want us to speak to Him, but He wants to speak to us. Jeremiah 33:3 tells us to "Call on Me and I will answer you and show you great and mighty things you do not know." You do not have to kneel every time you pray or use candles or even be quiet and bored. Prayer should be an exciting time of interaction between you and God. It was Hope MacDonald who said, "Prayer is nothing more than a conversation between two people who love and understand each other." What a great way to put it. Scriptural Support: Luke 11:1-4, Jude 1:2.

FIND A GOOD CHURCH

A good church can be characterized by several key components. Ask yourself the following questions:

- Does the church teach from the Bible?
- Can you sense genuine love from the people?
- Is the worship style something you can connect with?
- Is there ministry for your kids? Do they seem to connect?

Maybe this church is a little farther from home, but that's okay. It shows value to your family. I've known people who traveled over an hour each way for work, but thought it was strange to travel 20 minutes to church. Your spiritual development as a couple is more important than how much money you earn. And one more thing, don't expect churches to be perfect. None of us are perfect, but we are all being perfected with God's help.

ACT ON WHAT YOU KNOW

Knowing information will never change your life. It is incorporating that knowledge into every day life and into the decision making process that does bring about change. The brother of Jesus, James, made a profound comment about those who learn but never act on what they know: "And remember, it is a message to obey, not just to listen to. If you don't obey, you are only fooling yourself" (James 1:22 NLT). The Bible is not for mere information. It is for transformation into Christ-like character.

CONNECTING POINTS

- What can you do to strengthen your spiritual foundation?

- What changes would need to take place on your part and your partner's in order to become more spiritually compatible?

- Do your lives really reflect what you claim your faith to be?

TARZAN & JANE'S FUN FACT!

At 12 years old boys cry just as much as girls, but by age 18 women cry 4 times more than men due to their surge of estrogen.

Source: Discovery Channel's, "Science of the Sexes".

CHAPTER 40

Your Number One Marriage Priority

"You will always have time and money for what is first place in your life."

A NEW PASTOR MOVED INTO A TOWN, and he went out one Saturday to visit his parishioners. All went well until he came to one house. It was obvious that someone was home, but no one came to the door even after he had knocked several times. Finally he took out his card, wrote "Revelation 3:20" on the back, and stuck it in the door. Revelation 3:20 reads, "Behold, I stand at the door and knock. If anyone hears My voice and opens the door, I will come in to him and dine with him and he with Me." The next day, as he was counting the offering, he found his card in the collection plate. Below his message was written "Genesis 3:10" which reads, "So he said, I heard your voice in the garden, and I was afraid because I was naked and hid myself."

Priorities... we all have them; from our families to work to taking care of ourselves. It seems like everyone wants a piece of our time and money, but we must learn to keep first things first. We must refuse to major in the minors. We cannot ignore the most important things in life and expect to remain emotionally and relationally healthy.

Your number one marriage priority is... staying close to God! As a matter of fact, that is your number one priority in life. Now I realize that there are many people reading this book that do not consider themselves to be the religious type.

However, marriage is something that was invented by God, not man. If the Inventor of marriage created something, then He knows how to sustain it. The problem for many is that they accept God's gift of marriage apart from the Creator of marriage.

When God isn't in first place in our life, we put a lot of pressure on others, especially our spouse to meet deep-seated needs that only God can fulfill. Sure, your spouse can meet your romantic needs, sexual needs, the need for love and human relationship, but only God can fill needs no human being can meet.

God Gives Us What Humans Cannot

GOD GIVES US UNCONDITIONAL ACCEPTANCE

God will love you even when you screw things up. God will love you when you no longer have six-pack abs. People want to know if they will be loved and accepted unconditionally. Will you love me if I lose my six-figure income? What if my teeth aren't the whitest? What if my health deteriorates? God will love you unconditionally even when man doesn't. Our goal is to love our spouse with the same unconditional love and commitment God shows us.

GOD GIVES US OUR TRUE IDENTITY

I need to know who I am in Christ. If I don't know, then I will go after the applause of men and become addicted to man's approval. When we seek to please man rather than God, we live life without conviction and will compromise to keep others happy even if they don't have our best interests at heart.

GOD GIVES US REAL SECURITY

Sure, we can get a certain amount of security from human relationships. However, have you ever noticed people with gobs of money, an attractive spouse, popularity and fame only to find out how insecure they really are? There are people with millions living in fear of depravity.

GOD GIVES US A SPECIFIC PURPOSE

Not only do we have an eternal destination (heaven), but we also have been given a specific assignment (purpose) from God! God directs us into a life of service that benefits mankind. God has called everyone to a purpose. He will direct you to that job best suited for you; one where you can fulfill your purpose in life. This isn't always something of grandeur but one of effectiveness nonetheless.

GOD GIVES US PEACE

Only God give us an internal tranquility despite outward circumstances. When peace is absent, anxiety, fear, and shame appear. People do many things (some very bizarre) looking for true peace. Our Creator can keep us sane in a hostile world by imparting His peace.

WHEN GOD IS FIRST

YOU WILL NOT BE A HUMAN "NEED MACHINE"

Overly-needy people automatically become unattractive to us. When God is first place in our life, there is a peace and security that engulfs your entire persona. It is not something that is merely natural, but truly supernatural. Many people think the supernatural and being close to God makes you weird and unrelatable, but just the opposite is true. In fact, being close to God assists you in reaching others and being relevant.

True spirituality makes you a better husband or wife, a better boss or employee, a better person to be around. When God is distant or void in you life, your spouse will feel a burden they were never meant to carry, the burden of meeting your deepest needs that only God can fulfill. When we do not go to God to meet our deepest needs we automatically transfer that onto those closest to us to meet those needs. Consequently, we put unrealistic expectations on others and feel disappointed when they are unable to meet these unrealistic expectations.

YOU CAN DO WHAT IS HUMANLY UNTHINKABLE

When you are closely connected to God you will become more and more Christ-like. That means you can love the unlovely and pray for those who are mean-spirited. You can respond in kindness when someone treats you like a jerk. This does not come from mere human discipline. This is a result of God working through us. When God's power is working within, you are able to give to others who cannot give to us, and even do it with a great attitude. Remember, you cannot give what you do not have. God created marriage where it will not work the way He designed it without His involvement. When we are close to God He fills us with His love. It is impossible to love people the right way without God filling us with His love. The Holy Spirit makes a mean person nice, a weak person strong.

YOU HAVE TRUE CONVICTION IN LIFE

When we naturally felt like walking out on each other, God's power restrains us and keeps us in check. When you are close to God you have God's power available to you to overcome temptation, unhealthy generational behaviors and thinking patterns, and addictions. Staying close to God will help you stay morally clean in a morally sick world. Keeping God first releases His power into your life. As our friend and pastor, Joe Cameneti attests, "A depleted life is a defeated life." Stay filled up on God's Word and God's presence and you will be an overcomer instead of being overcome.

YOU CAN BE RIGHTLY RELATED WITH GOD

You will never be right with God if you are treating my spouse with contempt and arrogance (1 Peter 3:1-7). You will never be right with God if you ignore the very One who gives you the strength to do what is right. We are so depraved as human beings that we cannot do anything right without God's help.

YOU BEGIN TO EXPERIENCE GOD'S HEALING

When we stay close to God He heals us from the inside out. This isn't a one-shot deal but a process. God heals us of the pain of sin: the shame, the brokenness, the heartache and so on. God restores our joy, peace, and heart. If you let Him, God will deliver you from unhealthy thinking patterns, depression, and bad habits we may have picked up from our upbringing.

"Keeping God first is the key to experiencing God's best."
~ Joyce Meyer

ONE FINAL THOUGHT

Staying connected to God helps you stay broken and humble towards others especially towards your spouse. Whenever you choose to be broken, you are able to show vulnerability with your mate and give more grace towards them. As one woman admitted, whose husband had cheated on her, "At the end of the day, we're still married today because we're both broken. Had I not chosen that, we wouldn't be married."[144]

Brokenness means "I know without the grace of God I am doomed to failure and I know I have disappointed my spouse more than I can fathom. I choose to be a grace giver instead of a being a law giver." Choosing God means choosing life! With your cooperation and God's help, your marriage will go beyond your wildest dreams no matter how bad things look! Your future is bright!

"I sought the LORD, and he answered me; he delivered me from all my fears. Those who look to him are radiant; their faces are never covered with shame. This poor man called, and the LORD heard him; he saved him out of all his troubles." - Psalm 34:4-6 (NIV).

"So, you see, it is impossible to please God without faith. Anyone who wants to come to him must believe that there is a God and that he rewards those who sincerely seek him." - Hebrews 11:6 (NLT)

CONNECTING POINTS

- How can we put unrealistic expectations on our spouse?

- What are some things only God can give?

- Is there anything that is keeping you from serving God today?

- How can you keep God in first place in your life?

DO YOU HAVE LIFE?

"He who has the Son has life; he who does not have the Son does not have life."
- 1 John 5:12

Accepting Jesus Christ as your personal Lord and Savior guarantees life eternally in the security of heaven. Don't wait... turn to Him today! It is the most influential decision you will ever make.

TARZAN & JANE'S FUN FACT!

A man's sense of self is defined through his ability to achieve results. A woman's sense of self is defined through her feelings and the quality of her relationships.

The female brain is predominantly hard-wired for empathy. The male brain is predominantly hard-wired for understanding and building systems.

Source: Cambridge University psychologist and autism expert Simon Baron-Cohen

Daily Accountability Sheet
14 Questions to Ask Yourself Everyday

Today's Date: _____

1. Did I spend time in the Word of God?

2. Did I spend quality, uninterrupted, unhurried time in prayer?

3. Did I worship the Lord today in song and connect with His presence?

4. Did I speak positive words today to my spouse and over myself?

5. Did I listen to the right voices today, especially those in authority?

6. Did I keep my calling before me today?

7. Did I reach out to someone today with the Gospel?

8. Did I follow my health and wellness plan?

9. Did I follow my financial plan and use my money wisely?

10. Did I use my time wisely and on purpose?

11. Did I honor my mate today through my gracious words, acts of kindness and servant's attitude?

12. Did I spend some quality time with my kids today?

13. Did I violate any physical or emotional boundaries with the opposite sex?

14. Did I completely forgive everyone who has hurt or angered me?

_____
Signature

Where Do I Go From Here?

You may be in a relational mess but you must realize a few very important points before making any decisions, especially one you may regret. Hopefully you have completed reading *Me Tarzan, You Jane* in its entirety and have begun implementing the principles discussed in this book. There are also some important reminders:

- First, your relationship is fixable – it is NOT beyond repair.

- Secondly, you must realize that you are not alone.

- Thirdly, you must recognize the source of conflict and your part in it.

- Fourthly, you must be willing to change and keep on growing.

- Fifthly, you must get some outside help.

- Sixthly, you must commit to the process.

- Finally, you must recognize your need for Divine intervention.

Don't give up! Once you demonstrate humility and begin to repair the brokenness in you, your partner will take notice and your marriage will go to levels beyond your wildest dreams! We know it because we've lived it and we believe you will too!

Acknowledgements

We are so grateful to...

Steve's grandparents, Chester (late) and Lottie Narewski... You have demonstrated commitment, hard work, and tenacity and stayed married for nearly 61 years. What an incredible example you have been. You both are our heroes!

Steve's dear friend and mentor, Dennis Heber... You have watched me grow up from a teenager and have always been in my corner cheering me on. Your friendship, wisdom, and encouragement, and occasional corrections have gone a long way. You are truly a mainstay!

Our friend and former neighbor, Michele Minger... For generously allowing me (Steve) to use her camper on many occasions so I could find solitude to work on this project. Thanks for always being such an encouragement and prayer warrior!

To Bill and Janet Grey... For allowing us the use of your serene summer home in the picturesque countryside of Northeast Ohio. We accomplished so much in such a peaceful setting. Thank you so much for your kindness.

To Dr. R.A. and Victory Vernon... For being our friends and people we can be real with. You are generous, loyal and wise.

To Bishop Joey Johnson… Thanks for being there for us especially during our ministry transition. God brought you into our life at the right time! Thanks for creating a safe place for us!

To Jimmy and Karen Evans... For inspiring us to be better partners. Your messages, television program, and books have deeply impacted our lives and it can be traced throughout this book. Thank you!

To Paul Endrei… you have always shown us much kindness and have encouraged us along the way. Thank you from the bottom of our hearts.

To Gary and Patty Chimelewski... For allowing us to utilize your lovely Florida home and for doing such a great job on our publications. We appreciate your friendship.

To (Steve's) Aunt Nancy... What an awesome aunt you are! Thanks for always believing in us and cheering us on!

To Pastors Joe and Gina Cameneti... Thank you for your friendship, encouraging support and for being such awesome pastors.

To Pastors Jim & Debi... Thank you for being my (Jane's) pastors when I lived in California. You helped me grow in my faith. Thanks for always believing in Steve and I and embracing us the way you do.

To Pete English and Pat Wischmeier... You guys have been such a mainstay and encouragement to us, especially for Steve. Thanks for serving alongside us for over a decade!

To Pastors Louis and Tina Kayatin... Thanks for encouraging us and being there for us.

To Pastors Antwan and Nikisha... What dear friends you have turned out to be!

To Dr. Bill Truby... You have been a friend and a positive influence to me (Steve) over the years. We appreciate you and Sherry!

To Brian Del Turco... For your expertise helping us put this project together. We couldn't have done this without you!

To Rich Dolesh... For the tremendous job you did on the book cover and for sharing creative ideas with me early on in the project. We'd recommend Dolesh Edit Design to anyone.

To our friends... You know who you are! You have believed in us and never doubted us even when we weren't at our best. We are blessed with some of the most incredible friendships this world has to offer. From the bottom of our hearts we say "thank you!"

To the C3 Church Family... thanks for believing in us and releasing us to do what God put on our hearts to do without complaining. What dear people you really are... we couldn't have done this without you. Thanks a million!

To those who have been a source of encouragement along the way:

Gary & Jennifer Gole, Steve & Sharon Kelly, Ralph & Maria Criswell, The Ron & Dr. Lori Leonard, Robert Cameron, Ricky Griffin, Ray Intihar, Van Crouch, Mike & Cathy Victor, Clint Dix, Jeffrey & Zena Paul, John Merola, Stan & Amy Debro, Angela Cooley, Margie Carson, Pastor Neal & Amy May, Dan Weed [late], Dave & Judy Walker... just to name a few! Your friendship, acceptance and love reaches beyond what words can ever say. We love you all!

About the Authors

Steve Hutchinson has served as a church planter and Lead Pastor for over 17 years. He has also served in various capacities such as an Associate Pastor, Worship Director, Youth Pastor, Bible School instructor and Sports Director. He is currently serving as an author and traveling speaker.

His travels have taken Steve to many nations equipping people in the areas of leadership, marriage and faith. With a combination of biblical scholarship and humor, Steve Hutchinson is known for his relevant and down-to-earth style of communicating God's Word.

Steve holds a Bachelor's Degree in Pastoral Studies, a Master's Degree in Theology and is currently pursuing a Doctorate in Counseling. Steve and his wife Jane have authored a marriage enrichment book entitled, Me Tarzan, You Jane.

Jane Hutchinson is a gifted teacher and speech therapist.

Jane holds a bachelor's degree in Speech and Hearing along with a minor in Psychology. Jane also holds two Master's Degrees: one in Speech and the other in Audiology. Sensing the call of God in her twenties, Jane attended Rhema Bible Training Center and prepared for ministry.

Throughout the years, Jane has assisted her husband as a church planter, staff pastor and author. She has served in various capacities such as Children's Director, FIne Arts Director, Singles Coordinator, Women in Crisis Volunteer, and Director of Women's Ministries.

Steve and Jane have been tremendously blessed with four incredible children – Caleb, Luke, Christianna, and Faith Victorya. Together they passionately love God, love people, and love life!

Contact Information

For booking engagements, to help support this ministry, or to contact us for any other reason, please use the following information:

STEVE & JANE HUTCHINSON

Me Tarzan, You Jane
Marriage Builders

Mailing Address:
P.O. Box 1111
Hudson, OH 44236

Phone: (330) 351-3459
Email: office@MeTarzanYouJane.com

Website: www.MeTarzanYouJane.com

Endnotes

1. Pew Research, www.pewsocialtrends.org (November 18, 2010).

2. Richard Dobbins, *Narrowing the Risk in Mate Selection* (Akron: Emerge Ministries, 1985), 5-6.

3. From the U.S. Census Bureau, Survey of Income and Program Participation (SIPP), Median Duration of Marriages (2004 data): Duration of first marriage for those whose first marriage ended in divorce: Men: 8.1 years; Women: 7.8 years.

4. Phillip C. McGraw, *Relationship Rescue* (New York: Hyperion, 2000), 1.

5. Ibid., 3.

6. Ibid., 3.

7. Patricia Love and Steven Stosny, *How to Improve Your Marriage Without Talking About It* (New York: Broadway Books, 2007), 42.

8. McGraw, *Relationship Rescue*, 10.

9. John Townsend and Henry Cloud, *Boundaries in Marriage* (Grand Rapids: Zondervan, 1999), 39, 42.

10. Rabbi Arush Shalom, *The Garden of Peace: A Marital Guide for Men Only* (Jerusalem: Chat Shel Chessed Institutions, 2008), 17.

11. We all need a dose of self-awareness. We need to see ourselves accurately the way others know us to be.

12. Adapted from a teaching from Jimmy Evans.

13. John Maxwell, *Go For Gold* (Nashville: Thomas Nelson, 2008), 106.

14. Jimmy Evans, *Marriage On the Rock* (Amarillo, Texas: Marriage Today, 2004), 206.

15. Maxwell, *Go For Gold*, 106.

16. Ibid.

17. Ibid.

18. Ibid.

19. Ibid.

20. Ibid.

21. Ibid.

22. Ibid.

23. Ibid.

24. Ibid.

25. Adapted from the book *The 5 Love Languages* by Dr.Gary Chapman. You can also log onto to www.5lovelanguages.com to take the Love Language Quiz and discover your dominant love language.

26. Love and Stosny, *How to Improve Your Marriage Without Talking About It*, 142.

27. Ibid., 169, 177.

28. Ibid., 177.

29. Ibid., 170.

30. Ibid., 177.

31. John Tesh, *Intelligence for Your Life: Powerful Lessons for Personal Growth* (Nashville: Thomas Nelson, 2008), 85.

32. Scott Stanley, Daniel Trathen, Savanna McCain and Milt Bryan, *A Lasting Promise: A Christian Guide to Fighting for Your Marriage* (San Francisco: Jossey-Bass Publishers, 2002), 28.

33. Wikipedia: The Free Encyclopedia.

34. Townsend and Cloud, *Boundaries in Marriage*, 120.

35. Stanley, Trathen, McCain and Bryan, *A Lasting Promise: A Christian Guide to Fighting for Your Marriage*, 29.

36. Ibid., 32.

37. Ibid., 35.

38. Ibid., 35.

39. Ibid., 37.

40. Ibid., 38.

41. Joey Johnson, *Article on Conflict Level Communication*, 11.

42. David Augsburger, *Caring Enough to Confront* (Ventura: Regals Books, 1973; revised edition, 1981 by Herald Press), 30, 32.

43. Ibid.

44. Ibid.

45. Ibid.

46. Ibid.

47. Ibid.

48. Ibid.

49. The Holy Bible, Proverbs 11:17.

50. John Tesh Radio Show (June, 2011).

51. Love and Stosny, *How to Improve Your Marriage Without Talking About It*, 35.

52. British Medical Journal (1997).

53. AskMen.com, Donald Zimmer (March 30, 2009).

54. British Medical Journal (1997).

55. Ibid.

56. Ibid.

57. Ibid.

58. Ibid.

59. Ibid.

60. Ibid.

61. Ibid.

62. Ibid.

63. Ibid.

64. Ibid.

65. Ibid.

66. AskMen.com

67. Ibid.

68. Ibid.

69. Ibid.

70. Ibid.

71. Ibid.

72. Ibid.

73. Ibid.

74. Ibid.

75. Quoted from Pastor Joe Camenti's message, *The Male Sex Drive* (September 11, 2011).

76. Jay Dixit, http://www.psychologytoday.com/articles/200706/five-shocking-stats-about-men-and-sex (June 4, 2007).

77. McGraw, *Relationship Rescue*, 54.

78. Paul and Patti Endrei, *Glue: Sticking Power for Lifelong Marriages* (Tulsa: Vision Imprints Publishing, 2006), 203.

79. Tom W. Smith, *American Sexual Behavior: Trend, Socio-Demographic Differences, and Risk Behavior* (National Opinion Research Center, University of Chicago, GSS Topical Report No. 25, March, 2006).

80. Les Parrot, *Good Crazy Sex: Putting to Bed the Myths Men Have About Sex* (Grand Rapids: Zondervan, 2009), 90.

81. Ibid., 90.

82. Margaret Carlson, *The Mummy Diaries* (Time, October 7, 2002).

83. Parrot, *Good Crazy Sex: Putting to Bed the Myths Men Have About Sex*, 44.

84. Ibid., 44.

85. Sue Johanson, counselor and sex educator, statistical analysis from Salon.com (2000).

86. Archibald Hart, *The Sexual Man: Masculinity Without Guilt* (Dallas: Word, 1994).

87. Love and Stosny, *How to Improve Your Marriage Without Talking About It*, 75.

88. R.T. Michael, J.H. Gagnon and E.O. Lauman, *Sex in America: A Definitive Survey* (Boston: Little, Brown & Co,), 125.

89. William R. Mattox, Jr., *The Hottest Valentines: The Startling Secret of What Makes You a High-Voltage Lover*, Washington Post (February 13, 1994).

90. McGraw, *Relationship Rescue*, 54.

91. Parrot, *Good Crazy Sex: Putting to Bed the Myths Men Have About Sex*, 67.

92. Quoted from a message by Jimmy Evans.

93. Tesh, *Intelligence for Your Life: Powerful Lessons for Personal Growth*, 91.

94. Bill Hybels, *Marriage: Building Healthy Intimacy* (Grand Rapids: Zondervan, 1996), 52.

95. Evans, *Marriage on the Rock*, 66.

96. Jay Dixit, http://www.psychologytoday.com/articles/200706/five-shocking-stats-about-men-and-sex (June 4, 2007).

97. Rod A. Martin, http://aath.org/articles/art_martin.html.

98. Love and Stosny, *How to Improve Your Marriage Without Talking About It*, 36-37.

99. Ibid., 46-47.

100. Census Bureau (2001).

101. *Men's Health Magazine* (October, 2003).

102. Ibid.

103. Ibid.

104. Ibid.

105. Ibid.

106. Ibid.

107. Ibid.

108. Elizabeth Brown, *Living Successfully with Screwed Up People* (Grand Rapids: Baker, 1999), 50.

109. Ibid., 50.

110. Study conducted by Dr. Jan Halper of executives, entrepreneurs, and professionals.

111. Love and Stosny, *How to Improve Your Marriage Without Talking About It*, 90-91.

112. Ibid., 91.

113. Townsend and Cloud, *Boundaries in Marriage*, 189.

114. www.truthaboutdeception.com/cheating-and-infidelity/stats-about-infidelity.html

115. Jim Davis, *Outreach Magazine* (September 1, 2011).

116. Adapted from a message on marriage by Jimmy Evans.

117. Nina Chen, *Extramarital Affairs in the Workplace* article.

118. John Tesh Radio Show (December, 2011).

119. www.thinkexist.com/quotations/relationships

120. Love and Stosny, *How to Improve Your Marriage Without Talking About It*, 119.

121. Ibid., 119

122. Ibid., 191.

123. Gary Chapman, *Toward A Growing Marriage* (Chicago: Moody Press, 1979), 97.

124. Joyce Meyer, *Help Me! I'm Married* (Tulsa: Harrison House, 2000), 120.

125. Townsend and Cloud, *Boundaries in Marriage*, 120.

126. Emerson Eggerichs, *Love & Respect: The Love She Most Desires, The Respect He Desperately Needs* (Colorado Springs: Thomas Nelson, 2004), 5.

127. Love and Stosny, *How to Improve Your Marriage Without Talking About It*, 26.

128. Stanley, Trathen, McCain and Bryan, *A Lasting Promise: A Christian Guide to Fighting for Your Marriage*, 80-81.

129. Ibid., 81.

130. Shaunti Feldhahn, *For Women Only* (Sisters, Oregon: Multnomah, 2004), 133.

131. Stanley, Trathen, McCain and Bryan, *A Lasting Promise: A Christian Guide to Fighting for Your Marriage*, 105.

132. Jeff McElroy, *Prepared to Last* (Minneapolis: Life Innovations, 2006), 13.

133. Harley, Willard F., His Needs, Her Needs: Building An Affair-Proof Marriage (Fleming H. Revell Company, Old Tappan, New Jersey, 1986), 72.

134. Ibid., 126.

135. McElroy, 13.

136. Stanley, Trathen, McCain and Bryan, *A Lasting Promise: A Christian Guide to Fighting for Your Marriage*, 149.

137. Ibid., 144.

138. Ibid., 146.

139. Jeff and Debby McElroy, Peter Larson and David Olson, *Prepare to Last* (Dallas: Marriage Today, 2006), 59.

140. Main points adapted from a sermon from Jimmy Evans.

141. Paraphrase from a sermon by Jimmy Evans.

142. http://articles.moneycentral.msn.com/SAvingandDebt/ManageDebt/TheWorstKindOfDebt-ChargingTheGroceries.aspx.

143. Quote from Jimmy Evans sermon.

144. Trisha Davis, *Outreach Magazine* (September 1, 2011).

CPSIA information can be obtained at www.ICGtesting.com
Printed in the USA
BVOW031157190212

283266BV00009B/55/P